Academic Writing for Graduate Students

ESSENTIAL TASKS AND SKILLS

3RD EDITION

John M.
SWALES
&
Christine B.
FEAK

MICHIGAN SERIES IN ENGLISH FOR
ACADEMIC & PROFESSIONAL PURPOSES

The University of Michigan
Ann Arbor

♾ Printed on acid-free paper

ISBN: 978-0-472-03475-8

2025   2024   2023   2022   13   12   11   10

Contents

Introduction to the Third Edition

The Changing Scene

The second edition of *Academic Writing for Graduate Students* (henceforth *AWG*) was published in 2004. In the ensuing eight years, many of the important trends we identified in that edition's Introduction—in North America and elsewhere—have developed further. Email and the internet are now nearly universal, especially since the spread of wireless technologies. Graduate degrees available or partly available online have been increasing rapidly. The American tradition of requiring doctoral students to take courses has been adopted and adapted by more and more countries. Co-authorship of papers written by graduate students and their professors and/or advisors continues to increase. Doctoral students are attending and presenting at more conferences and are doing so at earlier stages in their PhD programs. As a result of these trends, graduate students and junior researchers are much more networked than they were 20 years ago; indeed, the 2010 book by Lillis and Curry, *Academic Writing in a Global Context*, provides compelling evidence of the advantages today of operating within and through networks. Several other scholars have also been emphasizing that academic writing today is much more of a collaborative activity than it used to be. The growth of research groups, writing circles, close mentoring, and email have all contributed to our growing understanding that writing is increasingly embedded in social and professional contexts (e.g., Bhatia, 2004; Molle & Prior, 2008). Although this book focuses on academic writing, we also recognize that it is often mediated by academic speech.

Further, those with overall responsibility for graduate education, such as graduate schools, are offering more workshops for graduate students, many of whom are often concerned with strengthening communication skills in some way. Finally, the traditional distinction between native and non-native speakers of English continues to erode. In the research world, in particular, there are today increasing numbers of "expert users" of English who are not traditional native speakers of that language. This has given rise, in recent years, to the English as a Lingua Franca (ELF) phenomenon whereby these expert users, as well as those with lower English language proficiency, communicate with each other on matters of research, scholarly, or business interest. One further piece of evidence for this trend is the increasing spread of English-medium post-secondary instruction at universities in non-Anglophone countries.

When *AWG* was originally published in 1994, the number of courses in academic writing for graduate students was both rather small and largely restricted to entering international graduate students. Nearly 20 years later, both the number and range of these courses have increased as graduate students move around the world in growing numbers and as recognition grows that increasing numbers of native speakers of English would welcome, for various reasons, some assistance with their academic writing. As part and parcel of these developments, research in English for Academic Purposes (EAP) has advanced, partly through dissertation-level studies on various aspects of academic discourse; leading examples of this trend are China, Iran, Italy, and Spain. It is clearly time for a third edition!

In the years between the previous edition and this one, there have also been changes in our personal circumstances. John officially retired in 2007, but he maintains a university office, interacts with doctoral students, and keeps busy as a researcher, materials writer, reviewer, guest lecturer, and conference speaker. Overall, he feels he is keeping up to date with events in the global world of EAP. Meanwhile, Chris has taken over and further developed the English Language Institute's advanced courses in dissertation writing and writing for publication. She also gives frequent workshops, both at Michigan and elsewhere, and is increasingly invited to speak at international conferences.

Approach and Organization

A third edition of an EAP textbook usually indicates that the first two have enjoyed some success. And this has been the case with *AWG*. As a result, we have largely retained the basic approach of the previous editions. This approach can be spelled out in this way.

- The book has evolved out of both research and teaching experience.
- It is as much concerned with developing academic *writers* as it is with improving academic *texts*.
- The book is conceived as providing assistance with writing *part-genres* (problem-solutions, methods, and discussions) and *genres* (book reviews and research papers).
- It is targeted at graduate students (although we have heard of its successful use with advanced undergraduates). These graduate students

may variously be internationals with limited experience writing academic English, "proficient users" with a first language other than English, and native speakers of English. The last group in particular may not need to pay as much attention to the *Language Focus* sections in this volume.

- The general approach is analytical and rhetorical: Users are asked to apply their analytical skills to the discourses of their chosen disciplines and to explore how effective academic writing is achieved. In effect, we are strong believers in this cycle, which is fashionably known as *rhetorical consciousness raising:*

Achievement   Analysis

Acquisition   Awareness

- The tasks and activities are richly varied, ranging from small-scale language points to issues of how graduate students can best "position" themselves as junior researchers.
- The book is fairly fast paced, opening with a basic orientation and closing with writing an article for publication.
- With the help of the accompanying *Commentary*, scholars and students should be able to use this volume profitably on their own.

We have also largely retained the original eight-unit organization because nearly all the reports we have received suggest that users are happy with it.

- The first four units are essentially preparatory; they pave the way for the more genre-specific activities in later units.
- Unit One presents an overview of the considerations involved in successful academic writing, with a deliberate stress on early exposure to the concept of positioning.

- Units Two and Three deal with two overarching patterns in English expository prose: the movement from general to specific and the movement from problem to solution.

- Unit Four acts as a crucial link between the earlier and later units since it deals with how to handle interpretation and discussion of data.

- Units Five and Six then deal with writing summaries and critiques, respectively.

- Finally, Units Seven and Eight deal with constructing a real research paper—that is, one that attempts to make an original contribution to the field.

Changes in the Text

Within this retained basic approach and structure, there are, however, also a number of important changes. Many of the older sets of data and older texts have either been updated or replaced. Even so, in response to user pressure, we have kept a number of instructor "favorites," such as the test-retest data in Unit Four. Although the range of disciplines represented remains large, we have, again in response to user requests, somewhat increased the material from the hard sciences and Engineering. Among other changes, an important one has been a sharp reduction in the attention to the grammar of definitions in Unit Two, which is now relegated to an appendix. The space created has allowed for a new closing section to this unit that deals with the kinds of specific-general texts that can be found in the humanities.

Throughout, new findings (both published and our own) from discourse analysis have been incorporated. Another important innovation has been our use of the Michigan Corpus of Upper-level Student Papers (MICUSP), which became freely available in 2009 (see www.elicorpora.info/). This corpus consists of an electronically searchable collection of 830 top-rated student papers at the University of Michigan, representing 16 disciplines and consisting of work submitted by final year undergraduates and graduate students in their first three years.

AWG has been designed as a first course in graduate-level writing and is most suited to the first two years of graduate education. For the later course work, there is *English in Today's Research World: A Writing Guide (ETRW)*, published by the University of Michigan Press in 2000. This has been replaced by some more specialized mini-volumes, all published by the University of Michigan Press (see www.press.umich.edu/esl/compsite/ETRW/).

As a result, *AWG* does not deal in depth with abstracts as a distinct part-genre, nor does it address free-standing literature reviews, writing introductions to term papers and other course work, or writing applications.

The Teaching Context

We have designed this textbook to be used by students who come from a broad range of disciplines. After all, this has been our primary experience as writing instructors at Michigan's English Language Institute. Even at our large research university, the logistic problems of organizing and staffing courses along disciplinary lines mean that such courses remain the exception rather than the rule. Although it is often believed that disciplinary courses are better or more efficient, it is our experience, especially with students in their second year or beyond, that a multidisciplinary class has several advantages over a monodisciplinary one. The former turns attention away from whether the information or content in a text is "correct" toward questions of rhetoric and language. In this way it encourages rhetorical consciousness-raising. It also leads to interesting group discussion among members who come from very different parts of the university. This kind of class can also create a special—and more tolerant and lighthearted—community among its members, since students are much less likely to be competing with others from their own departments.

Irrespective of whether the teaching context is multidisciplinary or not, *AWG* is a text that instructors should use selectively. Each unit has more material than can realistically be handled in a timely and efficient manner. Further, instructors should be encouraged to substitute activities and, more particularly, texts more suited to their own circumstances. In effect, we look upon our fellow instructors more as distant partners and collaborators in an educational enterprise rather than as people expected to obediently follow the course we have set out. In the same light, we have not tried to impose our own beliefs (which are by no means identical in every case) about how *AWG* should actually be taught. We have, therefore, relatively little to say about such matters as error analysis, peer feedback, task-based learning, or product-process approaches to teaching academic writing. So, rather than a traditional teacher's manual, *AWG* is supported by a companion volume carefully entitled *Commentary*. This consists of synopses of what each unit attempts to achieve, further discussion of certain points, and sample responses to the more controlled tasks. The *Commentary* should therefore also be useful for scholars and students using *AWG* in self-study situations. In addition, and again in response to numerous requests, we have expanded the number of teaching suggestions, which are now placed at various points in each unit.

Thanks to Others

Finally, we turn to those who have helped us prepare this third edition. We would like to acknowledge the insights of all those who took the trouble to write and publish reviews of the second edition or to provide feedback to us directly (including colleagues Deborah DesJardins, Mindy Matice, and Julia Salehzadeh at the University of Michigan English Language Institute) or via Kelly Sippell at the University of Michigan Press. Then there are the hundreds of graduate students who have taken ELI writing courses over the last eight years and who have taught us much about what works and what does not. We have also been able to benefit from the evaluations of our workshops at the University of Michigan and elsewhere, wherein we experimented with parts of this volume. Finally, we want to thank the developmental editor who offered valuable feedback that has strengthened the textbook and commentary in significant ways.

As intimated in the previous paragraph, a particularly significant player in the emergence of this volume has been Kelly Sippell, the dynamic ELT editor at the University of Michigan Press, who not only provided enthusiastic encouragement, but also kept the pressure on when it mattered most. Chris would like to thank Glen, who again willingly endured the uncertainty of her schedule and picked up the slack so that this book could be completed. She also wants to thank Warren and Brian for their newfound interest in her books and her mom, Ursula, for her support. And not to be forgotten are Karl and Angie, who have realized that *AWG* is actually a rather useful resource that they can turn to in their own academic writing pursuits. John is grateful to Vi Benner for once again putting up with the distractions arising from his co-authoring at home yet another book-length manuscript, even though he is "supposed" to be retired. We also both thank Vi for her careful reading of the proofs.

JMS & CBF
Ann Arbor, 2012

Acknowledgments

Grateful acknowledgment is given to these individuals and publishers for permission to reprint their work or previously published materials.

American Association for the Advancement of Science for Wuchty, Jones, and Uzzi, "The increasing dominance of teams in production of knowledge," *Science,* Vol. 316, no. 5827, pp. 1036–1039, Copyright © 2007. Used with permission.

Benny Bechor for "Navigation."

Prudencia Ceron-Mireles for her description of preeclampsia.

Elsevier for reprinting from: *Accident Analysis & Prevention,* Vol. 42, Neider, McCarley, Crowell, Kaczmarski, and Kramer, "Pedestrians, vehicles, and cell phones," pp. 589–594, Copyright © 2010, with permission from Elsevier; *Drug and Alcohol Dependence,* Vol. 99, Reissig, Strain, and Griffiths, "Caffeinated energy drinks—A growing problem," pp. 1–10, Copyright © 2009, with permission from Elsevier; *International Journal of Nursing Studies,* Vol. 40, no. 1, Pölkki, Pietilä, and Vehviläinen-Julkunen,"Hospitalized children's descriptions of their experiences with postsurgical pain relieving methods," pp. 33–44, Copyright © 2003, with permission from Elsevier; *Journal of Economic Psychology,* Vol. 21, Schwer and Daneshvary, "Keeping up one's appearance: Its importance and the choice of type of hair-grooming establishment, pp. 207–222, Copyright © 2000, with permission from Elsevier; *Journal of Economic Psychology,* Vol. 30, Casola, Kemp, and Mackenzie, "Consumer decisions in the black market for stolen or counterfeit goods," pp. 162–171, Copyright © 2009, with permission from Elsevier; *Journal of Safety Research,* Vol. 32, DePasquale, Geller, Clarke, and Littleton, "Measuring road rage: Development of the propensity for angry driving scale," pp. 1–16, Copyright © 2001, with permission from Elsevier; *Library and Information Science Research,* Vol. 33, Hall, "Review of *The critical assessment of research: Traditional and new methods of evaluation* by A. Bailin and A. Grafstein," p. 56, Copyright © 2011, with permission from Elsevier.

IEEE for "Counterfeit money detection by intrinsic fluorescence lifetime," Levene and Chia in *Lasers and Electro-Optics (CLEO) and Quantum Electronics and Laser Science Conference (QELS), 2010 Conference on Laser Electro-Optics: Applications,* pp. 1–2, Copyright © 2010.

IOP Publishing Ltd. for "Review of *Quantum field theory in a nutshell* (2nd edn) by A. Zee," by M. Peskin, published in *Classical and Quantum Gravity* 28: 089003, Copyright © 2011. Used with permission.

Yasufumi Iseki for "Reducing Air Pollution in Urban Areas: The Role of Urban Planners."

Patrick Kelley for reaction paper.

Kohlee Kennedy for reaction paper.

H.J. Kim for LOC chip text.

John Lebens for reaction paper.

Jiyoung Lee for "Comparison of the Actual CO2 Levels with the Model Predictions."

Pierre Martin for his textual outline.

Mei-Lan for her interview.

Michigan Audubon for "Occurrence of a Badger in Pictured Rocks National Lakeshore, Michigan," by Belant, Wolford, and Kainulainen, Vol. 14, no. 2, pp. 41–44, published in *Michigan Birds and Natural History*, 2007. Used with permission.

Physical Review for "Nuclear-Structure Correction to the Lamb Shift," by Krzysztof Pachucki, Dietrich Liebfried, and Ted W. Hänsch, Vol. 48, pp. R1–R4, Copyright © 1993.

Riley Publications, Inc. for "University-Community Agency Collaboration: Human Service Agency Workers' Views" by Mojisola F. Tiamiyu, *Journal of Multicultural Nursing and Health* 6, 29–36, Copyright © 2000. Reprinted with permission.

Royal Society of Chemistry for "Soft capacitors for wave energy harvesting," by Ahnert, Abel, Kollosche, Jorgensen, Kofod, in *Journal of Materials Chemistry*, 21, no. 38, 14492–14497, Copyright © 2011. Used with permission.

Royal Swedish Academy of Sciences and Springer for "Fog-water collection in arid coastal locations" by Schemenauer and Cereceda, *Ambio*, Vol. 20, no. 7, pp. 303–308, Copyright © 1991.

Sage Publications for Rabinovich and Morton, "Who says we are bad people? The impact of criticism source and attributional content on responses to group-based criticism" in *Personality and Social Psychology Bulletin* 36, 524–526, Copyright © 2010; for tables in Selwyn, "A safe haven for misbehaving? An investigation of online misbehavior among university students," Vol. 26, pp. 446–465. Copyright © 2008. Used with permission.

Hiroe Saruya for her description of nationalism.

SCImago for table and figure from SCImago Journal & Country Rank, retrieved from http://www.scimagojr.com.

Springer for "Does self-citation pay?" by Fowler, J. H. and D. W. Aksnes. *Scientometrics*, 72, pp. 427–437, Copyright © 2007.

Taylor & Francis Ltd for table from "Disciplinary discourse" by T. Becher in *Studies in Higher Education*, 12, no. 3, pp. 261–274, Copyright © 1987. Used with permission.

Figure adapted from "The effects of phase control materials on hand skin temperature within gloves of soccer goalkeepers," by Purvis and Cable, *Ergonomics*, Vol. 43, No.10, p.1484, Copyright © 2000; and for figure adapted from "Exercise and Cold" by T.D. Noakes, *Ergonomics*, Vol. 43, No.10, p. 1473, Copyright © 2000. Reprinted with permission.

John Wiley & Sons Limited for "Procrastinators lack a broad action perspective" by DeWitte and Lens, *European Journal of Personality*, Vol. 14, pp. 121–140. Copyright © 2000. Reproduced with permission.

Unit One

An Approach to Academic Writing

As graduate students, you face a variety of writing tasks throughout your chosen degree programs. Naturally, these tasks will vary from one degree program to another. They are, however, similar in two respects. First, the tasks become progressively more complex and demanding the farther you go in the program. Second, in general they need to be written "academically," although certain assigned writing in some fields may require personal reflection (such as teaching reflections) and thus may be somewhat more informal. In Units Two through Six of this textbook, we focus on the writing tasks that may be required in the earlier stages of a graduate career. In the last two units, we look a little farther ahead.

This opening unit is different from the others since it does not focus on a particular type of text. Instead, we try to help you reflect upon a variety of aspects of academic writing, ranging from style to some sociological, cultural, and rhetorical issues. Overall, we are primarily concerned with your "positioning" as a writer—the means by which you create in writing a credible image as a competent member of your chosen discipline. We begin with a focus on your writing strategies.

TASK ONE

Discuss these possible writing strategies with a partner. Put a check mark (✓) next to those writing strategies that you use a lot. If you rarely or never use some of the strategies, discuss why you do not.

_____ 1. Translating, if you use English as an international language

_____ 2. Spending a lot of time on gathering information or doing research and then quickly writing your paper from your notes, data sources, or outlines

_____ 3. Referring to one or more "model" papers in your discipline, noticing in particular such matters as how the papers are organized, how phrases are used, and where and why examples or illustrations are provided

_____ 4. Relying on a mentor (either native or non-native speaker) who "knows the ropes" and can anticipate how a particular written text might be received by a particular set of readers or reviewers, who may also be able to offer advice on which journal or conference a piece might be submitted to and why

_____ 5. Relying on friends who are not in your field to help you with phraseology

_____ 6. Developing a sense of the anticipated audience, particularly with regard to what needs to be said and what does not

_____ 7. Recognizing the need for some stylistic variation and acquiring the linguistic resources to achieve this

_____ 8. Finding useful phraseology from other, possibly published papers and using it to string your ideas together

_____ 9. Constructing an appropriate author "persona," so that you come across as a member of the disciplinary community

_____ 10. Concentrating on making sure your sentence-level grammar is accurate because that is the most important aspect of getting your ideas across

Understanding your writing strategies is important in becoming a confident writer. To help you explore your strategies further, we offer Task Two.

TASK TWO

Write a reflective paragraph in which you share your reactions to these questions.

1. What is your main writing strategy? Why do you use it? What one other strategy apart from those on the list do you use? Are your strategies dependent on the type of text you are composing?

2. Which of the strategies that you do not use would you most like to develop? And how might you go about developing it?

3. Do you think strategies listed in Task One apply equally well to all fields? How might they vary in importance for an author in Physics, History, Economics, Public Health, or Engineering? Which of them is most important in your own field?

As you may already realize, academic writing is a product of many considerations: audience, purpose, organization, style, flow, and presentation (see Figure 1).

FIGURE 1. Considerations in Academic Writing

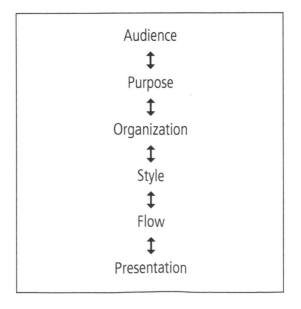

Audience

Even before you write, you need to consider your audience. The audience for most graduate students will be an instructor, who is presumably quite knowledgeable about the assigned writing topic and will have expectations with which you need to be familiar. Other possible audiences include advisors, thesis committees, and those who will review research you may want to present at a conference or publish in a paper. Your understanding of your audience will affect the content of your writing.

TASK THREE

Read these excerpts from two longer texts that discuss obtaining drinking water from salt water. Answer these general questions with a partner. For whom were they written? What aspects of each text helped you decide the audience? In what kind of publication would you expect to find these texts? Sentence numbers have been added here (and in subsequent texts throughout the book) for ease of reference. Then answer the more specific questions that appear on page 5.

A. ❶ People have been pulling freshwater out of the oceans for centuries using technologies that involve evaporation, which leaves the salts and other unwanted constituents behind. ❷ Salty source water is heated to speed evaporation, and the evaporated water is then trapped and distilled. ❸ This process works well but requires large quantities of heat energy, and costs have been far too high for nearly all but the wealthiest nations, such as Kuwait and Saudi Arabia. ❹ (One exception is the island of Curaçao in the Netherlands Antilles, which has provided continuous municipal supplies using desalination since 1928.) ❺ To make the process more affordable, modern distillation plants recycle heat from the evaporation step.

⑥ A potentially cheaper technology called membrane desalination may expand the role of desalination worldwide, which today accounts for less than 0.2 percent of the water withdrawn from natural sources. **⑦** Membrane desalination relies on reverse osmosis—a process in which a thin, semipermeable membrane is placed between a volume of saltwater and a volume of freshwater. **⑧** The water on the salty side is highly pressurized to drive water molecules, but not salt and other impurities, to the pure side. **⑨** In essence, this process pushes freshwater out of saltwater. (Martindale, 2001)

B. **❶** Reverse osmosis (RO) membrane systems are often used for seawater and brackish water desalination. **❷** The systems are typically installed as a network of modules that must be designed to meet the technical, environmental, and economic requirements of the separation process. **❸** The complete optimization of an RO network includes the optimal design of both the individual module structure and the network configuration. **❹** For a given application, the choice and design of a particular module geometry depends on a number of factors, including ease and cost of module manufacture, energy efficiency, fouling tendency, required recovery, and capital cost of auxiliary equipment. **❺** With suitable transport equations to predict the physical performance of the membrane module, it should be possible to obtain an optimal module structure for any given application. (Maskan et al., 2000)

1. How do the texts differ in terms of vocabulary?

2. How do the texts differ in terms of detail?

3. Where do the definitions of *reverse osmosis* appear? How do these definitions differ?

4. Do the texts appear to be well written? Why do you think so?

The differences in the two texts reflect some of the assumptions that the authors have made about the typical reader's familiarity with the subject. In the first text, the author assumes the reader is probably not familiar with reverse osmosis and thus provides a fair amount of background information along with a clear definition of the process.

TASK FOUR

Now write a short definition of a term in your field for two different audiences. One audience could consist of graduate students in a totally unrelated field, while the other could be students in your own graduate program. Exchange your definitions with a partner and discuss how they reflect differences in your chosen audiences.

Purpose and Strategy

Audience, purpose, and strategy are typically interconnected. If the audience knows less than the writer, the writer's purpose is often instructional (as in a textbook). If the audience knows more than the writer, the writer's purpose is usually to *display* familiarity, expertise, and intelligence. The latter is a common situation for the graduate student writer.

The interesting question that now arises is what strategy (or strategies) can a graduate student use to make a successful display. To explore this, let's consider the case of an international student who calls himself Sam in the United States. Sam is enrolled in a master's program in Public Health. He has nearly finished his first writing assignment, which focuses on the impact of video games on the cognitive development of children in the United States. This is a short five-page assignment rather than a major research paper. The deadline is approaching, and there is no more time for further data analysis. He wants to make a good impression with his concluding paragraph. He believes (rightly) that final impressions are important.

Sam (quite appropriately) begins his last paragraph by reminding his audience (i.e., his instructor) of what he has done in the paper.

He begins as follows:

Conclusion

The aim of this paper has been to examine the impact of video games on the cognitive development of pre-adolescent children in the United States. In particular I have examined the effects of video games on visual attention.

So far, so good. His first attempt at concluding his paper is as follows:

As I have explained, video games can indeed account for differences in cognitive abilities of pre-adolescents, specifically the ability to switch attention from one task to another.

He thinks, "This just repeats what I have already written; repeating makes it seem that I have nothing new or interesting here; my paper falls flat at the end." Sam tries again. "This time," he says to himself, "I will take my results, summarize them, and then try to connect them to some wider issue. That's a better strategy." Here is his second version.

As the tables show, pre-adolescent children who play video games score better on tests of visual attention than those who do not. This relationship was quite strong among children between 10 and 12 years of age, while for children aged 6 to 9 the association was not so pronounced. Children who were very good at playing video games, mostly those who are older, appear to be able to effectively switch attention. These findings support the conclusion of other studies that playing video games may not simply be a mindless activity; instead video games can enhance the cognitive skills of gamers.

Sam likes this version; however, he is also worried. He knows—but he has not said so anywhere in the paper yet—that there is a problem with the data he has been using. He knows that there are many types of video games and so the effects of one game on cognitive development may be quite different from those of another. For instance, shooting video games are not the same as sports video games. And even within the same game genre there is variation in terms of the skills that are needed to play. Luckily, he is not using his own research data for this assignment; he is using data that he has found in journal articles.

He now adds this to his concluding paragraph.

The conclusions presented here, however, should be interpreted cautiously. This is because the data presented here are based on analyses of two sports video games, which differ in terms of visual attentional demand from other types of video games, such as first-person shooting games that require an awareness of a full screen.

Sam is feeling somewhat unsure of his conclusion and is now asking himself the following questions: "Have I been too cautious in my conclusion when I use *appear to*, *may*, and *can*? Is it actually better to clearly state that there are problems with the data or to not mention this at all? Which strategy is better? Will I appear more or less capable by discussing the limitations of the data? And if I do discuss them, should I do so right at the end or at the beginning of my conclusions? In effect, how should I *position* myself as a junior graduate student?"

TASK FIVE

What advice would you give Sam? Consider the questions he raises about the strength of his points and the inclusion of limitations. Write this in a paragraph or two. Then edit or re-write his final paragraph to reflect your advice.

Organization

Readers have the expectation that information will be presented in a structured format that is appropriate for the particular type of text. Even short pieces of writing have regular, predictable patterns of organization. You can take advantage of these patterns, so that readers can still follow, even if you make some language errors.

Although our goal in this text is not to work on letter writing, we would like to begin our discussion of organization by looking at two letters that may, in fact, resemble letters or email you have received at some point in your academic career. Each letter has a clear, predictable pattern of organization. The first is a good-news letter.

	Parts
Dear Ms. Wong:	Greeting
Thank you for your interest in our university.	Acknowledgment
On behalf of the Dean of the Graduate School, I congratulate you on being accepted to the program in Aerospace Engineering to begin study at the master level. This letter is your official authorization to register for Fall 20XX. As a reflection of the importance the Graduate School places on the ability of its students to communicate effectively, the Graduate School requires all new students whose native language is not English to have their English evaluated. Specific details for this procedure are given in the enclosed information packet.	Good news Administrative matters
We look forward to welcoming you to Midwestern University and wish you success in your academic career.	Welcoming close that points to the future
Sincerely,	

TASK SIX

Read the bad-news letter, and label the four parts: greeting, preparation for bad news, bad news, and close. Where does the most important news appear (first? second?)? How does this compare to the good-news letter? How do the different purposes of the two letters influence the kind and placement of information?

	Parts
Dear Mr. Lee: Thank you for your interest in the graduate program in Industrial and Operations Engineering. We have now finished our rigorous review process for Fall 20XX applications. We received an unusually high number of applications for the Fall term and we unfortunately had to limit the number we could accept. While your background is impressive, I regret to inform you that your application to the program has not been accepted. Given your excellent qualifications, I trust you will be able to pursue your academic interests elsewhere and wish you luck in your further endeavors. Sincerely,	

You are already likely aware that academic writers employ a variety of organizational patterns. You are already familiar with external organization features, such as chapters, sections, and paragraphs. As you work your way through this book, you will become familiar with the various approaches to internal organization as well. One very common strategy that is foundational to academic writing is to organize information in terms of problems and solutions (Hoey, 1983). This pattern usually has four parts. Can you identify them in this next task?

TASK SEVEN

Draw boxes around and label the four parts of this problem-solution text (situation, problem, solution, and evaluation). After marking the text, answer the questions on page 12.

❶ As standards of living rise and the world's population grows, the demands for freshwater have been increasing. ❷ Along with this increase is growing pressure to protect this precious resource. ❸ Efforts to protect the water supply have traditionally focused on regulating industrial and municipal waste that is discharged into rivers and lakes. ❹ However, in recent years researchers have identified a new threat to world freshwater supplies. ❺ Studies have identified in freshwater around the world a number of medicinal drugs, ranging from painkillers such as acetaminophen, to antibiotics, to cholesterol absorption inhibitors. ❻ These drugs easily enter the water supply when they are eliminated through digestion or improperly disposed of by directly flushing them down a toilet. ❼ Although the amount of these drugs in freshwater supplies is small (a few parts per billion or trillion), their impact on the freshwater supply and on human health has yet to be established. ❽ Given this uncertainty, efforts are underway to address this problem. ❾ One simple, inexpensive approach involves educating consumers about proper medication disposal methods. ❿ This effort involves educating consumers to be made aware that medicines should not be poured into a sink or flushed, but should be discarded through local drug collection programs. ⓫ For example, many pharmacies collect unused or unwanted medicines and some communities have special medicine collection sites. ⓬ With increased education, consumers can dispose of medication properly and help protect freshwater resources.

1. How serious does the author perceive the problem to be? How did you determine this? To what extent is this a global problem?

2. What does the author think of the solution? What do you think of the solution?

3. What is one major problem in your field of study? Why is it important?

TASK EIGHT

Here is another passage with the same structure. Read it and answer the questions on page 13.

❶ Ghana is located on West Africa's Gulf of Guinea just north of the Equator. ❷ Unlike many poor West African countries, this country of 24 million has a growing economy that is expanding over 10% annually. ❸ This growth has largely been attributed to the 2007 discovery of a major oil field off the coast and to Ghana's position as a leading gold producer. ❹ Ghana has also emerged as an important center for e-waste recycling and disposal, an industry that contributes more than US$200 million into the economy. ❺ E-waste consists of electronic devices typically from Europe and North America that have been discarded, but still have some value. ❻ E-waste has been said to provide opportunities for employment, poverty alleviation, recycling business developments, and may even bridge the digital divide by contributing to the country's growing demand for information technology. ❼ However, this industry also poses environmental and health risks that cannot be ignored.

❽ The largest e-waste recycling and disposal center is located in the capital city of Accra and is adjacent to the Agbogbloshie Food Market. ❾ At this site recyclers disassemble electronics to retrieve valuable metals (for example, gold) or burn items covered with plastic (for example, computer wires) to recover metals such as copper and aluminum. ❿ These processes expose workers and others living near the e-waste site to toxic materials including plastics, lead, aluminum, and silica that are known to cause cancers and central nervous system damage among other health problems.

⓫ One way to address e-waste dangers is to install modern, sustainable recycling technology that can drastically reduce exposures to toxins. ⓬ One drawback to this approach, however, centers around who should be responsible for the cost of installing such systems. ⓭ Perhaps a more viable solution is for the manufacturers of electronics to reduce the amount of toxic materials used to make their products. ⓮ Thus, rather than placing all of the responsibility for safe handling of e-waste on the recyclers, the manufacturers could be persuaded to examine their own practices to determine ways to lower the risks associated with e-waste.

1. For what type of audience was this written?

2. What assumptions does the author make about the background knowledge of the audience?

3. What is the author's purpose?

4. How is the problem introduced?

5. To what does *this growth* in Sentence 3 refer? What are *these processes* in Sentence 10? To what does *this approach* in Sentence 12 refer? What is the effect of these particular expressions on the flow of ideas?

6. What does the author think of the two solutions?

7. If the writer had thought that the second solution would not work, what might she have written for the last sentence? In such a case, would this last sentence be enough to complete the text? If not, what would need to be added?

In addition to the problem-solution structure, some other ways of organizing information include the following.

- Comparison-contrast (see Unit Five)

- Cause-effect (focusing on one cause and multiple effects as in an earthquake or describing multiple causes and one effect as in an economic downturn)

- Classification [categorizing, as suggested by this example: "Earthquake effects on underground structures can be grouped into two categories: (1) ground shaking and (2) ground failure such as liquefaction, fault displacement, and slope instability." Note the cause-effect aspect of this as well.]

Research paper introductions in your field might also follow an established organizational pattern. Introductions are addressed in Unit Eight.

Style

Academic writers need to be sure that their communications are written in the appropriate style. The style of a particular piece should not only be consistent but also be suitable both in terms of the message being conveyed and the audience. A formal research report written in informal, conversational English may be considered too simplistic, even if the actual ideas and/or data are complex.

One difficulty in using the appropriate style is knowing what is considered academic and what is not. The grammar-check tool on your word processing program is likely not of much help in this matter since such programs are written primarily to find spelling and basic grammar errors and not to offer stylistic advice for *academic* writers. Moreover, what little stylistic advice is offered may not be right for what you are writing. For example, contrary to what your grammar checker might suggest, if you are describing a procedure or process, you *can* and probably even *should* use passive voice in many cases.

Deciding what is academic or not is further complicated by the fact that academic style differs from one area of study to another. For instance, contractions (e.g., *don't*) may be used in Philosophy but are not widely used in many other fields. And, as noted in a study by Chang and Swales (1999), some authors often use informal elements such as sentence-initial *but;* imperatives (as in the common expression *consider the case of . . .*); and the use of *I*. In the case of *I*, we see quite a bit of disciplinary variation. It is less commonly used in Computer Science papers (5.6 per 10,000 words in the Michigan Corpus of Upper-level Student Papers—MICUSP) but is frequent in Philosophy (53.9 occurrences per 10,000 words in MICUSP). Other fields lie somewhere in between those two. All this variation contributes to even more confusion when trying to determine what is "academic."

Finally, academic style is not used in all academic settings. Research based on the Michigan Corpus of Spoken Academic English (MICASE) shows that academic and research speech, in linguistic terms, is much more like casual conversation than written academic English. It is not uncommon to hear U.S. lecturers use words and phrases like *stuff, things, a bit, bunch,* or *a whole lot of,* which we would not expect to find in a written academic text. They may also use elaborate metaphors and other vivid expressions to enliven their speaking style. (For some examples of spoken academic English, check MICASE at www.elicorpora.info/.)

TASK NINE

Find and download two or three journal articles from your field that you think are well written. The articles do not necessarily have to be written by native speakers of English; however, they should be typical research articles in your field—not book reviews, editorial commentaries, or trade magazine articles from a publication with extensive advertising. If you are having difficulty deciding whether you have the right kind of article, ask your instructor for assistance. Bring your articles to class so that you can reference them and gain an understanding of the writing conventions in your field.

Cross-Cultural Differences in Academic Language

Over the past two decades, there has been considerable interest in tracing similarities and differences in academic language. Because of the dominating position of academic English prose and because of the wish of many people to acquire this variety of the language, the great majority of studies to date have compared some other academic languages with English academic prose. These languages include Arabic, Chinese, Finnish, French, German, Japanese, Korean, Malay, Polish, Spanish, and Swedish. Simplifying somewhat, the overall conclusions point in one basic direction: academic English, especially U.S. academic English, has several features that place it toward one end of a number of continua.

TASK TEN

Put a check mark (✓) next to the items that you think are typical of academic writing in English. If you are familiar with another academic language, also mark those points that you think are consistent and inconsistent in academic writing in that other language. Are the differences, if any, strong, or does it seem to you that the academic languages are more similar than different? To what extent should you incorporate the features in the list into your own writing?

U.S. academic English, in comparison to other academic languages, can be considered to

_____ 1. be more explicit about its structure and purposes (i.e., contains a noticeable amount of metadiscourse)

_____ 2. be less tolerant of asides or digressions

_____ 3. use fairly short sentences with less complicated grammar

_____ 4. have stricter conventions for subsections and their titles

_____ 5. contain more citations

_____ 6. rely more on recent citations

_____ 7. have longer paragraphs (in terms of number of words)

_____ 8. point more explicitly to "gaps" or "weaknesses" in the previous research

_____ 9. use more sentence connectors (words like *however*)

_____ 10. place the responsibility for clarity and understanding on the writer rather than the reader

Now let's explore some additional points that you can think about when working on your writing style. If you search for "academic style" on the internet, you may or may not be surprised at the roughly 260,000 hits. Clearly, a lot of people have a lot to say about this topic. You will find pages of things to do and not do (for instance, never use *I*, but do use references to support your points); pages telling you to forget about the "rules"; and other pages that describe what academic style is and is not (e.g., academic style is formal and not casual; it is not about using big words). Although many perspectives on academic style are available, much of the advice is vague, conflicting, and often based on personal preference rather than research. Thus, it should come as no surprise that, despite a sizeable amount of research, academic writing is in fact "poorly understood by teachers and students alike" (Lillis, 1999). So, where do we begin?

In this Language Focus section, we will present some more specific ideas about the characteristics of academic style for you to consider. You may wish to incorporate some of these points into your writing and ignore others. In the end, our purpose here is for you to think more about your stylistic choices as you write and to help you realize that good academic writers make many stylistic choices as they write.

Language Focus: The Vocabulary Shift—Verbs

English often has two (or more) choices to express an action or occurrence. The choice is often between a phrasal (verb + particle) or prepositional verb (verb + preposition) and a single verb, the latter with Latinate origins. In lectures and other instances of everyday spoken English, the verb + preposition is often used; however, for written academic style, there is a tendency for academic writers to use a single verb when possible. In some fields this is a very noticeable stylistic characteristic. Here is an example.

> Given our fast-paced society, people must routinely **put** creative solutions to unexpected problems **into practice.**

> Given our fast-paced society, people must routinely **implement** creative solutions to unexpected problems.

TASK ELEVEN

Choose a verb from the list to replace each verb in italics to reduce the informality of the sentence. Note that you may need to add tense to the verb from the list. Write down any other single verbs that you think could also work in the sentences.

consider   decrease   develop   investigate   reach
constitute   determine   eliminate   maintain   tolerate

1. Many software manufacturers in developed countries *put up with* widespread copyright violations in less developed countries and often even offer local versions of their products.

   _____

2. Scientists are *looking into* innovative drug delivery systems that can transport and deliver a drug precisely and safely to its site of action. _____

3. The purpose of this paper is to try to *figure out* what is lacking in our current understanding of corrosion and corrosion protection in concrete. _____

4. Researchers have *come up with* plug-in hybrid vehicles (PHEV) that can draw from two sources of energy: stored electrical energy from the grid and stored chemical energy in the form of fuel such as gasoline. _____

5. Rice and aquatic products *make up* a major part of the diet of the people in the Mekong Delta, Vietnam. _____

6. The use of touch screen voting systems could *get rid of* many problems associated with traditional paper-based ballots.

   _____

7. Worldwide consumption of pesticides has *gone up to* 2.6 million metric tons. _____

8. Although labor unions in the U.S. have been able to *keep up* their membership numbers over the last two decades, they have been losing their political strength. _____

9. The number of mature female green turtles that return to their primary nesting beach has *gone down* from 1,280 ten years ago to 145 today. _____

10. Many funding agencies worldwide are *thinking about* ways to give new researchers greater opportunities to receive grant money. _____

TASK TWELVE

In the space provided, write a few single verbs that could be used in place of the one in italics. In each case, try to find two or three possibilities and be prepared to discuss them.

1. Researchers have *come up with* a number of models to describe the effect of certain cola drinks on dental enamel erosion.

   _____

2. AIDS researchers have *run into* a variety of unexpected problems in their efforts to develop an effective vaccine.

   _____

3. Recent studies on car scrapping have *brought up* the important question as to whether CO_2 emissions can be significantly reduced by taking old cars out of service. _____

   _____

4. Problems with the new data management software *showed up* soon after it was launched. _____

   _____

5. In the past five years, many studies have *looked at* the effect of different grassland management practices. _____

   _____

Language Focus: The Vocabulary Shift—Nouns and Other Parts of Speech

English has a very rich vocabulary derived from many languages. Because of this, there may be more than one way to express an idea. When several alternatives are available, choose the one that most efficiently and accurately gets your point across.

You may have also noticed that in many academic texts there is an abundance of rather long noun phrases, which tend to carry a lot of meaning in a rather compact form. For instance, we can start with the word *language* and expand on the simple noun in this way.

language

↓

the language of scientific communication

↓

the international language of scientific communication

↓

English as the international language of scientific communication

↓

the emergence of English as the international
language of scientific communication

Thus, it is possible to write

> The emergence of English as the international language of scientific communication has been widely documented.

as opposed to

> English has emerged as the international language of scientific communication. This phenomenon has been widely documented.

The first example contains a very long noun phrase, a nominalization. Which of the two sentences do you prefer? Why? Which do you think would be more similar to writing in your field? What, if anything, do you think is gained or lost by nominalizing?

TASK THIRTEEN

Which of the italicized expressions might be more suitable for an academic paper? Can you think of additional alternatives?

1. Crash test dummies are *really important for / an integral part of* automotive crash tests.

2. According to a recent study *just about / nearly* 25% of all cell phone users view text messaging as an important source of entertainment.

3. There has been *a lot of / considerable* interest in how background sounds such as music affect an individual's ability to concentrate.

4. We obtained *robust / nice* results using structural bamboo rather than timber.

5. Consumer interest in electronic billing and payment is *getting bigger and bigger / increasing*.

Of course, when you are offered the choice between two alternatives, the more academic choice may be fairly clear. The more difficult task is making good language choices on your own. We have helped you a bit in this next part of the task by italicizing the phrases that you could change. You may need to make other changes so that the sentence is still grammatical.

6. The competition faced by U.S. growers from imports of fresh vegetables has *gotten more intense*.

_____

7. Many urban areas *do not have enough* land to build new public schools.

_____

8. Allergic reactions to local dental anesthesia *do not happen very often*.

_____

9. The doors on these ferries were *made bigger to make it easier to load and unload* vehicles.

_____

Language Focus: Other Stylistic Features

While you may prefer to closely follow the stylistic conventions of your field, you may also want to seek ways to "push gently at the boundaries of convention" (Casanave, 2010), more strongly position yourself, and create your scholarly identity. What follows are some other considerations that you can investigate and possibly incorporate in your academic writing style. These are not rules to follow, but rather choices you can make.

1. As indicated earlier, single authors in some fields use the first-person pronoun *I* (note that in some Engineering and hard science fields, single authors may choose *we,* given the collaborative nature of research in these areas). *We,* of course, is common in co-authored papers, which are increasingly the norm in publications. Research indicates that *I* or *we* can be used in academic writing, but many new authors are very reluctant to use *I.*

In this paper I argue that small incentives can lead to greater participation in surveys.	This paper argues that small incentives can lead to greater participation in surveys.

2. Again we remind you that in a few fields contractions may be common; in most they are not.

Export figures won't improve until the economy is stronger.	Export figures *will not* improve until the economy is stronger.

3. Some authors prefer some negative forms over others, believing that those on the right are more academic.

Not . . . any The analysis didn't yield any new results.	*no* The analysis yielded *no* new results.
Not . . . much The government didn't allocate much funding for the program.	*little* The government allocated *little* funding for the program.

Not . . . many	*few*
This problem doesn't have many sustainable solutions.	This problem has *few* sustainable solutions.

4. Some readers (for example, journal editors) object to the use of vague expressions such as *and so forth* and *etc*. These expressions may sometimes be used, but keep in mind that they are imprecise and require readers to "fill in" the missing information.

Micropumps can be used in drug delivery, lab-on-a-chip analysis, etc.	Micropumps can be used in drug delivery, lab-on-a-chip analysis, ink dispensing, and other specialized applications that require self-contained, low power, miniature pumps.

5. In many fields writers typically avoid addressing the reader as *you* (except, of course, if you are writing a textbook or other instructional materials). Note that this means you may need to use passive voice.

You can see the results in Table 1.	The results *can be seen* in Table 1.

6. Sometimes the use of a direct question can be a very effective means to draw your reader's attention to a point. This may be particularly useful when laying out an argument or research questions to be answered. However, indirect questions, such as those on the right, are likely more common.

Why has antibiotic resistance increased?	Many studies have investigated *why antibiotic resistance has increased.*
	or
	It is important to understand *why antibiotic resistance has increased.*
	or
	It remains unclear *why antibiotic resistance has increased.*

7. Adverb placement might be important. Often in academic writing adverbs are placed in mid-position rather than in the initial or final positions of sentences. In other contexts, English adverbs often occur at the beginning or end of sentences.

This model was developed by the International Monetary Fund (IMF) originally and was adapted by Lalonde and Muir (2007) later.	This model was *originally* developed by the International Monetary Fund (IMF) and was later adapted by Lalonde and Muir (2007).
Then the morphology of the samples was analyzed using a scanning electron microscope (SEM).	The morphology of the samples was *then* analyzed using a scanning electron microscope (SEM).

8. Consider whether you should split infinitives (*to* + verb). The prescriptive view of grammar condemns the use of split infinitives (placing an adverbial modifier between *to* and the infinitive as in *to sharply rise*). Although we would agree that split infinitives are not so common in some areas of academic writing, they are sometimes used, particularly to avoid awkwardness or ambiguity. (Both Chris and John regularly use split infinitives in their writing.)

We need *to adequately meet* the needs of those enrolled in the program.	We need *to meet* the needs of those enrolled in the program *adequately*.
Neural networks have the ability *to correctly classify* new patterns.	Neural networks have the ability *to classify correctly* new patterns.
The size of the container could be modified *to downwardly adjust* the portion size and amount of consumption.	The size of the container could be modified *to adjust* the portion size and amount of consumption *downwardly*.

The examples on the left came from published papers, while the versions on the right have been rewritten to eliminate the split infinitives. Can you guess why the authors chose to split the infinitives?

9. Use as many words as you need to express your points, but try not to use too many words. If you are wordy, readers may have difficulty following your point.

It may be difficult to make a decision about the method that should be used.	Choosing the proper method may be difficult.
There are some inorganic materials that can be used in tissue engineering by bioengineers in the process of tissue engineering that have been shown to be very promising.	Some inorganic materials have shown great promise in tissue engineering.

10. Consider using both active and passive voice. Both active and passive voices are used in academic writing; the key is to choose the right voice for the right purpose. Although grammar checkers may caution against using passive voice, it is commonly used in academic writing. (See Unit Three for more discussion.)

In summary, most of our comments about grammar and language have been designed to help you think about the sentence-level choices that may contribute to the development of your own style. The vocabulary shift and some of the other features we have mentioned are more important for maintaining a consistent academic style and for positioning yourself as knowledgeable and as an authority. In fact, you may remember that Sam wrote, *I have examined* . . . .

TASK FOURTEEN

Let's suppose that you want to follow the considerations listed in the Language Focus on pages 22–25. How would you revise these sentences?

1. You can use this model to optimize the water supply.

2. So, why did the bridge collapse? There're a lot of reasons.

3. In addition to herbs, animal products are employed in some forms of traditional medicine frequently.

4. So far there hasn't been much research on how conflict influences the level of trust and respect in a group.

5. There are several studies in Epidemiology that have shown that when people consume alcohol in moderate amounts they have a lower risk of developing heart disease in comparison to those people who drink a lot of alcohol.

6. Developed by computer scientists in the 1980s, data mining is a collection of methods aiming to understand and make money from the massive data sets being collected by supermarket scanners, weather buoys, intelligence satellites, and so on.

Work with a partner and look through the articles you chose for Task Nine. Can you find examples that demonstrate how the authors dealt with the stylistic considerations as well as the possible need to be cautious, as in the case of Sam? More importantly, can you offer explanations as to why certain stylistic choices were made and how these might relate to the author's purpose? Use the chart on page 27 to guide your analysis.

Article Analysis				
Do the articles contain examples of:	**Yes**	**In what part(s)?** **Give one or more example(s).**	**No**	**Do you think this is typical? (Yes, No, Unsure)**
I / we				
contractions				
more formal negatives				
etc., and so forth, and so on				
addressing the reader as *you*				
indirect questions				
mid-position adverbs				
split infinitives				
too many words to make a point				
passive voice				
may, appear to, or other language that softens a point				

TASK FIFTEEN

Now that you have become more familiar with some of the possible stylistic features of academic writing, write a one-page problem-solution text about a problem in a country that you are familiar with. Try to choose a problem unique to that country. Refer, if you like, to the text in Task Eight. Your audience is a group of professors and students interested in your selected country. Consider the style points on pages 16–25 as you write.

To conclude this extensive discussion on vocabulary and style, we now turn our attention to the use of the internet and online tools that may help you become more familiar with commonly used expressions or standard phraseology. Standard phraseology consists of expressions that are typical of academic writing across many disciplines. Many authors new to academic writing want to have some knowledge of these expressions as well as an understanding of what can be borrowed.

Using Google Scholar to Identify Potentially Useful Words and Phrases

1. Go to http://scholar.google.com/.
2. In the search box, place quotation marks around a phrase that you want to learn to use. For instance, you might want to find ways to use "In recent years there has been interest in . . . ." You might want to know what kind of modifiers can be used before *interest*. Place an asterisk * before *interest*. This search will yield the phrase along with words that come before *interest*. To narrow your search, you can add another topic. For instance, your area may be electric vehicles. Your search would then look something like this.

   "In recent years, there has been * interest in" "electric vehicle"

A search in 2011 produced one screen that included this information.

FIGURE 2. Sample Google Scholar Results

A novel design of a heat exchanger for a metal-hydrogen reactor
S Mellouli, F Askri, H Dhaou, A Jemni... - International Journal of ..., 2007 - Elsevier
... such as hydrogen which is especially attractive for **electric vehicle** use. Over the last decade, world wide interest in the use of hydrogen has led to much research interest on its storage and usage [1], [2] and [3]. **In recent years, there has been increasing interest in** using metal ...
Cited by 33 - Related articles - All 3 versions

A hybrid controller design for parallel hybrid electric vehicle
W Li, G Xu, Z Wang... - Integration Technology, 2007. ICIT' ..., 2007 - ieeexplore.ieee.org
... **In recent years there has been considerable interest in** using hybrid system theory to develop a systematic framework for the analysis and design of ... The hybrid **electric vehicle** systems contain interacting dis- crete and continuous dynamics, and exhibit simultaneously several ...
Cited by 7 - Related articles - Availability at UMichigan - Availability at UMichigan - All 3 versions

Design of interior PM machines for field-weakening applications
WL Soong, S Han... - Electrical Machines and ..., 2007 - ieeexplore.ieee.org
... **In recent years there has been increasing interest in** the use of concentrated winding stators for both interior [10] and surface PM rotors [8]. Surface PM machines using distributed winding ... The first application is for an **electric vehicle** traction motor. ...
Cited by 5 - Related articles - Availability at UMichigan - All 4 versions

Adaptive proportional–integral–derivative tuning sliding mode control for a shape memory alloy actuator
NT Tai... - Smart Materials and Structures, 2011 - iopscience.iop.org
... Robustness has gained more and more attention. **In recent years, there has been extensive interest in** self-tuning these three controller gains. For example, the PID self-tuning method based on the relay feedback technique was presented for a class of systems [32, 33]. ...
Related articles - Availability at UMichigan - All 4 versions

Design and test of a high-power high-efficiency loosely coupled planar wireless power transfer system
ZN Low, RA Chinga, R Tseng... - ... , IEEE Transactions on, 2009 - ieeexplore.ieee.org
... transfer. I. INTRODUCTION **IN RECENT** years, **there has been increasing interest** in research and development of wireless power technology [1] to eliminate the "last cable" after Wi-Fi becomes widely accepted. Wireless power ...
Cited by 13 - Related articles - Availability at UMichigan - All 2 versions

---

As you can see in Figure 2, adjectives that can modify *interest* are *increasing, considerable,* and *extensive.* To determine how common these adjectives are, you can then search for the complete expressions (e.g., "in recent years there has been increasing interest in").

Other ways to use the internet to search for specific language examples include WebCorp LSE (www.webcorp.org.uk/index.html), which searches all of the internet. You can also search online corpora with a specific focus such as MICUSP, the British National Corpus, the British Academic Written English (BAWE) corpus, or the Corpus of Contemporary American English (COCA). New corpora are being developed with great frequency, and you may want to periodically search the internet to see what is available. You can even create your own corpus of texts in your chosen field (or even from your own writing) that you can then analyze using online tools such as Compleat Lexical Tutor or freeware such as AntConc, a concordance program for Windows, Macintosh OS X, and Linux. While we cannot offer instruction on the use of these resources here, you will find that you can learn to use them well enough on your own with minimal effort.

Flow

Another important consideration for successful communication is flow—moving from one statement in a text to the next. Naturally, establishing a clear connection of ideas is important to help your reader follow the text. We have already tried to demonstrate good flow of ideas in the water passage in Task Three.

TASK SIXTEEN

Read the passage and discuss the questions on page 31 with a partner.

❶ In many countries around the world, it is customary for consumers of hospitality and other services to provide gifts of money (called "tips") to the workers who have served them. ❷ However, the specific service workers that are customarily tipped, and the amounts consumers give those workers, vary across nations. ❸ For example, in the United States consumers tip over 30 different service professions, while no service professions are tipped in Iceland (Star, 1988). ❹ In Mexico consumers tip restaurant servers 15% to 20% of the bill, but tip only 5% to 10% of the bill in Romania (Putzi, 2002). ❺ These variations in tipping norms are sources of uncertainty for international travelers and phenomena to be explained by hospitality and tourism researchers.

❻ International differences in tipping customs may be partially explained by differences in national values. ❼ According to Hofstede (1983), national values differ on four major dimensions—power distance, uncertainty avoidance, individualism, and masculinity. ❽ Power distance reflects a nation's acceptance of power and status differences. ❾ This value should be positively related to national acceptance of tipping because tipping gives customers power over servers (Hemenway, 1984; Lynn, 2000a).

Lynn, 2004.

1. How do you think the author establishes the relationship between the ideas?

2. Underline the grammatical subjects of Sentences 2–9. Can you find a link between each grammatical subject and the sentence that comes before it?

3. How would you explain the relationship between Sentences 1 and 2?

4. To what does *these variations* in Sentence 5 refer?

5. Which words are repeated in the text? Are you surprised by the amount of repetition of words in the text? Did you even notice this when you first read the passage?

6. What do you think Sentence 10 will discuss? Why?

Old-to-New Information Flow

Although your first instinct in establishing a smooth flow of ideas is to use logical connectors such as *however* or *furthermore*, many writers generally try to follow a progression from old or given information, which is in the subject position or early at the left end of the sentence, to new information, which is placed at the right end of the sentence. Placing relevant "old" information in early position establishes a content connection backward and provides a forward content link that establishes the context. Notice how this old-to-new pattern is established in this text.

❶ Research has shown that caffeine does indeed reduce sleepiness and can lead to better academic performance since students can spend more time studying. ❷ Despite its effectiveness in counteracting sleepiness, caffeine can have a negative impact on subsequent sleep, which for many students may already be compromised. ❸ Specifically, caffeinated beverages consumed near bedtime at night can prolong sleep onset and reduce sleep efficiency and depth, thus affecting both sleep quality and duration. ❹ Most of the research on how caffeine affects sleepiness/alertness has focused on coffee or no-doze pills. ❺ However, a new kind of caffeinated drink has become increasingly popular, namely functional energy drinks (FEDs). ❻ FEDs are marketed as products that can improve both mental and physical performance. ❼ In addition to containing caffeine, FEDs have other active ingredients such as taurine, glucose, and glucoronolactone. ❽ Exactly how these ingredients together affect alertness remains unclear.

The old-to-new pattern of information is established by starting a text with some familiar information. In the following sentence, you can repeat some information from the previous sentence (exact repetition, in the form of a synonym or variation on the part of speech). In the energy drink example, you can see the repetition of caffeine in Sentences 1 and 2.

> ❶ Research has shown that caffeine does indeed reduce sleepiness and can lead to better academic performance since students can spend more time studying. ❷ Despite its effectiveness in counteracting sleepiness, caffeine can have a negative impact on subsequent sleep,

To tie two sentences together, you can repeat information from the beginning of the first sentence, as in the case of *caffeine* in Sentences 1 and 2. Alternatively, you can pick up information from the end of the first sentence (since, once read, this new information is now familiar). An example of this is Sentences 5 and 6.

> ❺ However, a new kind of caffeinated drink has become increasingly popular, namely functional energy drinks (FEDs). ❻ FEDs are marketed as products that can improve both mental and physical performance.

Note also how passive voice in Sentence 6 is essential here. The point about marketing might not be well connected using active voice. An old-to-new pattern can also be achieved by using *this/these* + a noun, which refers back to some or all of the preceding sentence. An example of this can be seen in this possible Sentence 9.

> ❾ If this relationship could be explained, more effective FEDs could be developed.

If old-to-new cannot be easily maintained, writers will often opt to use a logical connector to make relationships clear, as in Sentences 4 and 5.

> ❹ Most of the research on how caffeine affects sleepiness/alertness has focused on coffee or no-doze pills. ❺ However, a new kind of caffeinated drink has become increasingly popular, namely functional energy drinks (FEDs).

Note that *a new kind of caffeinated drink* is new information that was not mentioned in Sentence 4. In order for the author to strongly establish the logical connection, the linking word, *however*, is added.

TASK SEVENTEEN

Work with a partner and answer these questions that focus on old-to-new flow of ideas.

1. The first sentence of a description of the biological clock follows. Given what you know about the old-to-new pattern of information, what are the two topics (or focal points) of the second sentence that the reader would likely expect?

> The biological clock is a master clock that dictates the day-night cycle of activity known as circadian rhythm.

Topic 1: _____

Topic 2: _____

2. In fact, the writer produced Sentences 2 and 3. How clearly are Sentences 1, 2, and 3 connected to each other? Explain your opinion.

> ❶ The biological clock is a master clock that dictates the day-night cycle of activity known as circadian rhythm. ❷ The suprachiasmic nucleus (SCN) was identified as the location of the clock in the brains of humans and animals. ❸ Specialized clock genes are activated and deactivated mainly by a pair of proteins, one of which turns on a group of genes and the other of which turns off a key gene in a feedback loop that has a 24-hour rhythm (specifically a 24-hour and 18-minute rhythm).

3. What do you think of this revision? How does this differ from the first version?

> ❶ The biological clock is a master clock that dictates the day-night cycle of activity known as circadian rhythm. ❷ The clock was identified in a part of the brain called the suprachiasmic nucleus (SCN). ❸ Within individual SCN cells, specialized clock genes are activated and deactivated mainly by a pair of proteins, one of which turns on a group of genes and the other of which turns off a key gene in a feedback loop that has a 24-hour rhythm (more precisely, a 24-hour and 18-minute rhythm).

4. In Sentences 4 and 5, the author wrote this:

> ❹ The biological clock functions regardless of the normal 24-hour cycle of light and darkness. ❺ Light is involved in resetting and regulating the clock.

Is the relationship between the two sentences clear? Could the author do anything to clarify how the two points are related? What? What about combining the two sentences into one?

Can you offer a revision here?

_____

_____

_____

_____

_____

5. Let's assume Sentences 4 and 5 are combined into one.

   ④ Although the biological clock functions regardless of the normal 24-hour cycle of light and darkness, light is still involved in resetting and regulating the clock.

   How well connected is this Sentence 5?

   ⑤ Sunlight resets the internal biological clock each day to synchronize the rhythms of activity of the clock genes, promoting the production of certain substances, such as hormones, which are necessary for maintaining good health.

6. What is the relationship between the information before *promoting* and the information after *promoting*? Should the author use a connector to make the relationship more clear?

7. In Sentence 6, the author wrote:

   ⑥ It was once thought that aging disrupts the biological clock.

   Does this sentence flow smoothly from Sentence 5? If so, why? If not, why not?

8. Here are the final three sentences of the biological clock definition. Do you think they should be in their own paragraph? Why or why not?

   ⑥ It was once thought that aging disrupts the biological clock. ⑦ But, recent research (Czeisler et al., 2005) has shown that the body temperature and hormone fluctuations of the elderly are as regular as those of the young. ⑧ Doctors can consider this valuable information in the treatment of sleep disorders in the elderly.

9. What do you think about the connection between Sentences 7 and 8? Can you think of a better connection?

10. **Now read these two texts on lasers in medicine. Which do you prefer? Why?**

A. ❶ Lasers have found widespread application in medicine. ❷ Lasers play an important role in the treatment of eye disease and the prevention of blindness. ❸ The eye is ideally suited for laser surgery ❹ Most of the eye tissue is transparent. ❺ The frequency and focus of the laser beam can be adjusted according to the absorption of the tissue. ❻ The beam "cuts" inside the eye with minimal damage to the surrounding tissue—even the tissue between the laser and the incision. ❼ Lasers are effective in treating some causes of blindness. ❽ Other treatments are not. ❾ The interaction between laser light and eye tissue is not fully understood.

B. ❶ Lasers have found widespread application in medicine. ❷ For example, they play an important role in the treatment of eye disease and the prevention of blindness. ❸ The eye is ideally suited for laser surgery because most of the eye tissue is transparent. ❹ Because of this transparency, the frequency and focus of the laser beam can be adjusted according to the absorption of the tissue so that the beam "cuts" inside the eye with minimal damage to the surrounding tissue—even the tissue between the laser and the incision. ❺ Lasers are also more effective than other methods in treating some causes of blindness. ❻ However, the interaction between laser light and eye tissue is not fully understood.

Language Focus: Linking Words and Phrases

As demonstrated in Task Seventeen, repetition and linking words and phrases can help a writer maintain flow and establish clear relationships between ideas. Table 1 lists some of the more common linking words and phrases, arranged according to their function and grammatical use.

TABLE 1. Linking Words and Phrases

Function	Subordinators (introduce a dependent clause that must be joined to a complete sentence)	Sentence Connectors (introduce a complete sentence or independent clause)	Phrase Linkers (introduce a noun phrase)
Addition		furthermore in addition moreover	in addition to
Adversativity	although even though despite the fact	however nevertheless	despite in spite of
Cause and effect	because since	therefore as a result consequently hence thus[1]	because of due to as a result of
Clarification		in other words that is i.e.	
Contrast	while whereas	in contrast however on the other hand conversely	unlike
Illustration		for example for instance	
Intensification		on the contrary as a matter of fact in fact	

[1] Note that *thus* may also be used in non-finite clauses of result, as in this example: *A fungus infected the fruit, thus causing a significant economic loss to the farmers.* See Unit Three for further discussion of this point.

Sentence connectors raise a small, but important, issue—namely, punctuation. Many general style guides and style guides for your specific area of study are available (online and in book form) that can provide detailed explanations of punctuation use. Therefore, we will limit our discussion to a few key points regarding semicolons (;), colons (:), dashes (—), and commas (,). (See Figure 3.)

1. Semicolons join two completely independent clauses or sentences and work much like a full stop.

   Air traffic delays due to high traffic volume have increased considerably over the last decade; these delays have become a major public policy issue.

2. Semicolons can be used with sentence connectors. In the following example, note the use of the comma after the connector.

   Increasing the size of airports is one solution to traffic congestion; however, this is a long-term solution whose benefits may not be seen for many years into the future.

3. Because semicolons are a "stronger" type of punctuation than commas (they mark a stronger break in the flow of ideas), they can be used to break sequences into parts.

   In recent years GNP growth rates have varied considerably for the countries in this study (China, 6%; U.S., 3%; Japan, 1%).

   Several researchers have examined whether capital income should be taxed in the steady state (Moriyama, 2003; Correia, 1996; Chamley, 1986).

4. Semicolons can be used to separate rather long items in a list.

   Some of the solutions to the air traffic delay problem include increasing the size of airports that routinely experience major flight delays; overhauling the air traffic control system so that more flights can be safely handled; and increasing landing fees (which are currently based on the weight of an aircraft) during peak periods.

FIGURE 3. Punctuation

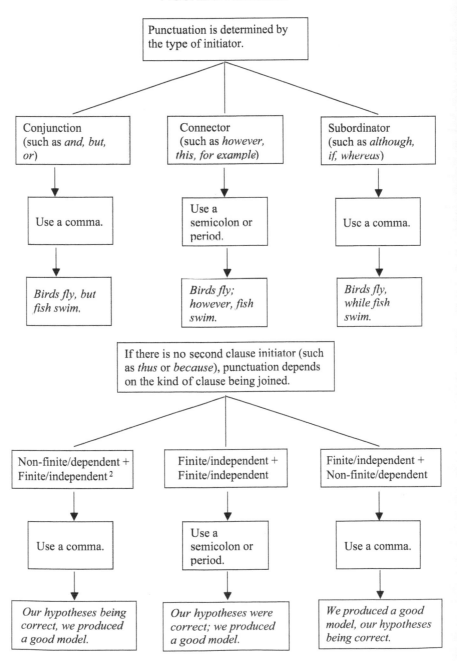

[2]A finite verb is a main verb that is inflected to indicate tense and person.

Although commas could be used in the preceding example, the length of the elements suggests that semicolons would work better; note the use of the semicolon before *and* toward the end of the sentence. Similar considerations apply to sentences that use a colon to introduce a list.

There are four main causes of airport congestion: bad weather, excessive volume, runway closures, and equipment outages.

There are four main causes of airport congestion: bad weather, such as a snowstorm, may ground planes; too many planes may be scheduled to arrive or depart within a short period; runways may be closed; and equipment may be out of service.

Sometimes a dash is used to introduce a list as well, but how you should choose between a dash and a comma is a matter of debate. Often dashes are used by authors to intrude into a sentence and to provide some additional information. Commas are used in a variety of situations. It is best to check a style manual for the many uses. For our purposes here, however, we will say only that commas are used with many of the subordinators.

Although weather is a major cause of airport delays, excess traffic volume is also a major factor.

5. Importantly, style manuals also have guidelines for semicolon uses. Refer to these for more information on semicolon use in your field.

TASK EIGHTEEN

Edit this passage by adding periods, semicolons, or commas where necessary.

Although most major companies provide their employees with email accounts as well as internet access many of these companies are concerned about potential abuse and monitor their employees' use of these media. In fact more than 75% of all major corporations report that they monitor their employees' use of email and internet access either by spot-checking or constant surveillance. Businesses have many reasons for monitoring email and internet use for example they may be concerned about protecting sensitive company information in addition they may be worried about lawsuits arising from sexual harassment because of mass mailing of offensive jokes they may also want to identify employees who are surfing the internet rather than working. In other words they are concerned about cyberslacking.

TASK NINETEEN

Supply linking words or phrases to enhance the flow of one of these passages. Look carefully at the punctuation to help you make an appropriate choice. Once you have made your choices, consider why the linking words are important and why an old-to-new pattern of information flow alone might not be adequate.

A. It has long been documented that individuals in an organization may voluntarily carry out tasks that are not part of their regular job duties. _____, individuals may go above and beyond the call of duty to help coworkers, prevent problems, or volunteer to stay late when not expected to do so. This behavior is intended to help others in the organization or the organization itself and is often referred to as organizational citizenship behavior (OCB).

_____ it is recognized that OCB is important for an organization to effectively function, there is debate among researchers as to how OCB can be encouraged and rewarded. This debate is further complicated when considering the role of OCB in multinational corporations pursuing global diversity. Most OCB research has focused on Western cultures; _____, whether these research findings can be extended to other cultures is not clear, _____ suggesting a need to investigate OCB as it exists in other cultures, particularly those described as "collectivist."

B. Shape Memory Alloys (SMA) are a group of metallic materials that can return to some previously defined shape or size when subjected to the appropriate temperature. When some SMA are cold they can be deformed at a low temperature; _____, when the material is heated above this temperature it undergoes a change in crystal structure, _____ causing it to return to its original shape. Some materials exhibit shape memory only when heated; others can undergo a shape change both when heated and when cooled. _____ many alloys are known to have the ability to "remember" their shape, only some may actually find widespread commercial use. Of particular interest are those that can recover sub-stantial amounts of strain or that generate significant force upon changing shape. _____, one common nickel and titanium SMA, Nitinol, has this ability and is being used in surgical implants, clamps, miniature valves and switches, and other devices.

This and Summary Phrases

As indicated earlier, *this/these* + a noun can be used to establish a good old-to-new flow of information. Consider the following sentences.

> Writing instructors know that students need to understand the differences between formal and informal language. *This understanding* can help students make strategic choices in their writing.

What does *this understanding* refer to? Consider the following sentences.

> In recent years, the number of students applying to PhD programs has increased steadily, while the number of places available has remained fairly constant. *This situation* has resulted in intense competition for admission.

What does *this situation* refer to? What is the effect of using *this* instead of *that?*

The phrases in italics contain a summary noun or word that refers back to the idea in the previous sentence. They summarize what has already been said and pick up where the previous sentence has ended. You may have noticed in your academic reading that *this* is not always followed by a noun—that is, *this* is unsupported or unattended. Keep in mind, however, that if there is a possibility your reader will not understand what *this* is referring to, your best strategy is to follow *this* with a noun so that your meaning is clear.

TASK TWENTY

Choose a noun to complete the second sentence of each set of sentences. More than one answer may be possible.

1. According to a recent survey, 26% of all American adults, down from 38% 30 years ago, now smoke. This _____ can be partly attributed to the mounting evidence linking smoking and fatal diseases, such as cancer.

   a. decline   b. decrease   c. drop   d. improvement   e. reduction

   Can you think of any other nouns that could complete the sentence?

2. Early in September each year, the population of Ann Arbor, Michigan, suddenly increases by about 25,000 as students arrive for the new academic year. This _____ changes the character of the town in a number of ways.

   a. increase   b. influx   c. invasion   d. jump   e. rise

   Can you think of any other nouns that could complete the sentence?

   _____

3. Nowadays, laptop computers are lighter, more powerful, and easier to use than they were five years ago. These _____ have led to an increase in the sales of these machines.

   a. advances   b. changes   c. developments   d. improvements

   Can you think of any other nouns that could complete the sentence?

   _____

As the task indicates, the noun that you choose to follow *this/these* can provide a strong interpretive signal that reveals your stance (see Unit Six). By revealing your stance you communicate not only what you know, but also what you think.

TASK TWENTY-ONE

Choose a summary word from the list to complete each sentence. Can you think of other possible summary words in addition to those on the list?

difficulty	estimation	problem	situation
disruption	finding	process	view

1. The traditional economic and consumer behavior models assume a rational, thoughtful consumer who gathers information about a good and then carefully makes a purchase. This _____ has recently been challenged, particularly because of the growing number of consumer choices.

2. Our pilot study has shown that wind turbines used to generate electricity can pose a threat to flying birds. This _____ suggests a need for further research on improving the safety of these mechanisms.

3. In soccer, goalkeepers routinely wear gloves that may restrict heat loss from the hands and cause discomfort. In order to alleviate this _____, special materials, called phase control materials (PCMs), have been incorporated into gloves to reduce the amount of heat inside the glove, thus maintaining a comfortable temperature.

4. Normal average human skin temperature is 37°C. At any lower environmental temperature, heat will be lost from the skin to the environment as the body attempts to heat up the air in direct contact with the body. This _____ is known as conduction.

5. Until adjustment of the body clock has occurred, individuals suffering from "jet lag" feel tired during the new daytime, yet are unable to sleep properly during the new night. For athletes in particular this _____ of sleep can affect mood and powers of concentration and might result in poorer training performances and competition results (Reilly et al., 1997b).

6. Until recently, the support needs of frail older people in Sweden have been met primarily by the state, with there being little expectation that the family would provide care. This _____ is now changing as increasing emphasis is being placed on the role of the family.

TASK TWENTY-TWO

Now try to find your own summary words that can complete these sentences.

1. Irrigation in sub-Saharan Africa is in most cases performed using a rope and bucket to raise and distribute water from a shallow open well. While this _____ has the advantage of being inexpensive, its low capacity and labor-intensive nature is decidedly a disadvantage.

2. Motor vehicle deaths in the U.S. declined from nearly 60,000 in 1966 to just over 40,000 in 2011, even though Americans drive millions more miles now and millions more vehicles are on the road. The death rate, which was 7.6 deaths per 100 million miles in 1950, declined from 5.5 in 1966 to 1.6 in 2011. This _____ can be attributed to the manufacture of safer vehicles with features such as airbags and antilock brakes.

3. Haigney concludes from his study that driving performance decreases when drivers use their cell phones. This _____ is consistent with recent reviews of the literature on driving distractions.

4. Although it seems that the construction of new roads and widening of existing roads should reduce traffic congestion, recent research has shown that these activities actually lead to increases in traffic. This _____ is known as the "induced traffic" effect.

5. In 1900, average life expectancy at birth was 47 years for individuals born in developed countries. In 1950, life expectancy was nearly 68. For newborns today, life expectancy is about 77 years. This _____, however, does not mean that humans are undergoing some physiological change. Rather, it is a result of advances in medicine and technology.

Summary expressions may be expanded into longer phrases to add clarity or interpretation. However, you should weigh the benefits of expanding the summary phrase. A long and possibly complicated summary phrase may actually be less effective.

Consider the opening sentences and Options a–d. Which of the options would you choose as the fourth sentence?

6. In Sub-Saharan Africa, only 20% of all households have access to financial services. In 2010, nearly 70 percent of Kenyan households either had no bank accounts or relied on informal sources of finance. In 2011, 13 commercial banks were operating in Benin, a country with a population of 10 million.

    a. This limits market exchanges, increases risk, and limits opportunities to save.

    b. This lack limits market exchanges, increases risk, and limits opportunities to save.

    c. This lack of formal financial services limits market exchanges, increases risk, and limits opportunities to save.

    d. This lack of formal financial services in parts of Africa limits market exchanges, increases risk, and limits opportunities to save.

Finally, we need to say something about whether it is better to use *it* or *this* to refer back to something stated earlier in the text.

TASK TWENTY-THREE

Which sentence in each set makes better sense following the main sentence? While all of the choices are grammatically correct, which one seems to better capture the connection?

1. Voice over Internet Protocol (VoIP) has been rapidly expanding over the past decade, growing at a rate of nearly 200%.

    a. It can be partially attributed to local telephone service providers, who were not specialized telecommunications operators, entering the VoIP market.

    b. This can be partially attributed to local telephone service providers, who were not specialized telecommunications operators, entering the VoIP market.

2. Our survey reveals an extremely high level of confidence that businesses are well equipped to prevent targeted cyber attacks by outsiders—94% of the businesses that responded described themselves as fairly or very confident.

   a. It suggests that the reality of the threats facing businesses has not been made clear.

   b. This unexpected finding suggests that the reality of the threats facing businesses has not been made clear.

3. Researchers have found that it is easier to start a traffic jam than to stop one. A small, but temporary, increase in the number of cars entering a highway can cause a bottleneck; however, after the number of cars decreases, traffic jams generally continue.

   a. It has been verified through the use of sensor data from Germany and the Netherlands.

   b. This has been verified through the use of sensor data from Germany and the Netherlands.

   c. This phenomenon has been verified through the use of sensor data from Germany and the Netherlands.

   d. This traffic phenomenon has been verified through the use of sensor data from Germany and the Netherlands.

Although up to this point we have emphasized *this* + noun, we know, in fact, that there are occasions when "unattended" *this* (no following noun) is perfectly reasonable. A study by Wulff et al. (2012) based on MICUSP demonstrated that unattended *this* is common with these verbs: *be* (overwhelmingly the most common), *mean, lead, result, have,* and *suggest.* As you can see, many of these verbs are short and simple and allow the author to offer an interpretation or explanation, as can be seen in the common phrase *this is because . . . .*

Presentation

Most instructors tolerate small errors in language in papers written by non-native speakers—for example, mistakes in article or preposition usage. However, errors that instructors think could have been avoided by careful proofreading are generally considered less acceptable. These include the use of an incorrect homophone (a word that sounds exactly like another, such as *too/to/two*); basic grammar errors (e.g., subject-verb agreement); and misspelled words, including those that are not identified in a computer spell-check routine. The issue of grammar errors is a complicated one since many instructors do not appreciate how difficult it is to master some aspects of English such as articles (*a, an,* and *the*) and prepositions. We believe that if the flow of ideas is good, small errors may not be noticed; when the flow of ideas is not strong—i.e., does not follow the old-to-new principle—grammar errors may be more pronounced. Thus, it makes more sense to us to focus more on content and information flow first and then tend to matters of grammar only after all other aspects of the paper are in good shape. Finally, your work is more likely to receive a positive response if you consider these questions.

1. Does the information flow in an expected manner?

   Look at the beginnings and ends of all sentences to see if there is a content bridge linking them backward and forward. If there is no content bridge, revise to establish one or consider adding a linking word or phrase.

2. Consider the overall format of your written work.

   Does your paper seem to have been carefully prepared? Are there clear paragraphs? Is the line spacing correct? Have you used standard fonts and font sizes? Have you tried to follow the style of your field (APA, MLA, IEEE, Chicago Style, to name a few)? If you are unsure of the style common in your field, be sure to learn which to use.

3. Proofread for grammatical accuracy.

   Do subjects and verbs agree? Have the appropriate verb tenses been used? Have the articles *a, an,* and *the* been used when necessary? Is *the* used too much? Do not automatically make changes based on suggestions from the grammar checker of your word processor. Some suggestions, such as changing from passive voice to active voice, may result in a poor connection of ideas.

4. Check for misspelled words, even if you have spell-checked your work.

   Has the correct homophone been used? Did the spell-checker miss anything?

TASK TWENTY-FOUR

Read this draft of a short discussion of earthquakes in Turkey and the instructor comments on pages 51–52. Discuss each comment with a partner and then decide whether it is R (reasonable) or U (unreasonable). If you are unsure, indicate this with a question mark (?). Consider then if and how you would revise the text. Finally, write a new draft, taking into account other advice given in the unit.

❶ Turkey is located in a region that is shaken by severe earthquakes. ❷ They occurred almost every year. ❸ Central Anatolian Fault Zone is one of the most active fault zones in the world, and it lies along the northern part of the country, going from south east to northwest. ❹ The reason of that most of these severe earthquakes causes a lot of damage and death of many people is not only the nature of the fault zone, but also that there are many cities and highways settled on it.

❺ Because many cities have been built on or within the vicinity of geologic fault. ❻ They are unquestionably prone to earthquakes. ❼ There are many earthquakes each year. ❽ The most serious damage occurred in August 1999. ❾ It affected a big area and caused approximately 20,000 people death and millions dollars physical damage in three cities. ❿ Too prevent such big damage and loss in the future, researchers have been researching the 1999 earthquake. ⓫ They looked at the excellent seismic records from recording stations near the epicenter of earthquake and saw that there were signs of earthquake. ⓬ They might help to develop some early warning systems to be aware of the upcoming shakings. ⓭ Even these can make warnings as short as 10 seconds before the shakings, if there is a well-planned evacuation plan, they may, at least, help to decrease the death toll of an earthquake.

Instructor's Comments

You have a good topic here and a good starting point. Your problem-solution organization is clear, which is very important. Here are a few suggestions for making your text even better.

____ 1. Although overall I understand the message you want to convey, I think it would help to add some more information in a few spots. For instance, in Sentence 9, "a big area" is rather vague. Can you be more precise? Also, in Sentence 9 you mention 3 cities were damaged. Should you give the names and the cost of the damage in each?

____ 2. In the first paragraph think about clarifying for your reader that the earthquakes originate in the Central Anatolian Fault Zone. Establish the connection. Also, what about including a map so that readers can see where the fault zone is?

____ 3. In Sentence 4 keep your focus on the earthquakes. Beginning the sentence with <u>the reason that the earthquakes cause a lot of damage</u> suggests that you have already stated that the earthquakes cause a lot of damage. Of course, readers should know that earthquakes cause serious damage, but I think you should say this. Consider beginning this sentence by saying that the earthquakes cause a lot of damage and then continue with your explanation.

____ 4. What do you think about giving some actual figures for the total cost of the damage and perhaps give an example of the most serious form of damage?

____ 5. In Sentence 11 you mention signs of the earthquake. What kind of signs?

____ 6. The connection of your points in Sentences 1–3 could be improved. I see what you're saying, but you could say it more efficiently. The point in Sentence 2 could be woven into Sentence 1. This would also eliminate the past tense in Sentence 2, which should not be used because you are making a statement of fact.

___ 7. I like the use of the word _excellent_ in Sentence 11 since this gives your reader a sense of what you think. You can position yourself better if you include some language that indicates your perspective; just reporting what others say or giving dry facts will not help you distinguish yourself. While _excellent_ is okay, I wonder whether you can find a better word here. What is it about the data that makes it excellent?

___ 8. Sentence 5 is not a complete sentence. _Because_ introduces a dependent clause that can't stand alone. Can you think of a way to connect this sentence to the following one? Or make some other change?

___ 9. In Sentence 6 can you really say _unquestionably?_ It seems a bit dramatic.

___ 10. Do you really need Sentence 7? I'm not sure it adds much. Sentence 7 just seems rather disconnected. Can you integrate the information somewhere else?

___ 11. In Sentence 9 the referent for the pronoun _it_ is not 100% clear. What is "_it_"?

___ 12. Sentence 9 describes a way to possibly minimize the destructiveness of earthquakes. Can you think of a smoother transition into the solution here? Something like _one way to . . ._ or _one possible method of . . ._?

___ 13. Can you find another word for _make_ in Sentence 13? I understand what you are saying, but we usually don't use _make_ with _warning_.

___ 14. Before turning in your next draft, be sure to check the overall old-to-new flow of ideas. Be sure content and organization are in good shape; then check the grammar; and then in your final step of proofreading, check the flow.

Positioning

Now that you are familiar with some characteristics of academic writing, you are ready to "position" or establish yourself as a junior member of your chosen field (see Figure 4).

FIGURE 4. Positioning

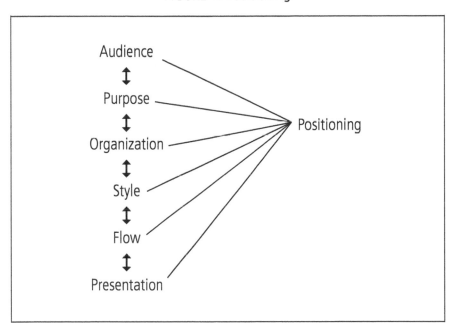

TASK TWENTY-FIVE

Mark these writing characteristics as H (helpful for positioning) or U (unhelpful for positioning). In some cases, there is room for disagreement. Explain your choices.

1. Choosing any writing style that you like   ——

2. Expressing enthusiasm and commitment   ——

3. Writing in a formal academic style   ——

4. Making broad generalizations throughout a text   ——

5. Being cautious about generalizations   ——

6. Using references to support your points   ——

7. Writing mainly from experience and personal knowledge ——

8. Reevaluating the work of authorities in the field   ——

9. Showing an awareness of the "hot" issues in your field   ——

Unit Two

General-Specific and Specific-General Texts

We have chosen to begin our focus on writing tasks with a type of text sometimes referred to as general-specific (GS). As the name suggests, the structure of these texts involves movement from broader statements to more specific ones. At the end of this unit, we will also introduce texts that move in the opposite direction, namely from specific detail to more general content. Such texts are common in a variety of fields such as Art History, History, and Literature, but you may find exemplars of this writing strategy in other fields where it may be helpful to orient the reader by providing "immediate contact" with an object or context (Bondi, 2007).

GS texts are quite common in graduate student writing, and they are comparatively straightforward. The GS pattern can be used at the paragraph level as well as for larger units of discourse, such as a series of paragraphs in a section or even the text as a whole. GS organization is often used to structure an introduction for a longer piece of writing. A GS pattern can help you produce

a. an answer to an examination question

b. a course paper

c. an opening paragraph of an assignment

d. background (or scene-setting) to an analysis or discussion.[1]

GS texts typically begin with one of the following: a short or extended definition, a generalization or purpose statement, a statement of fact, or some interesting statistics. While the overall movement is from more general

---

[1] Choices b, c, and d may also take the form of a descriptive or evaluative summary of previous studies. See Unit Five.

to specific, these texts can widen out again in the final sentence. The shape is
similar to that of a glass or funnel with a base (see Figure 5).

FIGURE 5. Shape of a GS Text

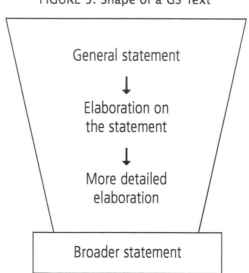

TASK ONE

Here are excerpts from a published paper entitled "Reality TV
Formats: The Case of Canadian Idol" from the *Canadian Journal of
Communication* (Baltruschat, 2009). Read them and answer the
questions on pages 57–59.

A. From documentaries to docu-soaps and game-docs

❶ The emergence of reality TV represents a shift from what
Kilborn (2003) calls the more "serious" representation of socio-
historical events to programming that is produced predomi-
nantly for entertainment purposes. ❷ Reality programs are
linked to different documentary forms, such as documentary
journalism, cinéma vérité traditions, and the observational documentary. ❸ However, due to elements of popular entertainment programming (e.g., talk shows, game shows, and soap
operas), reality TV ultimately creates its own generic map.
❹ Commenting on these programs, Hill (2005, p. 50) suggests

a fact/fiction continuum, which reflects the sliding scale of factuality. ⑤The continuum covers contemporary documentaries and popular factual entertainment ranging from docu-soaps and game-docs to makeovers and quiz shows.

1. How does the author take readers from the general opening emphasis on reality TV to the final focus on "docu-soaps and game-docs to makeovers and quiz shows"? Would you agree that the first sentence provides a more general point than the last one?

2. Take a closer look at the information flow. Underline the beginning (or opening) focus of each sentence. Except for Sentence 1, for each sentence opening, can you find a connection to some similar information in the previous sentence? If so, how does this contribute to the information flow?

3. Do you think the author could have started with this variation of Sentence 4? Why or why not?

④ In her research on reality TV, Hill (2005, p. 50) suggests a fact/fiction continuum, which reflects the sliding scale of factuality.

4. Read the next paragraph of the text. Does it logically flow from the first? How did you decide this?

B. ⑥ Similar to documentaries, reality programs aim for the "articulation of the authentic self" in order to depict "moments of truth" (Holmes, 2004, p 159). ⑦Tele-confessionals in designated video rooms and individual strategies for winning the game provide intimate accounts of unfolding events. ⑧ Also, slightly off-the-mark camera angles and out-of-focus shots contribute to a sense of immediacy and intimacy with characters and suggest a "fly-on-the-wall" experience for viewers. ⑨ Reality TV producers aim for this "tele-factuality" (Corner, 2002, p. 257), which is reflected in statements such as "the camera doesn't lie, [e]specially up close" (*Canada's Next Top Model*, Citytv, 2006). ⑩ Similarly, the executive producer of

Big Brother states, "I wanted it to look live and exciting. . . . [T]his was not meant to be a polished drama. *We were filming it for real*, and it was a virtue of the programme that viewers understood that" (Ruth Wrigley, cited in Ritchie, 2000, p. 11, italics added). ⑪ Indeed, Lewis (2004) refers to a "tele-reality" into which people from the "everyday world" are submerged to perform their role. ⑫ Viewers understand this blurring of boundaries between the public, private, and "adjacent realities" (Lewis, 2004, p. 295). ⑬ And they find pleasure in looking for moments of "truth" that may shine through improvised perform-ances (Hill, 2005).

5. Now compare Sentence 1 and Sentence 13. The text has moved from talking about reality TV in general to the very specific point about viewers' understanding of the genre and the "truth." Can you outline how the author has created this general-to-specific discussion?

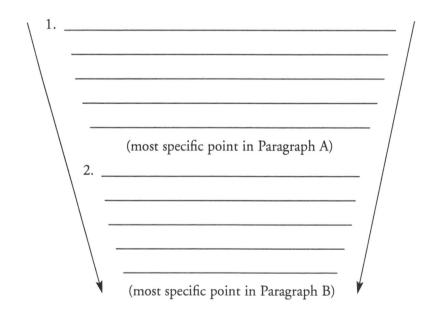

1. _____

_____

_____

_____

_____

(most specific point in Paragraph A)

2. _____

_____

_____

_____

_____

(most specific point in Paragraph B)

6. How much repetition of vocabulary is present in the text? Did you notice the repetition when you first read it or only after you began analyzing the text?

7. Why is *truth* in Sentence 13 in quotation marks?

8. Note that Sentence 13 begins with *and.* How common is *and* in sentence-initial position in your field? Are you comfortable using it? If not, can you suggest another linking expression?

9. Overall, how easy or challenging is this text to read? What features contribute to your opinion?

10. Does the text give the impression that the author is knowledgeable? Why or why not?

The GS passage on reality TV is not unlike a response to a paper assignment in a Communications or Sociology course. An assigned topic might be something like this.

> Are reality TV programs similar to or different from traditional documentaries?

Alternatively, the passage could also have been the opening paragraph to a different assignment—perhaps one asking students to analyze a reality TV program. Or it could have been an assignment focusing on the aims of reality TV.

Central to creating a GS text is your strategy for information flow. You want to be sure that the text is indeed becoming more specific. Let's look more closely at how this is accomplished in this text on plug-in hybrid electric vehicles.

❶ The increasing popularity of electric vehicles (EVs) and plug-in hybrid electric vehicles (PHEVs) is attributed to the savings in fuel costs compared to conventional internal combustion engine (ICE) vehicles. ❷ EVs and PHEVs save energy due to the employment of reverse regenerating braking during the deceleration cycle. ❸ This energy is typically stored in batteries and/or ultracapacitors (UCs). ❹ The incorporation of on-board energy storage systems (ESS) and generation in PHEVs has been facilitated and dictated by the market demands for enhanced performance and range.

Amjadi and Williamson, 2009.

This text is a good example of old-to-new information flow. In Sentences 1 and 2 the old information is electric vehicles. Sentence 2 also introduces *energy* as some new and more specific information. *Energy* is then picked up in Sentence 3 as old information, and the sentence introduces *ultracapacitors* as new information. *Ultracapacitors* marks a clear narrowing of the topic, which in Sentence 4 now focuses on on-board energy storage and generation. In just a few sentences, the topic narrowed from the broad focus on electric vehicles to energy storage as well as performance and range of electric vehicles. This has been accomplished by strategically picking up some new information at the end of one sentence and providing more information on the new topic.

TASK TWO

Discuss with a partner how well the author moves the information from general to specific.

❶ The tragedy of the commons refers to the tendency to overuse common resources without controls or regulations. ❷ The tragedy of the commons was described in terms of herders sharing a common parcel of land (Hardin, 1968). ❸ Although the tragedy of the commons is an old concept, it remains a serious problem in the world. ❹ Most of the present environment and natural resource issues can be tied to this concept. ❺ Today this concept is applied to "global" commons such as transboundary pollution, tropical deforestation, and climate change. ❻ According to Dietz, Ostrom, & Stern (2007), environmental resources should be governed to protect the commons. ❼ Sustained research on both domestic and international policies (Dietz et al., 2007) is also necessary to determine the appropriate regulatory policies.

As in many GS texts, the electric vehicle passage (and the one on page 60) began with a general statement. General statements of fact or tendency can often be useful starting points of papers and sections of papers. In fact, our small study of a subset of student papers in MICUSP[2] revealed that this was overwhelmingly the most common choice of openings among students. Other common ways to begin a paper include providing some interesting statistics, a quotation, or a definition.

Opening with General Statements

General statements can include those providing facts as well as broad statements made about a topic that are usually, but not necessarily always, true. Here are a few examples.

> Individuals in organizations exhibit a wide range of behaviors, from the minimalist who does the least possible to maintain membership to those who go beyond expectations, engaging in extra-role behavior to promote the effective operation of the organization or to benefit others.

> In the last decade, tremendous strides have been made in the science and technology of organic light-emitting diodes (OLEDs).

> Medical tourism is growing in countries such as Thailand, Malaysia, and the Philippines.

Generalizations that you anticipate readers are likely to accept can be effective opening sentences. By beginning with information that is generally accepted, you begin with something familiar to the readers, and ease them into your paper. While you may worry whether starting with familiar information is a good strategy, in many fields this may be preferred over starting with a highly challenging or provocative claim. Why do you suppose this is?

After making a general statement, some support or explanation for the statement should be offered, which, as we have discussed, helps move the passage from general to specific. Support can take the form of specific detail or perhaps a citation to earlier work. Whether you begin a GS text with a general statement or a definition is a matter of personal preference. However, sometimes one may be a strategically better choice than the other.

---

[2] The Michigan Corpus of Upper-level Student Papers is available at www.elicorpora.info/.

Suppose, for instance, the topic assigned is "The English Language." Now, if we were to write on this topic as linguists and the audience was a professor in Linguistics, we might open the text with a definition.

> English is a language that belongs to the West Germanic subgroup of the Indo-European language family. It began its history as a distinct tongue in England around 500 ACE.

However, in other circumstances, depending on your purpose, it may be a better strategy to start with a generalization.

> In comparison to many of the world's better-known languages, English is relatively new. Indeed, the English of 600 years ago can be understood only by specialists.

> Although Chinese has the greatest number of native speakers, English is the most widely distributed language in the world today. This position derives from the fact that English is widely taught as a second language in schools and widely used in international communication as a lingua franca.

TASK THREE

Three pairs of sentences are shown on page 63, each consisting of a definition and a generalization. When would it be better to begin a text with the first sentence in each pair rather than the second?

<u>Example</u>

    A. Plug-in hybrid electric vehicle (PHEV) technology is considered a potential near-term approach to addressing global warming and U.S. dependency on foreign oil in the transportation sector as the cost, size, and weight of batteries are increasingly reduced.

    B. A plug-in hybrid electric vehicle (PHEV) combines the propulsion capabilities of a traditional combustion engine with an electric motor.

Sentence A may be good for either expert or non-expert readers. The information in Sentence A seems broadly accessible since readers should be familiar with global warming and dependency on foreign oil. Although most definitions often work for an audience that is unfamiliar with the topic to be addressed, the definition in Sentence B might be too technical for a broad audience. So, it seems that Sentence B would be best for an audience familiar with concepts like propulsion and traditional combustion engines. In the end, audience matters.

1. a. Since their introduction, social network sites (SNSs) such as MySpace, Facebook, RenRen, and Bebo have attracted millions of users, many of whom have integrated these sites into their daily practices. As of this writing, there are hundreds of SNSs, with various technological affordances, supporting a wide range of interests and practices.

   b. According to Messinger et al. (2009) a social networking website is a platform in which members can (a) easily create "profiles" with information about themselves, and (b) define their "trusted" circle of friends.

2. a. Since their discovery in the late 1970s, hydrothermal vents associated with mid-oceanic ridges have fascinated scientists of various disciplines.

   b. A hydrothermal vent is a fissure in a planet's surface from which geothermally heated water emerges (Lal, 2008). Such vents are commonly found near volcanically active places, areas where tectonic plates are moving apart, and new crust is being formed.

3. a. Folk art is often defined as an art form created out of everyday materials by untrained artists.

   b. Folk art distinguishes itself from what is commonly known as fine art in that it has been and remains an important link in cultural transmission.

Opening with Statistics

Statistics can be particularly effective openings to GS texts because they can sometimes generate reader interest in the text, as demonstrated by this excerpt from a student paper written for a mechanical engineering course.

> In the United States in 2006, 4,784 pedestrians were killed in traffic accidents. Because a larger percentage of Americans use private vehicles than walk or use public transportation compared to people in many countries in the European Union and around the world, less attention is given in the U.S. to pedestrian safety than in these more pedestrian-friendly countries. In addition, though numerous efforts have been made to improve vehicle passenger safety (air bags, crumple zones, et cetera), no similar effort to protect pedestrians has been initiated. While pedestrians were involved in just over 1% of all traffic accidents in 2006, these vulnerable road users accounted for over 12% of all traffic fatalities.

MICUSP File MEC.G1.03.1

TASK FOUR

Discuss with a partner whether opening a GS text with some statistics is possible in your field of study. Why are such openings potentially interesting for readers? Now look at this GS opening from a student paper in Economics and answer the questions on page 65.

> ❶ Between 1992 and 1995, an international lysine cartel that included five companies illegally colluded on prices around the world. ❷ Lysine is an amino acid used as a feed additive for enhancing muscle growth in livestock. ❸ Prior to the collusive agreement, worldwide sales of lysine were over $600 million annually and this figure increased by $200 million following the price-fixing arrangement.

MICUSP File ECO.G0.02.2

1. What message is the author trying to convey in the first three sentences?

2. The purpose of this paper was to examine the extent to which economic models on collusion describe collusion in the lysine industry. Do you think this is an effective opening? Why or why not?

3. What is the purpose of Sentence 2? How important is this sentence?

Opening with Definitions

Definitions are a common way of getting started; they are "hooks" from which GS paragraphs can be hung. Such paragraphs typically open with full-sentence definitions. Textbooks, in contrast, often introduce the definitional information as a minor part of the sentence, as in this example:

> The majority of corporate profits, or earnings after all the operating expenses have been deducted, are subject to tax by the government.

Textbook definitional information is used to clarify terms that may be unfamiliar to the reader. However, this is not your task if your audience is already familiar with the terms and expects you to write a text that demonstrates your understanding of concepts.

In the next part of this unit, we will highlight certain aspects of the structure of these key definitional sentences. We will then consider more extended definitions, contrastive definitions (e.g., organic versus inorganic chemistry), and comparative definitions (i.e., discussions of the advantages and disadvantages of competing definitions).

Writing a Definition

The term *definition* comes from the Latin word *definio*, which means "to limit or bound; to interpret ideas or words in terms of each other; to understand one thing by another." A definition sets the boundaries for a word's meaning. As you are aware, one term can have different meanings depending on the context. The dictionary definition of *cold*, for example, usually has something to do with low temperature or a deficiency of heat. But *cold* is a relative term whose meaning changes with context. In the following text, how does the author define *particularly cold* for the reader?

> Only when environmental conditions are particularly cold, for
> example during winter conditions at latitudes above about 50°
> in either hemisphere, or when cold is associated with windy and
> especially wet conditions, or when the athlete exercises in cold
> water for prolonged periods, does the risk arise that the athlete will
> lose heat faster than he or she can produce it.
> Noakes, 2000.

Words and phrases may also have different meanings depending on the field of study. For example, *tone* has several definitions. In Music, a *tone* can be a sound of distinct pitch, quality, and duration; while in Linguistics, *tone* can refer to the rise or fall of the voice on a particular syllable (as in Chinese). In Interior Design, *tone* may be a color or shade of color. And, finally, *tone* in Physiology may be used to describe the normal state of elastic tension or partial contraction in resting muscles.

Apart from disciplinary differences in the meaning of a term, meanings may differ within some fields of study; this is not uncommon in the social sciences and the humanities. In these fields the definition of a term may not be agreed on by members of the discipline; there may be multiple or competing definitions, each of which has merit. An awareness of these differences may be critical for your reading as well as your writing. Indeed, to quote Boggs (2009), "Definitions are curious things. On the surface, one resembles another, sometimes more closely, sometimes less. Beneath their surface, however, lurks the essential quality that differentiates one definition from another, a quality that makes that definition unique to its referent."

To illustrate, while we may all have an understanding of *fast food*, definitions of the concept differ for different research purposes and it may be necessary to clearly state the definition so as to avoid misunderstanding or criticism. Even within the sciences there is a need for clarifying concepts such as high blood pressure, for which there are no universally accepted pressure readings (which in turn can complicate comparisons of study outcomes). Even in the sciences there are occasionally debates regarding the meaning of important concepts such as noise. We will return to the issue of multiple definitions later.

To sum up, we suggest that you offer a definition of a term or concept if one or more of the following apply

1. the term or concept is perhaps unfamiliar to your readers

2. you need to display your understanding for a course paper or examination

3. the origin of the term is interesting or sheds light on the meaning (as in our definition of *definition* earlier)

4. there is a lack of agreement on or some ambiguity surrounding the meaning

TASK FIVE

List some terms in your own field with meanings different from those in everyday life. In Engineering, you might consider the word *chip* or *jitter*. In Business, Computer Science, or Automotive Engineering, you might consider the word *crash*. Engineers may also consider *noise*. What about a *cloud*? Now define one or two of those terms as we did for *tone* in Linguistics and Physiology.

Some Common Ways to Define in Academic Writing

Definitions are common in student papers and published papers. Definitions may simply be short, parenthetical additions to a sentence or perhaps a larger part of a paper. The extent of the definition depends on the purpose of the paper, the level of familiarity your audience has with the subject, and the extent to which there is an agreed-upon definition of the concept. Here are some common ways to define.

1. short definitions or "glosses" that give information about a term in a word or phrase and are placed within either parentheses or commas in a sentence; phrasal definitions signaled by such devices as *i.e.* or phrases such as *known as, defined as,* and *called*

2. sentence definitions, which are brief and somewhat similar to a dictionary definition

3. extended definitions, which are longer and more detailed than definitions found in dictionaries

Language Focus: Verbs in Defining and Naming

Here we offer a few points on verb choices for you to consider when you offer an explanation of a term.

a. The verb *name* itself is uncommon and seems restricted to a focus on the name itself.

> This new species was named *Ascochyta mycoparasitica*.

b. The verb *denote* is common but seems largely restricted to matters of notation.

> Any rotational velocity is usually denoted by *f*. Any vector in this paper will be denoted by a bold letter.

c. The verb *call* can be used in definitions, but using it in full sentences can be tricky. One danger in written papers is that it can give the impression of stating the obvious, as in this example.

> A book containing lists of word definitions is called a dictionary.

While this kind of definitional explanation may be fine when provided by the instructor, it may not work so well when writing for experts. Notice the general-to-specific order of information and the use of the passive in the following examples.

> This new method is called activity-based costing, or simply ABC.
>
> Fig. 15 shows two simple mirrors, bending around the light. The configuration may be called a two-dimensional corner reflector.

d. With more than a million hits on Google Scholar, the phrase *known as* would appear to be fairly common in definitional sentences.

> Another principle source of heat is the natural increase in temperature as the depth increases. This is known as the geothermal gradient.

e. The verb *define* is widely used and often represents a safe option, especially in more elaborate explanations and for terms or concepts that can be defined in more than one way.

> Shadow work may be defined as those subsistence activities engaged in by the homeless which are outside of the regular employment system, but not necessarily outside of the market system altogether (Ilich, 1981).

> For the purposes of this study, fast food is defined as food sold by a franchised restaurant chain offering both dining and take-out facilities with no "table" service (e.g., McDonald's).

> One important product attribute is perceived product sophistication, which I define here as the degree to which a product exhibits the latest technological advances.

In the preceding examples, what expressions suggest to you that other definitions may be possible?

f. Finally, the verb *refer to* is widely used in definition sentences in academic writing.

> The natural gas contained in coal formations is generally referred to as coal bed methane.

> Individuals may go above and beyond the call of duty to help coworkers, prevent problems, or volunteer to stay late when not expected to do so. This behavior is intended to help others in the organization or the organization itself and is often referred to as organizational citizenship behavior (OCB).

> Reductionism primarily refers to inappropriate simplification.

Identify the uses of the passive voice in the first two sample definitions. Why do you suppose passive voice was used?

Finally, remember that it is possible to simply place a short definition in parentheses after a term, as in this example.

> DNA microarrays (or gene chips) are an extremely powerful new tool in the field of genomics-based biotechnology.

TASK SIX

Identify and underline the definitional elements in each passage.

1. In addition to the examination of historical records, a study of the geologic record of past seismic activities, called paleo-seismology, can be used to evaluate the occurrence and size of earthquakes in the region. Geomorphic (surface landform) and trench studies may reveal the number of past seismic events, slip per event, and timing of the events at a specific fault.

2. The uncertainty associated with the energy obtained from other types of non-utility generators (NUGs), i.e., thermal and hydro, is relatively small compared to that associated with wind.

3. Average raw scores on IQ tests have been rising for years (Flynn, 1984, 1987, 1999), by an estimated three IQ points per decade (Neisser, 1998). This rise, known as the Flynn effect, has received much attention, though its exact nature was recently questioned.

4. Phytoremediation is the direct use of living green plants for *in situ*, or in place, risk reduction for contaminated soil, sediments, and groundwater.

5. Procrastination refers to deliberately putting off one's intended actions.

6. Software watermarking is a process in which identifying information is embedded into a file, enabling authors to control the distribution of and verify ownership of their digital information. The purpose of software watermarking is to protect the intellectual property that belongs to the author.

TASK SEVEN

Skim one or two journal articles in your area of study (perhaps the texts you examined in Task Fourteen of Unit One), looking for definitions. Highlight any definitions you find and try to categorize them as one of the types described. In which section of the article did you find the definitions? Why? Bring your findings to class.

A Brief Look at the Elements of Formal Sentence Definitions

Let us now look at formal sentence definitions. As we said earlier, sentence definitions are often a useful starting point for a GS paragraph. In a formal sentence definition, such as the examples that follow, the term being defined is first assigned to a class or group to which it belongs and then distinguished from other terms in the class. The class word is a superordinate—a category word one level of generality above the term. Some common superordinates, or class words, are *technique, method, process, device,* and *system* (Pearson, 1998).

> Annealing is a metalworking process in which a material is
> subjected to elevated temperatures for a period of time to
> cause structural or electrical changes in its properties.

To what class does annealing belong? How is it different from other members of the class, such as hammering or welding? So what we have here is this structure:

Term	*is/are*	*a/an* class	*that/wh-*word[3] + distinguishing detail
A solar cell	is	a device	that/which converts the energy of sunlight into electric energy.

Notice the use of the indefinite articles *a* and *an* in the first part of these definitions. Also note that the distinguishing information in the restrictive relative clause can be introduced by either a full or a reduced relative clause. (For more information on the grammar of definitions, see Appendix One.)

---

[3] Although some style manuals recommend using *that* instead of *which* in restrictive relative clauses, research shows that *which* continues to be used in definition statements. Therefore, we have used both *which* and *that* in the sample definitions presented in this unit.

Now notice also that in a full relative clause, the relative pronoun can be preceded by a preposition. The relative pronoun *which* must be used in this type of restrictive relative clause. This construction is common in formal academic writing.

> Organizational learning is a process through which firms develop new knowledge or insights.

> A bioactive material is a material on which bone-like hydroxyapatite will form selectively after it is immersed in a serum-like solution [1] and [5].

TASK EIGHT

Complete the definitions by inserting an appropriate preposition.

1. A thermometer is an instrument _____ which temperature can be measured.

2. Photosynthesis is a process _____ which sunlight is used to manufacture carbohydrates from water and carbon dioxide.

3. A credit bureau is an organization _____ which businesses can apply for financial information on potential customers.

4. An anhydride is a compound _____ which the elements of water have been removed.

5. An eclipse is a celestial event _____ which one body, such as a star, is covered by another, such as a planet.

6. An axis is an imaginary line _____ which a body is said to rotate.

7. Mentoring is a means _____ which professional values are imprinted and transmitted from one generation to the next.

8. Demography is a discipline that is concerned with changes in population size and the degree _____ which fertility (i.e., births), mortality (i.e., deaths), and migration (i.e., movement into and out of an area) contribute to these changes.

9. Energy balance is a state _____ which the number of calories eaten equals the number of calories used.

10. "Hotelling" is a new type of office design _____ which employees who mostly work at home or in the field are not given permanent offices but, rather, shared, temporary space as needed.

Whereby is commonly used in formal writing instead of *by which*, *by means of which*, and *through which*.

> Collective bargaining is a process whereby employers agree
> to discuss work-related issues with employee representatives.

Here are two final pieces of advice about writing formal definitions. First, if possible, avoid using any form of your term in the definition. Using the term itself in the definition can result in a circular or uninformative definition.

> Erosion is a process during which the surface of the earth
> erodes. →
> Erosion is a process during which the surface of the earth is
> degraded by the effects of the atmosphere, weather, and
> human activity.

Some authors, however, prefer to repeat the term (or a form of the term) to achieve clarity.

> Queries may be one-time queries or recurrent queries. A
> recurrent query is a query that an application submits to
> request that a sensing/actuation task be carried out or that
> an event be detected repetitively with a given frequency and
> for a given duration.

Second, if possible, use *when* and *where* in definitions only if necessary. These may seem overly informal to readers.

> Pollution is when the environment becomes contaminated as
> a result of human activity. →
> Pollution is a form of environmental contamination resulting
> from human activity.

> A fault is where there is a fracture in the earth's crust and the
> rock on one side of the fracture moves in relation to the rock
> on the other side. →
> A fault is a fracture in the Earth's crust in which the rock on
> one side of the fracture moves in relation to the rock on the
> other side.

TASK NINE

Write a one-sentence definition for one of the following terms or one term from your own field. Make sure you provide enough specific detail to distinguish your term from other members in its class.

a bridge	a conductor	a piano
a computer virus	a carcinogen	a syllabus
a laser	a migraine	arsenic (As)

Exchange and discuss your definition(s) with a partner.

Extended Definitions

So far we have dealt only with sentence definitions. In some cases, one sentence may be enough before continuing with a GS passage. However, in others, it may be relevant and important to expand the definition, particularly in a course paper. In this way, you can demonstrate your knowledge of a concept more fully. An extended definition usually begins with a general, one-sentence definition and then becomes more specific as additional details are provided. There may be a need to focus on aspects such as components, types, applications, history, or examples.

TASK TEN

Read the following extended definitions. Discuss with a partner the kind of information that has been included. Does the definition mainly discuss components, applications, history, examples, or something else?

1. A microscope is an optical instrument with which the apparent size of an object can be enhanced. A simple microscope consists of a double convex lens and a magnifying glass. A compound microscope, on the other hand, will contain more than one of each of these lenses, which are situated at the ends of a cylinder.

2. Pollution is a form of environmental contamination resulting from human activity. Some common forms of pollution are wastes from the burning of fossil fuels and sewage running into rivers. Even litter and excessive noise or light can be considered forms of pollution because of the impact they can have on the environment.

3. Perspective is a technique in art that is used to represent three-dimensional objects and depth relationships on a flat surface. Modern linear perspective (which involves making objects seem smaller the more distant they are from the observer) was probably first used in the 1400s by the artist Masaccio and the architects Filippo Brunelleschi and Leon Battista Alberti in Florence, Italy. Before this time, artists paid little attention to realistic perspective. In recent decades, many modern artists have returned to the practices of early artists and have abandoned realistic perspective.

4. An acrylic plastic is a polymer which can take a high polish, is clear and transparent, and can be shaped while hot. Because of these and other characteristics, acrylic plastic is used in situations where glass is not suitable or desirable, for instance, in certain types of windshields.

An extended definition may also include information regarding operating principles or causes and effects. A description of operating principles is also known as a *process analysis*. A process analysis has some unique characteristics, which will be discussed in greater detail in Unit Three, but we provide this example to illustrate.

Lateralization is a developmental process during which the two sides of the brain become specialized for different functions. As a child develops, the two sides of the brain become asymmetric in that each side controls different abilities. Language, for instance, is controlled by the left side of the brain and certain types of pattern recognition by the right. However, there is some disagreement as to when this specialization is complete. Some researchers believe the process is not complete until puberty, while others maintain that the brain is lateralized by age five.

Extended definitions may also include information about many other features, such as rarity and cost. You can even go beyond the type of specific detail just described and display your breadth of understanding by discussing problems, exceptions, and future predictions, as demonstrated by this text written by one of our students.

> A lab on a chip (LOC) is a microfluid device that integrates a variety of laboratory functions onto one chip that may be as small as a few centimeters or millimeters. The chips can be fabricated by standard photolithography and time controlled wet etching on a glass slide. Similar to electronic circuits that route the flow of electricity on computer chips without external controls, the microfluidic circuits etched onto a material regulate the flow of fluid through their devices without instructions from outside systems. A lab on a chip can analyze a volume of liquid 10,000 times (or more) smaller than that required for a conventional analytical instrument. A further advantage is that the work of an entire lab can be done on a single chip. Given their size and time-saving advantages LOC technologies will become key instruments in the process of diagnosing and fighting disease.
>
> H. J. Kim, minor editing

The LOC text was written by a student who knew the concept well enough to not need citations to other work; our examination of MICUSP, however, reveals that most students rely on one or more citations in their extended definitions, the reasons for which are taken up in Unit Eight. Some students use quoted material, but many use their own words so as to reveal their understanding. Note the use of citations in these two texts. In each case, the authors chose to use their own words and placed the original author and date in parentheses.

> Insomnia is defined as inadequate or poor sleep based on the quality of sleep, number of wakings in a night, length of time sleeping, and length of time spent awake during the night (Vincent et al., 2006). Causes of insomnia can be transient or chronic (Schenck, 2008).

Transient insomnia is related to sickness, stress, and traveling. Chronic insomnia is a disruption in sleep every night for more than 6 months. If untreated, insomnia can increase the risk for severe depression. When patients are treated for insomnia, they often report little change, even when sleep patterns improve. These poor sleep habits are also correlated with anxiety and increased worrying (Jansson-Fröjmark & Lindblom, 2008).

To accomplish the necessary increase in effluent* quality, the city government selected to upgrade to a membrane bioreactor (MBR) system. MBRs can be defined as systems that integrate biological treatment of wastewater with membrane filtration techniques. They offer several advantages compared to conventional biological treatment systems, including improved biodegradation efficiency, higher loading rates, lower sludge production, improved effluent quality, and smaller plant size. Additionally, MBRs eliminate settling problems, which are often troublesome in wastewater treatment (Cicek, 2002), and are more automated, allowing for less operator monitoring. Disadvantages associated with MBRs are mainly cost related, due to expensive membrane units, frequent membrane cleaning, and high energy demands.

In each text, the author used non-integral citations, placing the original author and date information in parentheses. In doing so, the focus remains on the content rather than the source of the information. The choice of citation form, therefore, can be very important in establishing a good flow of ideas.

---

*outflow from a sewer or sewage system.

TASK ELEVEN

Now read the extended definition by one of our students and answer the questions.

❶ Navigation is a process by which means of transport can be guided to their destination when the route has few or no landmarks. ❷ Some of the earliest navigators were sailors, who steered their ships first by the stars, then with a compass, and later with more complicated instruments that measured the position of the sun. ❸ We are reminded of this by the fact that the word navigation comes from the Latin word for "ship." ❹ However, the history and importance of navigation changed radically in the 20th century with the development of aircraft and missiles, which fly in three dimensions. ❺ Today, both ships and aircraft rely heavily on computerized navigational systems, known as Global Positioning System (GPS), that can provide a continuous, immediate, and accurate report of position. ❻ In fact, the capabilities of GPS render the older positioning technologies impractical and obsolete.

Benny Bechor, minor editing

1. What type of information is included in each of the sentences in the definition?
2. How is the passage organized?
3. What tenses are used for which sentences? Why?
4. Sentence 3 begins with *we*. Is this appropriate?
5. The term *navigation* is also used in connection with the internet. How and under what circumstances could this connection be included in the discussion?

Notice how the paragraph moves from a very general statement at the beginning to specific details and then "widens out" again in the final sentence to describe the current status of navigation. As noted at the beginning of this unit, this pattern is quite common in paragraphs of this type.

TASK TWELVE

Here are the sentences of a GS passage on an unusual but interesting topic. Work with a partner to put them back in the correct order. Write 1 next to the first sentence, 2 next to the second, and so on.

Palindromes

_____ a. The term itself comes from the Ancient Greek word *palindromos* meaning "running back again."

_____ b. Another good and more recent example is "draw pupils lip upward."

_____ c. Now, however, computers have allowed word puzzlers to construct palindromes that are thousands of words long, but these are simply lists of unrelated words that do not have meaning when taken together.

_____ d. A palindrome is a word or phrase that results in the same sequence of letters no matter whether it is read from left to right or from right to left.

_____ e. One of the classic long palindromes is "A man, a plan, a canal, Panama."

_____ f. Before we had computers, long palindromes used to be very hard to construct, and some word puzzlers spent immense amounts of time trying to produce good examples.

_____ g. Some common English words are palindromes, such as *pop, dad, noon,* and *race car.*

TASK THIRTEEN

This task presents a draft of a definition along with some instructor comments (see page 81). Revise the text after reading the comments. Re-write the entire passage to reflect the changes that you think are reasonable.

❶ Automotive airbag is occupant restraint system. ❷ It provides protection for occupant of vehicle in crash. ❸ Although airbags may seem to be somewhat recent innovation, rapidly inflating air cushions designed to prevent crash injuries existed for quite some time. ❹ Before being used in the automobiles. ❺ In fact researchers filed very first patents for inflatable safety cushion to be used in airplanes during World War II.

❻ A recent study by the National Highway Traffic Safety Administration concluded that airbags save nearly 1,000 lives annually. ❼ In the future even more lives will be saved as new airbag technologies are developed. ❽ Currently, for example, research is being done on as many as six different types of airbags that will offer protection in a wider range of accidents beyond front-end and side-impact collisions.

❾ Automotive airbag technology developed between 1940 and 1960 was quite similar to that of airbags currently in use. ❿ Those early airbag systems were very difficult to implement and costly. ⓫ The main concern for design engineers at the time centered on storage. ⓬ And the efficient release of compressed air. ⓭ The housing of the system had to be large enough for a gas canister. ⓮ The canister had to keep the gas at high pressure for a long period of time. ⓯ The bag itself had to have a special design. ⓰ It would deploy reliably and inflate within 40 milliseconds. ⓱ The solution to these problems came in the early 1970s with the development of small inflators. ⓲ Inflators used hot nitrogen instead of air to deploy the bag. ⓳ It allowed the widespread installation of airbags in vehicles beginning in the 1980s.

Instructor's Comments

Your draft looks pretty good. Tenses are just fine, but there still are a few things you need to work on.

1. Consider beginning with a formal sentence definition, as we discussed in class.

2. Take a look at the organization of the text. It seems to me that your text would flow better if you organized according to situation-problem-solution-evaluation in your definition.

3. Some of your sentences are incomplete and/or should be joined with another sentence to improve the flow of ideas. See specifically Sentences 3 and 4, 9 and 10, 15 and 16, and 17 and 18.

4. Add some connectors to improve the flow. Consider using a connector in Sentence 10. Sentences 13, 14, and 15 might also need connectors.

5. Your use of articles is generally good except for the first paragraph. Check each noun, and remember to consider whether it is a count or non-count noun as you make your choices about articles (a, an, the, Ø).

6. Sentence 19 would be clearer if you used this + summary word instead of it.

7. In Sentence 18, consider adding some description of nitrogen as a harmless gas. Use a short definition within the sentence.

8. In Sentences 6 and 8, consider placing the adverb in mid-position.

TASK FOURTEEN

Complete one of these tasks.

1. Write an extended definition of an important term or concept in your field of study. If you use references, be sure to use your own words and provide a citation to the sources. We ask you to use your own words so that your instructor will have an opportunity to give you feedback and to make sure that you do not engage in inappropriate borrowing (see Unit Five).

2. Write an extended definition for a key innovation or discovery in your field. For example, this could be a process, an approach to doing something, or a device. Include the following information: a sentence definition of the innovation, when the innovation came about, the importance of the innovation, the problem that the innovation addressed, and some discussion of how the innovation changed your field.

Definitions to Demonstrate a Distinction between Two Objects or Concepts

So far, we have concentrated on developing a text starting from the definition of a single term. Often, however, you may be asked to display your knowledge about two (or more) related terms. Consider, for example, the following pairs.

a thesis	a dissertation
a scanning electron microscope (SEM)	a transmission electron microscope (TEM)
concrete	cement
ceramic materials	composite materials
cirrus clouds	cumulonimbus clouds
a pulsar	a quasar
formal English	informal English
an LED	an OLED

If you were asked in an in-class examination to explain the differences between the members of each pair, how many could you do?

Read this draft of a contrastive definition. The draft focuses on patents and copyrights, the differences between which may not be clear to non-lawyers.

A patent, in law, is a right that grants an inventor sole rights to the production, use, or sale of an invention or process for a limited period of time. The inventor is guaranteed the possibility to earn profit for a reasonable period, after which the public is guaranteed eventual free use. On the other hand, a copyright is a form of protection which grants an originator of artistic work exclusive use of the artistic creation for a specific period of time. Copyrights are issued to authors, playwrights, composers, artists, and publishers, who then have control over publication, sale, and production of their creations for a period of time.

This is a good start, but the two terms have been presented rather independently. The passage does not reveal the writer's understanding that there is one major characteristic linking patents and copyrights—namely, that they both have a legal basis. The writer has also not made clear the distinction between the two. One way to do this would be to say

The former deals with . . . ,   while the latter is
                                     concerned with . . . .

Other contrastive connectors are provided in Unit Five (see page 226).

TASK FIFTEEN

Discuss with a partner how you could re-write the patent/copyright passage using *the former* and *the latter*. The missing information could be placed at either the beginning or the end of the passage. Which strategy would result in the more effective presentation? Can you suggest other changes that might improve the passage?

Now look at the two suggestions from our students. Discuss how they differ and which one you prefer.

A. Patents and copyrights are forms of legal protection concerned with the rights of an individual who has created something. The former grants an inventor sole rights to the production, use, or sale of an invention or process for a limited period of time, while the latter grants an originator of artistic work exclusive use of the artistic creation for a specific period of time. Patents guarantee an inventor the possibility of earning profit for a reasonable period, while the public is guaranteed eventual free use. Copyrights, however, are issued to authors, playwrights, composers, artists, and publishers, who then have control over publication, sale, and production of their creations.

B. Patents and copyrights are forms of legal protection that grant inventors or artists exclusive rights to their creations for a limited period of time. Patent and copyright owners are guaranteed the possibility to earn a profit and have control over their creations, while the public is guaranteed eventual free use. However, the former deals only with the creator of an invention or process, while the latter is concerned with authors, playwrights, composers, artists, and publishers.

Did you notice how the second contrastive definition naturally makes use of contrastive connectors?

Variations in Definitions

As we said earlier, sometimes a definition of a term or concept is not fixed. There may be a lack of agreement as to a precise definition, or perhaps there are competing perspectives. While not as common in the hard sciences, this is something that students in other fields may encounter. If competing definitions exist for a term that you will be using, a good strategy is to acknowledge some of the different definitions, but then make clear to your reader the definition you will adopt. Notice how the authors of the examples express the lack of agreement surrounding a term.

> For two decades, and particularly during the 1990s, authors and practitioners concerned with vulnerability as related to food security and famine have engaged in a lengthy attempt to define vulnerability and develop methods to measure it. Nonetheless, just what the term means and how it informs assessment methods remain unclear.

> Preeclampsia has been defined as a pregnant condition characterized by arterial hypertension, proteinuria, and edema during the second half of pregnancy. Although this definition seems simple and includes the main clinical signs, actually there is a wide diversity in the use of this term in clinical and epidemiological studies, leading to difficulties in comparing research outcomes.
>
> Prudencia Ceron-Mireles, minor editing

> For centuries scholars have attempted to define, explain, and theorize nationalism. Despite their efforts, it seems there is little agreement on the definition of this concept among researchers.
>
> Hiroe Saruya, minor editing

Here are some skeletal phrases that you could use to present the definition that you have chosen.

> While debate exists regarding a precise definition of . . . , the stance adopted in this paper is that . . . .

> For the purposes of this paper, . . . refers to/is defined as/is considered to be . . . .

> Here we define . . . as . . . In this paper I have adopted [author's] definition of . . . .

> This paper follows [author's] definition of . . . .

TASK SIXTEEN

Take a look at this discussion of road rage and answer the questions on page 87.

❶ The term "road rage" was first coined in 1988 (Fumento, 1998) and is defined in the *Oxford English Dictionary* as "violent anger caused by the stress and frustration of driving in heavy traffic." ❷ Some researchers suggest that this definition is not entirely accurate. ❸ For example, road rage has been described as a cultural habit of retaliation that occurs as a result of frustration and can occur independent of heavy traffic (James & Nahl, 1998). ❹ Some have even gone so far as to label road rage a mental disorder (Schmid, 1997). ❺ Classifying this cultural phenomenon as a mental disorder may be a stretch, but there is substantial evidence that some drivers become very angry when confronted by an adverse driving event. ❻ Elevated levels of anger may prompt aggressive and other risk-taking behavior, behavior that can increase accident risk, and risk of other negative behavior such as physical assault between drivers or arguments with passengers (Deffenbacher, Oetting, & Lynch, 1994).

DePasquale et al., 2001.

1. How many and what kinds of different definitions of road rage do the authors include? Why?

2. How is the text organized? Does it seem to be a GS text?

3. What verb tenses are used? Why?

4. In Sentence 5, what is *this cultural phenomenon?*

5. In which sentences do the authors seem to be cautious about their claims? Which words or phrases suggested that the authors were hedging (i.e., being careful)?

6. What do the authors mean when they say, *Classifying this cultural phenomenon as a mental disorder may be a stretch?*

7. What is the purpose of the second sentence (i.e., *Some researchers suggest that this definition is not entirely accurate*)?

8. What do you think the authors are going to write about next? Their data? Their method? Their hypothesis? Something else?

TASK SEVENTEEN

Read through the discussion of procrastination, which views the term from a variety of perspectives. Answer the questions on pages 88–89. Does it seem like a competing or a contrastive definition, or is it another kind?

❶ Procrastination refers to deliberately putting off one's intended actions. ❷ This means that procrastinators intend to perform an action at a certain moment, but do not engage in it at the moment that it was planned. ❸ Instead, they postpone it, or even never do it at all. ❹ This phenomenon is defined at the behavioral level (not doing what was intended) as well as at the cognitive level (postponing decisions) and does not refer to the possible causes of the dilatory behavior. ❺ There may be several reasons for putting off one's intentions, some of which we are not interested in, such as illness, technical problems, and so on. ❻ Moreover, sometimes procrastination might even be functional (for instance, postponing a decision because crucial information is lacking, as in Ferrari, 1994). ❼ Two types of procrastinator have been described: the optimistic procrastinator and the pessimistic procrastinator. ⑧ Optimistic procrastinators put off their intentions but do not worry about doing so (Milgram et al., 1992). ⑨ They are confident that they will succeed in the end, regardless of their engagement in the intended action now or later. ⑩ Moreover, they overestimate their progress and their chances to succeed and underestimate the time needed to achieve their goal (Lay, 1987, 1988). ⑪ In contrast, pessimistic procrastinators do worry about their dilatory behavior (Milgram et al., 1992). ⑫ They are aware of the fact that they get behind schedule. ⑬ Nevertheless, they still procrastinate because they do not know how to deal with the task (Lay, 1987, 1988). ⑭ They feel incompetent and are afraid that their involvement in the task will prove their incompetence. ⑮ Therefore, they procrastinate to avoid unpleasant experiences.

Dewitte and Lens, 2000.

1. What elements make the passage seem "academic"?

2. Why do the authors include the general discussion of procrastination in Sentences 1–6?

3. What is the purpose of Sentence 7? Is this sentence helpful to a reader? Why?

4. Underline the sentence connectors in the text. What kinds of connector did the author use (see page 37)? How do these affect the flow of ideas?

5. In Sentence 4 there is a summary phrase. What does *this phenomenon* refer to?

6. Why do you suppose the authors used *sometimes* and *might* in Sentence 6?

7. If, during the revision process, you thought that the passage would be improved by breaking it into two paragraphs, where would you put the paragraph break?

8. The authors have chosen to place the references to previous work in parentheses. What would be the effect of clearly making the reference part of the sentences, as in this example?

They are aware of the fact that they get behind schedule. Nevertheless, Lay (1987, 1988) states that they still procrastinate because they do not know how to deal with the task.

How do writers refer to previous work in your field? Do they use numbers, parentheses, or something else? If you do not know, check a journal in your field.

9. What might the authors of this text discuss next?

10. What question (or questions) might this passage be part of an answer to?

11. What field do you think the passage is from?

TASK EIGHTEEN

We offer two choices here. Write an extended definition of a term for which there are competing definitions. Or write a contrastive definition for a term in your field. Remember to use citations if you refer to sources.

Discussions of Schools of Thought

Many fields have controversies that have led to competing schools of thought. Examples are schools of thought in Economics, the different categorizations of intelligence, or disagreements about the origins of the universe. Passages outlining these schools of thought often involve highlighting contrasts. Notice how this is done in the sample text in Task Nineteen.

TASK NINETEEN

Read this comparative definition and answer the questions on page 91. This passage is more complex than others presented so far. Use a dictionary to check the meanings of words you do not know.

Theories of Humor

❶ Generally speaking, humor is a quality in an event or expression of ideas which often evokes a physical response of laughter in a person. ❷ It is an evasive quality that over the centuries has been the subject of numerous theories attempting to describe its origins. ❸ There are essentially three main theories of humor, each of which has a number of variants: the superiority theory, the incongruity theory, and the relief theory. ❹ The superiority theory, which dates back to Aristotle, through Thomas Hobbes (1651) and Albert Rapp (1951), describes all humor as derisive. ❺ In other words, people laugh at the misfortunes of others or themselves. ❻ Humor is, therefore, a form of ridicule that involves the process of judging or degrading something or someone thought to be inferior for a variety of reasons such as speech patterns, or clumsiness.

❼ While the superiority theory can describe some forms of humor, it cannot account for others. ❽ For instance, word play and puns are not humorous because of misfortune, but because of inconsistency. ❾ This incongruity as opposed to degradation is thought by others to be the source of humor. ❿ The incongruity theory maintains that humor originates from disharmony or inappropriateness. ⓫ Koestler (1964), for example, argues that humor involves coexisting incompatible events. ⓬ In other words, when two opposite or opposing ideas or events exist at the same time, humor may emerge. ⓭ This may involve finding something inappropriate in something that is appropriate, which gives rise to a cognitive shift. ⓮ Take, for instance, this joke. ⓯ "Two fish are in a tank. ⓰ One turns to the other and asks, 'Do you know how to drive this thing?'" ⓱ The play on the word *tank* can result in laughter.

⓲ Although the incongruity is widely accepted, this theory cannot explain instances where neither superiority or incongruity are the bases for humor. ⑲ To account for humor that appears to be a form of release from psychological tension, theorists developed relief theory. ⑳ According to relief theory, humor provides relief from anxiety, hostility, aggression, and sexual tension. ㉑ Humor gratifies repressed feelings that operate on an unconscious level. ㉒ Strong proponents of this theory were early psychologists, such as Freud, Dewey, and Kline.

㉓ More modern theories of humor are essentially variations of one of these three traditional ones. ㉔ For instance, Duncan (1985), in his superiority theory, states that humor is linked to social status. ㉕ Deckers and Buttram (1990) expand incongruity theory to include elements of schema theory. ㉖ In their view, distinctions between and within schemata* are necessary for an understanding of humor. ㉗ While each of these theories can explain some aspect of humor, none can successfully be applied to all instances of humor.

1. In which sentences are the different theories introduced?

2. What verb tense is used to introduce the theories of the various researchers? Why do you suppose this is?

3. Underline the sentence connectors in the passage. Why were they used?

4. What do you think might follow this discussion of humor theories—a presentation of the author's own definition of humor, an analysis of one event using the different theories, or something else?

5. Do you think that the whole passage is a GS text, that part of it is, or that none of it is?

6. Does the passage mention a modern version of relief theory?

7. Do you think that the author of this passage (Chris) has positioned herself as neutral, or do you think she has a preference? If you think she has a preference, what do you think it is? Why do you think so?

*Schemata is the plural of schema; it comes from ancient Greek.

We return to the writing of comparative summaries in Unit Five.

TASK TWENTY

Write a general-specific paragraph on your first language or on a topic from your field of study. Begin with either a definition or a generalization. Alternatively, write a "different schools of thought" text of relevance to your field.

Specific-to-General Organization

We began this unit by exploring GS texts, and in this final section we return to the notion of general and specific, but in terms of specific to general (SG). SG patterns are also possible in academic writing and, in fact, are fairly common in some fields such as History and Art, as well as some medical genres, most notably in case reports, and legal genres, in case notes. SG texts begin with a specific focus and then progressively become more general. The specific focus could be an event, a piece of art, an individual (e.g., a patient in a case report in Medicine), or organization (e.g., a company in a Business case study). The SG pattern, as you can well imagine, looks something like that shown in Figure 6.

FIGURE 6. Shape of an SG text

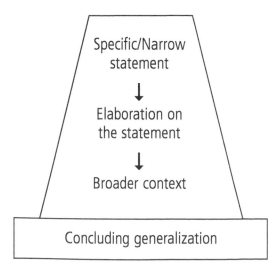

Specific/Narrow
statement

↓

Elaboration on
the statement

↓

Broader context

Concluding generalization

Let's look at how one student in Mechanical Engineering organized this SG text as part of an introduction to a paper on using MEMS accelerometers to monitor human falls. The full text can be found in MICUSP.

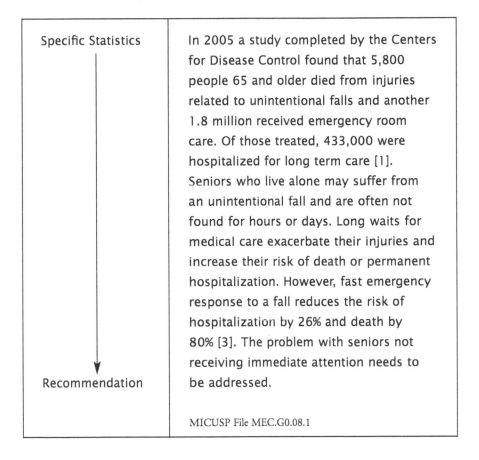

Specific Statistics	In 2005 a study completed by the Centers for Disease Control found that 5,800 people 65 and older died from injuries related to unintentional falls and another 1.8 million received emergency room care. Of those treated, 433,000 were hospitalized for long term care [1]. Seniors who live alone may suffer from an unintentional fall and are often not found for hours or days. Long waits for medical care exacerbate their injuries and increase their risk of death or permanent hospitalization. However, fast emergency response to a fall reduces the risk of hospitalization by 26% and death by 80% [3]. The problem with seniors not receiving immediate attention needs to
Recommendation	be addressed.
	MICUSP File MEC.G0.08.1

TASK TWENTY-ONE

Read the text about Figure 7 and discuss the questions on page 96. Note here that we have numbered independent clauses as sentences for ease of discussion.

FIGURE 7. La Gamin by F. Preiss (circa 1925)

❶ The illustration shows a small statue of a young woman with elegant legs, slender arms and a small head capped by short, curly hair. ❷ It is 25 cm. high. ❸ The flesh is carved from ivory and the clothes and shoes are cast in bronze; ❹ the figure stands on a base made of Brazilian green onyx. ❺ The figure is signed "F. (Fritz) Preiss." ❻ Although the statue is not dated, it was almost certainly created some time during the 1920s. ❼ Some 90 years later, *La Gamin* is in excellent condition: The ivory is not stained or cracked; the bronze retains its original patina; ❽ and there remain traces of brown in the hair and rose-red on the girl's cheeks. ❾ Several copies of this statuette are known to exist.

⑩ Johann Philipp Ferdinand ("Fritz") Preiss was born in Erbach in Germany in 1882[4] and, as a boy, was apprenticed as an ivory carver. ⑪ In 1906, he and Walter Kassler established a workshop in Berlin, which reopened in 1920, following the First World War. ⑫ Preiss died in 1943 and the workshop, records and stock of the company were destroyed by fire in a bombing raid in 1945.[5] ⑬ As a result, our information about Preiss and his work remains limited.

⑭ Preiss and the Romanian-born Demetre Chiparus remain today the two most important and famous of the Art Deco makers of small bronze and ivory figures. ⑮ These are mostly of young women, sometimes nude, sometimes as dancers and sometimes in athletic or sporting poses. ⑯ Original figures by these two men have become highly collectible and so can command several thousand dollars; ⑰ in consequence, numerous fakes have been produced.

⑱ *La Gamin*[6] beautifully captures the spirit of the 1920s, particularly in terms of female freedom and emancipation.[7] ⑲ Gone were the complex underclothes, long dresses, and long hair of the pre-WWI era; ⑳ instead we find slender athletic bodies, close-cut hair, short skirts and loose, light tops. ㉑ It was these new fashions that made energetic dances such as the Charleston and sports such as golf and tennis possible for young middle-class women. ㉒ *La Gamin* today stands confidently before us, with her hands in her pockets (surely unusual at that time), optimistically looking out on a brighter future, representing the sophistication of her time.

---

[4] B. Catley. (1978). *Art deco and other figures.* Woodbridge, U.K.: Baron Publishing.

[5] C. Proudlove. *Chiparus and Preiss—doyens among Art Deco sculptors.* http://writeantiques.com/chiparus-and-preiss-doyens-among-art-deco-sculptors.

[6] The traditional name for the figure is *gamin*, which is a slang French term for a young man, the expected female equivalent being *gamine*. It is possible that the title tries to capture the "tomboy" aspect of the sculpture.

[7] E. Knowles, *Femmes Fatales*, www.ericknowles.co.uk/Femmes_Fatales.htm.

1. Briefly describe the topic of each paragraph.

   Paragraph 1: _____

   Paragraph 2: _____

   Paragraph 3: _____

   Paragraph 4: _____

2. Which paragraph do you think is the most descriptive and which most evaluative?

3. Which paragraph do you think is the most interesting and successful, and why?

4. How well does the author "translate" the visual into the verbal at the beginning?

5. Has the author made a connection between the statue and the historical/cultural context? Do you think this is the author's overall purpose? Or is it mainly to engage in a formal analysis of the work so as to offer a fresh look at it? Is it to raise a social issue? Is the goal to discuss how the artist's life influenced the art?

6. What do you think of the title of this text? What, if any, changes might you suggest?

7. What do you think *onyx* and *patina* might mean in the first paragraph?

Often in SG texts the strategy is to give specific examples or details that provide a foundation for and justify the investigation of a larger concern. Notice how this next text from a history journal draws the reader in by starting with a story about a woman, but by the end of the second paragraph focuses on the broader topic of reconstructing the Communist state in East Germany after World War II. Before you read the text, discuss whether you think young people in particular feel the need to be part of organizations that have strong ideological agendas.

A Duty to Forget? The 'Hitler Youth Generation' and the Transition from Nazism to Communism in Postwar East Germany, c. 1945–49

McDougall, A. (2008).
German History, 26(1), 24–46.

❶ The short story for the year 1949 in Günter Grass's "My Century" relates an encounter at a conference between the narrator, a West German man, and a woman he had known in his childhood in Stettin (then part of the Third Reich), who subsequently grew up in Communist East Germany. ❷ In the course of the story, we learn that the woman, Inge, had once been a zealous functionary in the National Socialist girls' organization, the League of German Girls (BDM), winning "promotion after promotion" and remaining loyal to the Nazi cause until the bitter end. ❸ After "an eighteen-month grace period" at the end of the Second World War, she then became an equally active and successful functionary in the East's Communist-led youth organization, the Free German Youth (FDJ). ❹ Inge, the West German narrator notes, appeared to be "perfectly at ease" in explaining her rapid switching of allegiance from one political system to another.[1]

❺ Inge had many real-life equivalents in the Soviet-Occupied Zone of Germany (SBZ) after the Second World War. ❻ Hundreds of thousands of young East Germans made just such a speedy transition from the brown shirt to the blue, from one mass youth organization—the two branches of the Nazi youth movement, the Hitler Youth (HJ) and the BDM—to another, the FDJ, in the mid- to late 1940s. ❼ Members of this "Hitler Youth generation"[2] played the decisive role in reconstructing the Communist state that ultimately emerged in East Germany from the ashes of the Third Reich.

---

[1] Grass, Günter, (1999), *My century*, Houghton Mifflin: New York, pp. 123–127.

[2] The term *Hitler Youth generation* refers to the generation of Germans born between 1919 and 1931, the oldest of whom could have joined the HJ in 1933 (the year in which the Nazi Party came to power) and the youngest of whom would have joined the HJ in early 1945. This paper focuses primarily on the younger part of the HJ generation (those born between circa 1925 and 1931), whose ranks contain the vast majority of young East Germans who experienced both the HJ and the FDJ. The generic term *Hitler Youth generation* will be used here to refer to former members of both the HJ and the BDM (i.e., both gendered branches of the Nazi youth movement).

Do you think the transition from the specific instance to the broader issue is successful? Historians may also describe a specific historical incident, what led up to it, and what the consequences were. This then is followed by some evaluation of the incident's historical significance.

TASK TWENTY-TWO

Here are the first and third paragraphs of a historical text. Read them carefully so that you are able to write the second paragraph.

The Meeting at Plombières

Paragraph One

On July 19, 1858, Cavour, the Prime Minister of the small northern Italian kingdom of Piedmont, left his holiday place in Switzerland and traveled to the small spa town of Plombières in northeastern France, arriving there at nightfall on the following day. On July 21, Cavour had a secret three-hour meeting with Emperor Napoleon III of France. During the meeting, the Italian statesman and the French emperor devised a plan for forcing the Austrians out of northern Italy.

Paragraph Two

Paragraph Three

Although Cavour did not live to see the unification of Italy—he died at the early age of 51—he remains, along with Garibaldi and Mazzini, one of the three key figures in the struggle for Italian independence. Not surprisingly then, most Italian towns and cities have one of their principal streets or main squares named after Count Cavour of Piedmont.

Now, write the second paragraph, making use of academic resources you find on the internet (remember, if you use or quote directly from source material, you will need to indicate this, making sure to use quotation marks around borrowed words). Here are some questions that might guide you.

1. What (briefly) had Cavour achieved as prime minister up to 1858?

2. Who was Victor Emmanuel?

3. What did Napoleon III want in exchange for helping the Piedmontese expel the Austrians?

TASK TWENTY-THREE

In every field of study, research that once seemed promising is abandoned. Concepts, models, chemicals, drugs, teaching methods, stylistic or design trends, and treatments are left behind for newer directions that offer more promise or are more in line with current needs. For instance, the causes of diseases such as cholera and the plague were once attributed to miasma or "bad air" and described in terms of miasma theory. In Astronomy, the steady-state theory of the expansion of the universe has been replaced by the big bang theory. In the field of nutrition, it was once thought that all fats were harmful, but now researchers know that some fats are better than others and have protective effects. Choose a concept, approach, design, stylistic trend, or line of research that was once widely accepted but has fallen out of favor. Explain the area and the reason it has been abandoned. Use some references, if you need them, but be sure to use your own words throughout your discussion. Organize in terms of GS or SG.

Unit Three

Problem, Process, and Solution

In Unit Two we mainly explored one common kind of underlying structure to academic writing, that of general-specific movement. This structure will prove useful in later units when producing data commentaries (Unit Four) or writing introductions to research papers (Unit Eight). In this unit, we explore and practice a second underlying structure in academic writing, that of problem-to-solution (PS) movement, which we introduced briefly in Unit One and touched on in Unit Two. This structure will again prove useful later when writing critiques (Unit Six) and Introductions (Unit Eight). So, clearly this structure is one of the more important ones in academic writing, especially if you consider how much academic research activity is aimed at solving problems, which may be discussed in published research articles, various kinds of research proposals, and case reports in certain fields, to name a few examples. Beyond looking at the overall organization, we have built into the problem-solution structure some discussion of process descriptions. In many cases, it makes sense to see describing the parts of a process as the steps required to provide a solution to some problem. Alternatively, a problem may be described in terms of a process—for example, how malware infects a mobile phone or how a tsunami (tidal wave) forms.

As we have seen, general-specific passages tend to be descriptive and expository. In contrast, problem-solution texts tend to be more argumentative and evaluative. In the former, students and junior scholars will most likely position themselves as being informed and organized and in the latter as questioning, perceptive, and convincing. We say this because you may need to convince your reader that your problem is indeed a problem and/or that your solution is reasonable.

The Structure of Problem-Solution Texts

We begin this unit with a passage on a topic that is likely of interest to you and others who want or perhaps need to publish. Although it is written from the perspective of research in Biomedicine, we think it raises some points that are relevant for all junior scholars.

TASK ONE

This passage discusses the need for junior scholars or novices to receive training in scientific writing. Before you read, discuss the first question with a partner.

1. How important is it for you to publish in journals in your field? Why? What are some challenges that novices may face?

Scientific Writing of Novice Researchers: What Difficulties and Encouragements Do They Encounter?
Shah, J., BA, MS; Shah, A., MD, MPH;
Pietrobon, R., MD, PhD, MBA. (2009).
Academic Medicine, 84, 511–516.

❶ Clear communication of research findings is essential to sustain the ever-evolving biomedical research field. ❷ Serving as the mainstay for this purpose, scientific writing involves the consideration of numerous factors, while building up an argument that would convince readers and possibly enable them to arrive at a decision. ❸ Those who report research must attend to the soundness of the subject matter, to the nature of the intended audience, and to questions of clarity, style, structure, precision, and accuracy. ❹ These factors, along with the weight of responsibility to the scientific community, make scientific writing a daunting task. ❺ Consequently, many researchers shy away from this critical element of research, which may impede the progress of science and their own scientific careers.

⑥ The ability to accurately and effectively communicate ideas, procedures, and findings according to readers' expectations is the primary skill required for scientific writing. ⑦ Additionally, skills such as the ability to relate and interlink evidence, to lend permanence to thoughts and speech, to enable one's writing to serve as a future reference to others, and to protect intellectual property rights[1] need to be developed and tempered* over a period of time. ⑧ These skills are necessary for all researchers, but especially for novice researchers in the beginnings of their careers so that they do not face failure and lose valuable time learning these skills later.

⑨ Individuals entering the research field with no or little experience with past publications qualify as novice researchers. ⑩ Even clinicians intending to explore and publish findings about research questions based on their clinical practice need to learn these skills to effectively contribute to health care.

⑪ Instruction in scientific writing and subsequent publication in peer-reviewed journals will help novice researchers refine their ideas and increase their expertise, because the act of writing is itself a valuable tool for learning and for fostering the scientific thought process[2]—this aligns with the principles of the writing to learn movement.[3,4] ⑫ Effective writing skills help new scientists take part in the ongoing, ever-evolving scientific conversation.[5] ⑬ The practice of scientific writing develops habits of reflection[2] that make for better researchers, and publication in respected journals strengthens the scientific process, while playing a crucial role in career advancement.

---

*made stronger through experience.

2. The passage includes the four parts of the standard problem-solution text, as shown in Table 2. Which sentences belong to each part? What is the general point being discussed in each part?

TABLE 2. Parts of a Problem-Solution Text

Situation	background information on a particular set of circumstances	
Problem	reasons for challenging the accuracy of the figures; criticisms of or weaknesses surrounding the current situation; possible counterevidence	
Solution	discussion of a way or ways to alleviate the problem	
Evaluation	assessment of the merits of the proposed solution(s)	

Note that sometimes an incomplete solution is offered; an incomplete solution may introduce a new problem, which then needs to be addressed. This type of text may look different (see Table 3).

TABLE 3. Variation of a Problem-Solution Text

Situation	background information on a particular set of circumstances
Problem	reasons for challenging the accuracy of the figures; criticisms of or weaknesses surrounding the current situation; possible counterevidence
Partial solution	discussion of a way or ways to alleviate the problem
Evaluation	assessment of the merits and limitations of the proposed solution(s)
New solution	discussion of a new way or ways to alleviate the problem
Evaluation	assessment of the merits of the proposed solution(s)

3. Do you agree or disagree with the opening sentence? Why or why not? What would be the reaction if the statement were about a field other than biomedicine? Why do you suppose the authors chose this as their starting point?

4. What is your reaction to the point made in Sentence 7?

5. Put a check mark (✓) next to the aspects of the text that contribute to the authors' attempts to convince you. How convinced are you that novices should receive instruction in scientific writing?

_____ a. the problem-solution organization

_____ b. the flow of ideas

_____ c. references to other published papers (indicated by the superscripted numbers at the ends of some of the sentences)

_____ d. claims that are stated cautiously (see Unit Four)

_____ e. the explanation of the causes of the writing challenges

6. Where do you think the authors are more convincing? Is it in stating the problem or in suggesting the solution? Why?

7. Put a check mark (✓) next to the items that you think could strengthen the text and would lend support to the argument.

_____ a. a quote from a study that shows the progress of science is slowed because researchers do not write up their work

_____ b. some statistics indicating that writing instruction is beneficial

_____ c. some data on the relationship between writing (publishing) and career advancement

_____ d. an explanation of the writing to learn movement mentioned in Sentence 11

8. Do you have any experience of your own to contribute to the discussion? Have you been involved in a publication? Would you agree or disagree with the authors' point that scientific writing involves the creation of an argument?

Language Focus: Mid-Position Adverbs

In the section on style in Unit One (beginning on page 14), we noted that adverbs tend to occur within or near the verb in formal academic writing. In this Language Focus, we develop the point further. First, look at this occurrence from the text in Task One (Sentence 2).

> . . . scientific writing involves the consideration of numerous factors, while building up an argument that would convince readers and *possibly* enable them to arrive at a decision.

You might wonder why it matters where the adverb is placed. After all, you could, following the rules of grammar, place *possibly* at the beginning or the end of the main clause.

> . . . *possibly* scientific writing involves the consideration of numerous factors, while building up an argument that would convince readers and enable them to arrive at a decision.

> . . . scientific writing involves the consideration of numerous factors, while building up an argument that would convince readers and enable them to arrive at a decision *possibly*.

While grammatically acceptable, the placement of adverbs in sentence-initial position in written academic texts is rather uncommon (Virtanen, 2008). More importantly, if the adverb is in sentence-final position, this may have an unintended effect on the reader. Specifically, if you recall from Unit One, the old-to-new pattern of information flow places the new information at the end of the sentence. Information at the end is therefore a reasonably good candidate for the beginning focus of the next sentence (Virtanen, 2008). In our example, then, the placement of *possibly* at the end could create the expectation that the next sentence will explore why the authors are not fully committed to the point.

> . . . scientific writing involves the consideration of numerous factors, while building up an argument that would convince readers and enable them to arrive at a decision *possibly*. While some readers . . . , other readers . . . .

Alternatively, it might suggest that the author is not convinced by the point just made. Thus, the placement of the adverb can influence your reader's ability to anticipate the development of your ideas.

TASK TWO

Find a single adverb to replace the phrase in italics and then place the adverb in mid-position.

1. The provisions of the law must be applied *with care*.

2. Part II of this paper describes the laws of the U.S. that pertain to agricultural biotechnology *in only a couple of paragraphs*.

3. Myopia, which is referred to as shortsightedness *most of the time*, is a common cause of visual disability throughout the world.

4. This study revealed that American and Japanese thresholds for sweetness and saltiness did not differ *a lot*.

5. *As a rule*, pulsed semiconductor lasers do not use the broad gain bandwidth to full advantage in the generation of subpicosecond pulses.

6. Environmental managers are faced with having to determine the extent of environmental contamination and identifying habitats at risk *on a regular basis*.

7. The water supply lines must be inspected to prevent blockages *now and then*.

8. Although many elaborations of this model have been developed over the years, *to a considerable extent* all of them have followed the traditional specification in presupposing that an individual will choose to make a tax report.

The text on novice writers includes a few references to other published papers to support the claims (Sentences 7 and 11–13). Whether and why to include references is a matter of some complexity and is dealt with in Unit Eight. Here we simply point out that a well-placed and well-chosen reference can give credibility to your points. In this next task, pay attention to the references and consider why they were included.

TASK THREE

Now consider this passage and answer the questions on page 108.

The Role of English in Research and Scholarship

❶ The problem of accurately assessing the role of English in contemporary research has been suggested as residing in the pro-Western and pro-Anglophone bias in major databases such as the Web of Science. ❷ Thus, to more accurately determine the predominance of English as the language of research and scholarship, studies have examined published articles describing small-scale empirical research papers. ❸ These early examinations of small studies suggested that the role of English was exaggerated. ❹ They concluded that "a more accurate percentage for English as the language of publication would be around 50% rather than 80%." ❺ These studies, however, failed to recognize that over the last thirty years many leading European (and Japanese) journals have switched from publishing in German, French, Dutch, Swedish, Japanese, etc., to new editorial policies that increasingly require submissions written in English. ❻ As long ago as 1978, Lippert listed 33 German journals from the health and life sciences which by 1977 had changed their titles and editorial policies from German to English. ❼ More recently, comparable accounts have been produced for German chemistry (Wood, 2001), Swedish medical research (Gunnarsson, 1998), and French geology (Dressen, 2002). ❽ This new data, together with studies showing the increasing Anglicization of doctoral dissertations in many countries, now suggests that the figure of 80% (or higher) may be more accurate than previously believed. ❾ Even so, there is also evidence that the dominance of English may be causing a counterreaction, especially in situations where local concerns and interests encourage publication in local languages. ❿ Rey-Rocha & Martin-Sempere (1999), for example, have shown this to be the case for earth scientists in Spain. ⓫ Clearly, further research is necessary to fully understand the dominance of English in academia.

1. Which sentences indicate the beginnings of the four parts of a problem-solution text: situation, problem, solution, evaluation?

2. If you were to divide this paragraph into two, where would you divide it? Would you opt for two paragraphs or three? Why?

3. Can you produce a version of an opening sentence from your own discipline using the following phrase?

   The problem of . . . was suggested as residing in . . . .

4. Underline all the time expressions in the passage. What conclusions can you draw?

5. What is your opinion regarding the dominance of English in publication? What kinds of studies would, in your opinion, actually resolve the debate?

6. Do you have information to share about the language policies of journals in another country?

Procedures and Processes

The text on the role of English is a typical research question example of a problem-solution text. In essence, it uses the problem-solution structure to review the current state of knowledge. This review approach allows the author to raise a question about the current state of knowledge and to offer a possible or partial answer. However, some "classic" problem-solution texts are more technical in nature and may describe procedures and processes. We see this in the passage in Task Four.

TASK FOUR

Read the passage and answer the questions on pages 110–111. The passage is a problem-solution text about an area in Chile that has a desert climate—the Atacama Desert.

Clouds and Fog as a Source of Water in Chile

❶ Many of Chile's poor, northern coastal villages have suffered for years from water shortages, despite the abundance of cloud cover and fog in the region. ❷ When the cold air from the Pacific Ocean's Humboldt Current mixes with the warm coastal air, a thick, wet fog, called *camanchaca* by the Andes Indians, forms along with clouds (Darak, 2008). ❸ However, rather than developing into rain, the fog and clouds quickly evaporate in the hot sun. ❹ This lack of rainfall has imposed severe hardships on communities. ❺ They cannot grow crops and must carefully ration their water, which is often delivered by truck.

❻ To address this problem scientists in the 1990s implemented an interesting solution on El Tofo mountain near the village of Chungungo. ❼ Using conventional technology, they redevised a centuries-old method to capture the water droplets of the fog in a process referred to as fog harvesting (Schemenauer and Cereceda, 1991). ❽ In this method, triangular-weave polypropylene nets are attached to support posts to serve as water collectors. ❾ Each of these nets is designed to collect approximately 40 gallons of water each day. ❿ When the fog develops, droplets of water are trapped in the nets and join to form larger drops that then fall into a trough. ⓫ From the troughs the water drains through filters into a series of underground tanks. ⓬ The water is then piped to a 25,000-gallon storage tank, where it is chemically treated to kill disease-causing organisms. ⓭ Finally, the water flows to individual households, just as in traditional water systems. ⓮ This collection system can supply as much as 2,500 gallons per day, enough for a small community to drink, wash, and water small gardens. ⓯ The water is not only clean, but far less expensive than water delivered to the area. ⓰ Moreover, it is collected at no apparent cost to the environment.

⑰ Despite the initial success of fog harvesting in Chungungo, the system is, unfortunately, no longer in use (de la Lastra, 2002). ⑱ The availability of water led to a tripling of the population from 300 to 900, putting pressure on the water supply (IDRC, 2003). ⑲ Because the community lacked a clear commitment to the project (see Diehl, 2010, for a full explanation), they did not add new nets to increase the water supply, and instead petitioned for water to be piped in from 20 km away. ⑳ Although the village abandoned this viable alternative technology, the Chungungo experience has led to successful implementation of fog harvesting initiatives in other mountainous coastal areas of Chile, Ecuador, Mexico, and Peru, providing much needed fresh water to small communities.

1. This passage has three paragraphs rather than four. Why?

2. This passage contains a process description in Paragraph 2. Make a sketch or timeline of the process.

3. What is the predominant verb tense used in Sentences 7 through 16? Why is this?

4. Underline the instances of passive voice in Paragraph 2. Why was passive used?

5. Underline the adverbs in Paragraph 2. How many of them are mid-position adverbs?

6. Identify the phrases consisting of *this* + noun in the text. How many are *this* + summary? Does the placement of *this* + summary noun tell us anything?

7. How is the solution introduced?

8. In the end, what is the overall evaluation of the system? What evaluative language can you find in the final paragraph?

9. As you may have noticed, the passage is a bit short on details. Put a check mark (✓) next to the details you think would help the writer create a text that displays expertise and familiarity with the topic. Some details are better candidates than others. Where in the passage would you place the details?

_____ a. the dimensions of the nets

_____ b. the brand name of the netting

_____ c. where the netting can be purchased

_____ d. the method of connecting the mesh to the posts

_____ e. the time of day the fog comes in

_____ f. the size of the fog water droplets

_____ g. a description of the post material

_____ h. the trough material

_____ i. the storage tank materials and dimensions

_____ j. the duration of the fog season

_____ k. the time needed to construct the system

10. This passage could be extended to provide information on maintenance of the fog collection system. This would include a discussion of the importance of regular inspection, cleaning, and repair of the nets, troughs, and tanks. Where would you place this information?

11. Where might you add the following information about cost?

> The cost of operating and maintaining the system, which averages nearly $12,000 annually, is quite low compared to other means of providing water.

12. What is your reaction to the discussion of the eventual failure of the water collection system in Chile?

We were in fact able to locate a published journal article written by two of the researchers who promoted the fog harvesting system. The full article was published in a journal called *Ambio*, a multidisciplinary journal focusing on topics ranging from Ecology and Hydrology to Environmental Economics and Meteorology. Task Five provides the section that describes fog harvesting.

TASK FIVE

Read the text and discuss the questions on page 113 with a partner.

Fog-Water Collection in Arid Coastal Locations
Schemenauer, R. S., and Cereceda, P. (1991).
Ambio, 20(7), 303–308.

FOG HARVESTING

Fog is composed of liquid droplets. Fog, in the simplest terms, is a cloud which is touching the ground and the type of fog is determined by the physical process which has created the fog. When a cloud with a base some distance above the sea or the land moves over a mountain, the mountain is covered by fog. Fogs produced by the advection of clouds over higher terrain tend to have higher liquid contents (8) than do fogs produced at the land or sea surface (9) and it is these high elevation fogs that are of primary interest for the production of water in arid lands.

The collection of fog droplets depends on the diameter of the droplets, the wind speed and nature of the collection surface. Fog droplets have diameters which are typically from 1 to 3μm in diameter. The mean volume diameters at the high elevation (780 m) site in Chile are in the 8 to 12μm range and droplet concentrations are typically 100 to 400 per cm³. Fog droplets are collected by a simple impaction process. An object (collector) is placed in the path of the droplets and as the droplets approach the surface, some flow around the object and some strike the surface. Enormous numbers of fog droplets must be collected since it requires about 10 million to a drop the size of a match head.

The efficiency of the large polypropylene meshes used in Chile has been both measured in the field and modeled (10). The meshes are woven from a flat polypropylene fibre 1 mm wide and 0.1 mm thick into a mesh with triangular openings approximately 1 cm on a side. A double layer of mesh is used in Chile. The collection efficiency at the center of a 12 m by 4 m collector was found to increase with wind speed up to 3.5 m s⁻¹ (the upstream wind speed) and then remained constant at about 65%. But the collector as a whole has a lower efficiency of closer to 20% due to lowered efficiencies away from the center of the mesh and due to water losses in the system. The array of fog water collectors is completely passive. Water drips from the bottom of the meshes into plastic troughs and then a gravity flow system delivers the water through a network of pipes to the point of use.

1. How would you describe the information given in the first two sentences? Would you say it is common knowledge, knowledge familiar to most journal readers, or expert knowledge? What does the inclusion of this information perhaps reveal about the authors' assumptions regarding potential readers?

2. What similarities and/or differences in terms of content do you see between the text in Task Four and this text? Why do you suppose these differences exist?

3. At the end of the excerpt from the article, the authors describe how the water reaches the users. What verb tense did they use? How does this compare to the process description in Task Four?

4. Think about the word *fog*. Is this word typically count or non-count? The excerpt uses a plural form.

   Fogs produced by the advection of clouds over higher terrain tend to have higher liquid contents (8) than do fogs produced at the land or sea surface (9) and it is these high elevation fogs that are of primary interest for the production of water in arid lands.

   What do you think about the use of *fogs*? Why did the authors use it?

5. One way to expand your academic vocabulary is to identify expressions that you think would contribute to your own writing. These are usually chunks of language (2 to 4 words) that do not convey original content but are like skeletons upon which you can build a point or an idea. One such expression in the first paragraph is "____ *produced by* ____ *tend to* ____." Using this stretch of language as a starting point, students from various fields could write these sentences.

   Layering *produced by* deformation *tends to* have sharply defined dark and light layers.

   The vinegar *produced by* this method *tends to* be of inferior quality due to uncontrolled conditions.

   The introduction of technologies *produced by* research *tends to* be a minor source of innovation in industry.

   Can you find any phrases in the excerpt that you might be able to use in your own writing?

The fog harvesting texts discuss some causes and effects, the topic of the next Language Focus (pages 115–116). Before exploring cause and effect in more detail, we turn your attention to Task Six.

TASK SIX

Work with a partner and underline the language that establishes a cause-and-effect connection.

❶❼ Despite the success of fog harvesting in Chungungo, the system is, unfortunately, no longer in use (de la Lastra, 2002). ❶❽ The availability of water led to a tripling of the population from 300 to 900, putting pressure on the water supply (IDRC, 2003). ❶❾ Because the community lacked a clear commitment to the project (see Diehl, 2010, for a full explanation), they did not add new nets to increase the water supply, and instead petitioned for water to be piped in from 20 km away. ❷⓿ Although the village abandoned this viable alternative technology, the Chungungo experience has led to successful implementation of fog harvesting initiatives in other mountainous coastal areas of Chile, Ecuador, Mexico, and Peru, providing much needed fresh water to small communities.

You likely noticed *because* and the verb phrase *led to* as a means to show a cause and effect, but perhaps less familiar to you are *–ing* verbs that can also be used to establish a causal connection.

Language Focus: *–ing* Clauses to Indicate Cause and Effect

In order to help your reader understand a problem and/or a solution, you may need to use expressions to highlight causes and effects. For example, the well-known relationship between supply and demand in the field of Economics can be conveyed as a cause-and-effect statement. Such statements can take many forms. Here are a few.

> An increase in demand *causes* a rise in prices.
>
> The tsunami was *triggered by* a very powerful earthquake.
>
> Researchers worldwide are *increasingly pressured to* publish in English language journals, *thus leading to* a decline in publications written in languages other than English.

The last sentence contains a *thus + –ing* clause of result. Such clauses of result can be particularly useful as alternatives to traditional logical connectors like *therefore* and *as a result.* Compare the sentences in each set.

> a. The magma flows into the pores of the rocks; as a result, the rocks rupture.
>
> The magma flows into the pores of the rocks, *thus* causing them to rupture.
>
> b. A current is sent through the material. As a result, the electrons are polarized.
>
> A current is sent through the material, *thus* polarizing the electrons.

Note that *thus* is optional in *–ing* clauses of result and that sometimes writers also use a preliminary subordinate clause to set the scene for the process.

> c. When the ABS controller senses that a wheel is about to lock up, it automatically changes the pressure in the brake lines of the car. As a result, maximum brake performance is achieved.
>
> When the ABS controller senses that a wheel is about to lock up, it automatically changes the pressure in the car's brake lines to prevent the lockup, *(thus)* resulting in maximum brake performance.

Optional subordinate clause	When the ABS controller senses that a wheel is about to lock up,
Main clause	it automatically changes the pressure in the brake lines of the car to prevent the lockup,
(optional thus/thereby) –*ing*	(thus) resulting in maximum brake performance.

This structure is particularly useful in problem-solution texts because it can be used to express the next step in the process, a resulting problem, or a resulting solution. Here is a simple example.

Process: Prices rise, thus leading to a drop in demand.

Problem: Prices rise, thus increasing the chance of hyperinflation.

Solution: Prices rise, thus increasing earnings that can then be reinvested in the enterprise.

TASK SEVEN

Read the sentences containing *-ing* clauses of result. Would you expect to find these sentences in the problem, solution, or evaluation part of a text? Discuss your decisions with a partner.

1. The laser light forms an EM field, thereby slowing the vibration of the atoms. _____

   _____

2. When manufacturing output drops, demand for business loans falls, leaving banks with a strong lending capacity.

   _____

   _____

3. Contact among humans, livestock, and wildlife may increase, thus creating opportunities for the emergence of new livestock diseases.

   _____

   _____

4. Users have access to information, thus supporting smarter purchasing decisions that affect a company's bottom line.

_____

_____

5. The propellant evaporates, leaving behind only the desired product.

_____

_____

Re-write each sentence without the –*ing* clause and instead use a traditional linking word or phrase to indicate a causal relationship. See Table 1 on page 37 if you need some ideas.

TASK EIGHT

Combine the ideas presented in each of the statements by using an -*ing* clause of result. Work with a partner.

1. Technical improvements in resource efficiency can lower demand for resources. This results in lower prices.

2. Avatars can use graphics capabilities to build new artifacts individually or collaboratively in real time. This leads to the creation of an effect referred to as "immediacy of artifacts."

3. The payment processing division of the bank announced that its systems had been breached by unknown intruders. Because of this breach, the personal information belonging to about 1.5 million cardholders was compromised.

4. The plants extract nickel and zinc; hence, the soil is left uncontaminated.

5. Rainfall levels plummeted. A slow, but steady, loss of grasses occurred. As a result, the region was transformed into a desert.

6. Countries sign treaties on the use of "free resources" such as air and ocean fish. Serious ownership questions arise; therefore, it is difficult to enforce any agreement.

TASK NINE

Read the passage, which has been divided into three parts. Choose the item that best completes each part. Each of the choices is grammatically correct; however, not all will work equally well. Before making your choices, consider the flow of the entire passage, not just the individual items.

1. Since the onset of air travel in the early 1900s, aircraft collisions with birds and other wildlife have been an ongoing threat to human safety. These collisions, known as wildlife strikes, occur on average nearly 20 times per day and have damaged or destroyed more than 400 aircraft

   _____.

   a. ; as a result, the average cost is $117,787 per incident

   b. , resulting in an average cost of $117,787 per incident

   c. . These collisions have resulted in an average cost of $117,787 per incident

2. Over the last 40 years the number of wildlife strikes has been increasing. Two years ago, 7,600 strikes were reported. Last year that number rose to 8,000. Over the last decade there has been a threefold increase. Several factors have contributed to this growing threat. First, most airlines are replacing older three- or four-engined aircraft with quieter, more efficient aircraft with two engines

   _____.

   a. ; thus, aircraft have less engine redundancy and a greater likelihood of engine failure in a collision with wildlife

   b. , resulting in less engine redundancy and a greater likelihood of engine failure in a collision with wildlife

   c. , which has resulted in less engine redundancy and a greater likelihood of engine failure in a collision with wildlife

3. Second, wildlife management programs have contributed to growth in the populations of many species of wildlife that are often involved in strikes. For example, the once-endangered Canada goose population has grown by more than 10% each year for the last 30 years. Canada geese and other birds, such as gulls, have expanded into urban and suburban areas, including airports. Third, the number of commercial and non-commercial flights has more than doubled over the last two decades _____.

   a. ; therefore, the parallel increases in wildlife populations and air traffic contribute to a higher probability of a wildlife strike

   b. . This concurrent increase in wildlife populations and air traffic contributes to a higher probability of a wildlife strike

   c. , contributing to a higher probability of a wildlife strike

Language Focus: Passive Voice

In most technical solutions, it is necessary to describe a process or a method. In the passages in Tasks Four and Five, the explanation of how the water is collected provides this necessary information. In addition, when you are describing the method you used to carry out some research, you will essentially be writing a process description. We have looked at adverbs in process descriptions; it is now time to turn to verbs.

The passive voice often plays an important role in process descriptions. We can see why in this example. Look at these brief notes about how influenza vaccines are produced.

Three sample virus strains	The virus strains most likely to cause disease are identified and three are selected for vaccine development.

Selected virus strains	Manufacturers inject the virus samples of each selected strain into separate batches of fertilized eggs to amplify the amount of virus. Each virus strain is grown separately inside the eggs over the course of several days, after which it is harvested, inactivated, and purified.
Inactivated virus strains	The three virus strains are then combined to create the vaccine, blended with a carrier fluid and dispensed into vials.

These steps are descriptive and not intended as a set of instructions. If the goal is to offer instructions, imperative forms are used to indicate the necessary steps, as shown in this example of how to inoculate eggs with the influenza virus.

Inoculation of eggs in flu vaccine development

1. Place eggs into egg trays with the blunt end up, and label eggs with a specific identification number. Allocate 3 eggs for each specimen.
2. Wipe the blunt end of each egg with 70% ethanol and punch a small hole in the shell over the air sac.
3. Aspirate 0.6 ml of processed specimen into a tuberculin syringe with a 22 gauge, 1 1/2-inch needle.
4. Hold the egg up to the candler and locate the embryo. Insert the needle into the hole in the shell and, using a short stabbing motion, pierce the amniotic membrane and inoculate 100 µl of the specimen into the amniotic cavity. Withdraw the needle by about 1/2 inch (1.25 cm) and inoculate 100 µl of the specimen into the allantoic cavity. Remove the needle.

However, if we are interested not in providing guidance for actually performing a particular task, but in explaining how something is done—as in a process—we would be more likely to write this.

First, the virus strains most likely to cause disease are identified and three are selected for vaccine development. The virus samples of each selected strain are injected into separate batches of fertilized eggs to amplify the amount of virus. Each virus strain is grown separately inside the eggs over the course of several days, after which it is harvested, inactivated, and purified. The purified virus strains are then combined to create the vaccine, blended with a carrier fluid and dispensed into vials.

Source for flu vaccine content: World Health Organization, 2011, *Manual for the Laboratory Diagnosis and Virological Surveillance of Influenza.* Geneva.

Notice that each sentence now refers to a particular stage in the process: the identification stage, the preparation stage, and the dispensing stage.

What would be the effect if the process were described using the active voice? As you can see from the following passage, the focus on the stages is lost and the emphasis shifts to the agent (the person doing the steps—the researchers or technicians). If the person performing the activity is part of the sentences and becomes the link of familiar or old information, the process itself is backgrounded (less in focus).

First, researchers identify the virus strains most likely to cause disease and select three for vaccine development. Technicians inject virus samples of each selected strain into separate batches of fertilized eggs to amplify the amount of virus. Technicians grow each virus strain separately inside the eggs over the course of several days, after which they harvest, inactivate, and purify it. The technicians then combine the purified virus strains to create the vaccine, blend it with a carrier fluid and dispense it into vials.

Of course, there may be some occasions when different agents are an important part of different steps in the process.

Technician 1 injects virus samples of each selected strain into separate batches of fertilized eggs to amplify the amount of virus. Technician 2 grows each virus strain separately inside the eggs over the course of several days, after which the technician harvests, inactivates, and purifies it. Technician 3 then combines the purified virus strains to create the vaccine, blends it with a carrier fluid, and dispenses it into vials.

However, this now looks more like a job specification or duty roster than a process description. If information about the agent is important—which is uncommon—it would be better to describe the process in the following way.

> The virus samples of each selected strain are injected by Technician 1 into separate batches of fertilized eggs to amplify the amount of virus. Each virus strain is grown separately inside the eggs over the course of several days, after which it is harvested, inactivated, and purified by Technician 2. The purified virus strains are then combined by Technician 3 to create the vaccine, which is then blended with a carrier fluid and dispensed into vials.

According to research studies, using *by* + a human agent is rather uncommon in formal academic writing, except when describing the history of the field, as in these examples.

> The theory of transformational grammar was first developed *by Noam Chomsky.*
>
> The Bayesian method has been used *by statisticians* for many years to aid decision making on the basis of limited information.

In fact, we are more likely to find *by* + process or *by* + a non-human agent.

> The impact velocity can be obtained *by calculating* the difference of the arrival times of the two waves.
>
> This enzyme is used *by the cancer cells* to replicate.
>
> The increased mobility provided *by this new joint* allows wearers of the finger prosthesis to hold a cup, to pick up a piece of paper, and in some cases to write again.

Do the three *by* phrases in this next short passage introduce a process or a non-human agent?

> The rate at which heat will be lost by conduction from the body will be determined by the magnitude of the temperature gradient—the steeper the gradient, the greater the heat loss— and the rapidity with which the cooler air in contact with the skin is replaced by colder air.

The *by* + process statements provide no details. Such *by* phrases are typical in published journal articles, especially in the Methods section (see Unit Seven) of articles in the sciences. However, sometimes further information is useful. For instance, when you are writing a paper for a class, it might be to your advantage to make the *by* phrases more informative.

The passive voice allows you to keep the focus on the something other than the agent and also allows you to maintain a good flow of ideas. Thus, it is reasonable to use passive constructions in sections other than a process description.

TASK TEN

Expand these statements, making them more informative by replacing the noun phrase with one or more verb phrases. Here is an example.

Teaching can be improved by in-service training. →
Teaching can be improved by asking teachers to attend a range of short courses throughout much of their careers.

1. Bacteria found in meat can be killed by radiation.

2. Possible harmful effects of drugs can be reduced by testing.

3. Information on political preferences can be obtained by polling.

4. Cultures are partly preserved by ceremony and ritual.

5. Changes in land use can be detected by remote sensing.

6. The spread of infectious diseases can be controlled by vaccination programs.

TASK ELEVEN

Read this text that discusses energy harvesting as a means to achieve a clean power generation process that has a long lifetime. Underline the instances of the passive voice. Then discuss with a partner whether you think passive was the right choice. Notice there are three instances of unattended *this* in the passage. Would you add a noun phrase to any of them? Why or why not?

A Piezoelectric Frequency-Increased Power Generator for Scavenging Low-Frequency Ambient Vibration
Galchev, T., Aktakka, E.E., Kim, H., and Najafi, K. (2010).
IEEE 23rd International Conference on Micro Electro Mechanical Systems, 1203–1206.

❶ Rapid advances in silicon-based wireless microsystems technology over the past few decades has [sic] led to devices with unprecedented performance and utility with low power consumption. ❷ These technological advancements have led to the recent pervasiveness of wireless technology. ❸ However, for these systems to truly become ubiquitous, the issue of power has to be addressed. ❹ Batteries power most of these devices. ❺ However, they typically cannot last the entire lifetime of the device, and periodic replacement or recharging is needed. ❻ This is preventing different applications of wireless devices from being feasible.

❼ Energy scavenging from ambient sources can enable many new uses for wireless microsystems. ❽ While several ambient energy sources have been explored, kinetic energy is one of the most prevalent [1, 2]. ❾ However, the vast majority of the reported devices are designed to operate at mechanical resonance and at high frequencies (>30 Hz), limiting them to scavenging vibrations from periodic sources such as motors and other man made machinery. ❿ This leaves out a number of applications that are prime candidates for energy scavenging such as wearable or implantable devices, environmental monitoring applications, wireless devices for agriculture, and various security and military uses. ⑪ This is because the kinetic energy in these applications is not periodic and occurs less often.

Flow of Ideas in a Process Description

Unit One introduced the concept of flow, focusing mainly on old-to-new information flow, sentence connectors, and summary words. A good flow of ideas can also be achieved by combining or linking verb phrases. In the clouds and fog passage in Task Four (pages 109–110), there were no occasions where two or more passives were linked in the same sentence. Often, however, this may be desirable, as in our example of the flu vaccine.

> Each virus strain is grown separately inside the eggs over the course of several days, after which it is harvested, inactivated, and purified.

Some care needs to be taken when linking verbs in this way because this can sometimes lead to an unfortunate ambiguity. How are these sentences ambiguous, and what can you do about it?

1. The liquid is collected and kept for 24 hours.

2. The sample is collected and stored in a sterile container.

3. In consumer research, individuals are selected and interviewed by telephone.

TASK TWELVE

Consider these two versions of a passage discussing treatment for water birds after an oil spill. Underline the parts in Text B that differ from Text A, including the linked passives. Why does B have better "flow" than A? Consider old-to-new information flow as well as other devices to establish a good flow of ideas that were discussed in Unit One.

A. ❶ Once a bird has been brought to a rehabilitation center, basic procedures are followed. ❷ The bird is sedated, if necessary. ❸ The bird is examined to detect broken bones, cuts, or other injuries. ❹ Oil is flushed from its eyes and intestines. ❺ Heavily oiled birds are then wiped with absorbent cloths to remove patches of oil. ❻ Stomach-coating medicines may be administered orally to prevent additional absorption of oil inside the bird's stomach. ❼ The bird is warmed. ❽ It is placed in a quiet area. ❾ Curtains are hung around the area to limit the bird's contact with people.

B. ❶ Once a bird has been brought to a rehabilitation center, basic procedures are followed. ❷ First, the bird is sedated, if necessary, and examined to detect broken bones, cuts, or other injuries. ❸ Next, oil is flushed from its eyes and intestines. ❹ Heavily oiled birds are then wiped with absorbent cloths to remove patches of oil. ❺ Stomach-coating medicines may be administered orally to prevent additional absorption of oil inside the bird's stomach. ❻ The bird is then warmed and placed in a quiet area. ❼ Finally, curtains are often hung around the area to limit the bird's contact with people.

In addition to the linked passives, good flow is also achieved in Text B through the use of several time adverbials that help establish the sequence of events—*once, first, next, then,* and *finally.* (See also the time adverbials in the passage in Task Three.)

Participles

You may also have noticed, through the flu virus examples, that flow can be maintained by taking the *-ed* participle in the passive construction and using it as an adjective.

> First, the virus strains most likely to cause disease are identified and three are *selected* for vaccine development. The virus samples of each *selected* strain are injected into separate batches of fertilized eggs to amplify the amount of virus. Each virus strain is grown separately inside the eggs over the course of several days, after which it is harvested, inactivated, and *purified*. The *purified* virus strains are then combined to create the vaccine, blended with a carrier fluid and dispensed into vials.

By using *selected* and *purified* as adjectives, the writer establishes a strong connection between the sentences and indicates a newly acquired characteristic of the virus. This form of repetition contributes to the overall old-to-new flow of ideas.

TASK THIRTEEN

Improve the flow of ideas for the process descriptions by adding a time adverbial, linking passive, or using an *-ed* participle. There may be several possibilities. To help you, we have identified the process being partially described.

Example

Phytoremediation—using plants to remove metal from the soil

Original

The plants are selected. The plants are planted at a particular site based on the type of metals present and other site conditions. The plants are allowed to grow for some time. The plants are harvested. They are either incinerated or composted to recycle the metals.

<u>Revision</u>

The plants are selected and planted at a particular site based on the type of metals present and other site conditions. After the plants have been allowed to grow for some time, they are harvested and either incinerated or composted to recycle the metals.

1. Oil spill cleanup

The oil is skimmed from the surface using a boom. The oil is pumped into a tank for recycling.

_____

_____

2. Banana virus infection

Banana trees become infected with the banana bunchy top virus. In the early stages of the disease, the banana trees produce fruit that is deformed. Eventually, in later stages of the disease, the plants yield no fruit at all.

_____

_____

3. Tempering glass

The glass is cut to size. It is inspected to determine if it has any imperfections. The glass is heated to over 600°C. The glass is cooled in a step known as quenching.

_____

_____

4. Coronary bypass surgery

A vessel is taken from the leg. The vessel is grafted to the aorta and the coronary artery beyond the narrowed area. The vessel allows blood to flow to the heart muscle.

_____

_____

5. Geyser eruption

> Water from rain or melted snow percolates into the ground through cracks. The water is heated by the underlying rocks to temperatures well above the boiling point. The water does not boil. It becomes superheated. It also becomes pressurized. The water bursts out of the ground in an explosive steam eruption.

_____

_____

6. Now re-write the instructions for inoculating eggs with influenza virus as a process description. For convenience, we provide the text again here.

Inoculation of eggs in flu vaccine development

a. Place eggs into egg trays with the blunt end up, and label eggs with a specific identification number. Allocate 3 eggs for each specimen.

b. Wipe the blunt end of each egg with 70% ethanol and punch a small hole in the shell over the air sac.

c. Aspirate 0.6 ml of processed specimen into a tuberculin syringe with a 22 gauge, 1 1/2-inch needle.

d. Hold the egg up to the candler and locate the embryo. Insert the needle into the hole in the shell and, using a short stabbing motion, pierce the amniotic membrane and inoculate 100 µl of the specimen into the amniotic cavity. Withdraw the needle by about 1/2 inch (1.25 cm) and inoculate 100 µl of the specimen into the allantoic cavity. Remove the needle.

Active Voice in Process Descriptions

So far we have emphasized the use of the passive voice in process descriptions. Part of the reason for this is that until now we have concentrated on processes that involve human action. There are, however, many natural processes that take place without direct human intervention. In such cases, active voice is often used, or there may be a mix between active and passive, depending on the process.

TASK FOURTEEN

Read this problem-solution text and then discuss the questions on page 131. Note the frequent use of active voice in the process.

❶ Coral reef ecosystems are well known for their beauty and diversity. ❷ Found throughout tropical and subtropical regions of the world, they are often thought to be the marine equivalent of terrestrial rainforests. ❸ During the last several decades, however, coral reefs have been undergoing alarming changes as a result of environmental stresses, the most serious of which is whitening or bleaching. ❹ Although the mechanism of bleaching is not fully understood, this phenomenon is linked to the breakdown of the symbiotic relationship between the coral and an algae known as *zooxanthellae*. ❺ The algae, which give the coral its color, live inside the coral and perform photosynthesis, sharing the food that they produce. ❻ When the coral is stressed as a result of increases in temperature or the amount of light, the zooxanthellae carry out too much photosynthesis and in response the coral expels the algae. ❼ The loss of the algae exposes the white calcium carbonate skeletons, thus leaving the coral unable to grow or reproduce. ❽ Coral can survive for brief periods of time without the zooxanthellae, but if the reef environment does not return to normal, the coral dies.

❾ Coral reefs require from 30 to 100 years to recover from bleaching, if they recover at all. ❿ Researchers are now investigating whether this recovery time can be accelerated. ⓫ One approach currently under study involves transplanting healthy coral into a bleached reef. ⓬ However, thus far, the process has seen limited success.

1. Identify the situation, problem, solution, and evaluation.

	Sentence Numbers
Situation	
Problem	
Solution	
Evaluation	

Which of these sections receives the greatest treatment? Why?

2. What linking words and phrases are used to indicate cause and effect?

3. In Sentence 10, the author wrote *are now investigating*. Why was the progressive used?

4. Also, Sentence 10 includes a passive construction—*can be accelerated*. Why was this used rather than the active?

5. In Sentence 2 the author wrote... *they are often thought to be the marine equivalent of terrestrial rainforests.* How would the meaning change if the author had omitted the phrase in the passive voice (i.e., *they are often thought to be*) and opted for *they are the marine equivalent of*?

If a process description employs verbs that indicate a change of state, such as *expand, rise, cool, fracture,* and *form,* active voice is often used.

The Sun *rises* in the east and *sets* in the west.

Most metals *expand* and *contract* with variations in temperature.

The beam *fractures* when the load upon it becomes too great.

Tropical storms *can form* only in areas of high humidity and temperature. First, the warm sea *heats* the air above its surface. The warm, moist air then *rises* above the sea, creating a center of low pressure.

When demand *increases*, prices are likely to rise.

Can you think of some other examples?

There is a close parallel between process descriptions and descriptions of methods in research papers (see Unit Seven). If there is a difference, it is that process descriptions deal with standard procedures, while methods descriptions are typically new modifications or developments of earlier methods.

TASK FIFTEEN

Researchers have been trying to develop artificial muscles for medical purposes and have recently developed a way to re-create muscle action using a type of artificial silk. Here is a set of instructions for the preparation of the material, followed by information on how the material simulates actual muscle. Write a problem-solution text that uses the information as part of the solution. Use your imagination to create a situation and problem that could be solved through the use of an artificial muscle. Be sure to include all the required parts of a problem-solution text and to present the process in an appropriate manner, using passive voice and sequential connectors. Show cause-and-effect relationships where appropriate.

1. Cook the Orlon. Orlon is a form of artificial silk.

2. Boil the Orlon until it turns into a liquid rubbery substance.

3. Pour the solution onto Plexiglas to form a thin film.

4. Vacuum away excess water from the film. Allow the film to dry.

5. Cut the dried film into 2 centimeter–wide strips. Bake it in a 90°C oven. The material is ready for use after it has been baked.

6. Prepared Orlon has a structure similar to that of human muscle fiber and is naturally negatively charged with electricity.

7. If you apply acid to the material, you introduce a positive charge and you cause the ions to attract. This attraction contracts the material like a muscle.

8. If you apply a base material, you introduce a negative charge, the ions repel, and the muscle expands.

TASK SIXTEEN

In the articles from your field of study that you chose for Task Nine in Unit One, can you identify a Methods section? Does it describe a series of procedural steps that the authors followed? If so, is the description mainly written in the active or passive? Is it written in present tense? How is the flow of information maintained? In particular, are there time adverbials at or near the beginning of some sentences?

TASK SEVENTEEN

Write a process description of your own choice. If possible, choose a topic that you can later incorporate into a full problem-solution text. Consider choosing a topic in your field.

Language Focus: Indirect Questions

In one important sense, this unit has focused on formulating questions (problems) and evaluating the answers to those questions (evaluations). For example, if we look back at the text in Task Fourteen, we can see an example.

> ⑩ Researchers are now investigating whether this recovery time can be accelerated.

You probably noticed that in both cases the writer has opted to use an indirect question rather than a direct question. As you know, indirect questions follow the standard word order (the subject followed by the verb). They do not require that the subject and the verb be inverted, as in a direct question. Indirect questions also end with a period rather than a question mark. Here is an example.

> Direct question: What was the response rate?
> Indirect question: The editor asked what the response rate was.

The main difficulty in using indirect questions involves remembering that the subject and verb should not be inverted. Both research and experience suggest that not inverting is learned relatively late. The use of a "question word" may automatically trigger the inversion and lead to these incorrect forms.

> It is unclear what will be the price of oil next year.
>
> It is unclear what will the price of oil be next year.

The correct form, of course, would look like this.

> It is unclear what the price of oil will be next year.

TASK EIGHTEEN

The verb *to be* is missing from these statements. Insert it in the correct position and in the correct form.

1. The question remains whether it possible to develop a reliable earthquake warning system.

2. We need to know what precautions being taken to prevent the spread of the disease.

3. There is some question as to whether the current crisis can eventually overcome.

4. It has not been determined how these policies likely to affect small businesses.

5. It might also be of interest to investigate to what extent persistence a major factor in graduate student success.

6. Another issue raised by this study is whether and to what extent poverty and environmental degradation linked.

7. The process uses the CPU power it needs, depending on what it doing and depending on what other processes running.

8. The research investigated whether time money and found that $V = \{W[(100-t)/100]\}/C$, where V is the value of an hour, W is a person's hourly wage, t is the tax rate, and C is the local cost of living.

Indirect questions have a number of functions in academic writing; for example, they can be used in explaining purpose.

A questionnaire was distributed to determine whether . . . .

However, perhaps their most important use has been illustrated in Task Eighteen. They are often used to "problematize" issues, cases, phenomena, statements, and so on. For this reason, they are particularly common in problem-solution texts—first as one way of introducing the problem and then as one way of offering a (critical) evaluation of the solution. In Task Nineteen you will have an opportunity to use indirect questions.

Although we have stressed indirect questions as a way of introducing or discussing problems, we do not want to imply that this is the only way. In some cases, direct questions may be possible.

However, is the data reliable?

Keep in mind, however, that you should limit your use of these in academic writing, as we stated in Unit One. Another common way to introduce a problem is to use an adversative sentence connector, such as *however* or *nevertheless* (see Table 1 on page 37). Notice how each of these examples is somewhat negative.

However, this system/process/idea has its problems.

Nevertheless, few solutions have been found to . . . .

Despite this, little progress has been made in . . . .

Nevertheless, the problem remains as to how . . . .

However, there remains the issue of reliability.

Even so, this model has some serious limitations.

Even so, researchers still have to find a way to . . . .

TASK NINETEEN

One of us (John) interviewed a student writing up her first research paper for her master's in Social Work. Mei-Lan said she was interested in learning more about the Chinese elderly living in the United States. She said that she had chosen this topic because many people believed that Chinese communities traditionally had always looked after their elderly and, further, that these old people would not easily accept help from outsiders. She wondered whether this was still true in the United States. She also observed that the available research had mainly been conducted in the larger Chinese communities in the major cities on the east and west coasts. She therefore decided to study small communities in the midwest. John then asked her about her methods.

JS: How did you find your subjects?

ML: I used friends and friends of friends in the local Chinese community to introduce me.

JS: How did you collect your data?

ML: I used face-to-face interviews. I wanted one-on-one situations since I was afraid that if family members had been there, my interviewees might not have been truthful about their feelings and experiences.

JS: Did you have to get permission from the review board?

ML: Yes, because I was dealing with human subjects.

JS: Did you have any problems with this?

ML: No, not at all. Interview methods are usually quickly approved.

JS: How many people did you interview?

ML: I only managed to interview about ten. Not much time, and not all of my contacts worked out. I also got some refusals. So, this was just a small-scale pilot study. There were not enough subjects for any statistical analysis.

JS: How long did the interviews last, and did you use a fixed list of questions?

ML: About an hour. I had some questions but did not always use them all. I guess my data could be said to be based on what sociologists call "semi-structured" interviews.

JS: Did you use English?

ML: The interviewees used whatever language they were most comfortable with—Mandarin, Taiwanese, or English. I think this was a strong point in my method.

Now write up Mei-Lan's investigative procedure. Maintain a formal style. You may decide to include only some of the information contained in the preceding conversation or re-order it.

Introducing the Solution

Looking back at the texts we have examined, we see these solutions introduced.

> To address this problem in the village of Chungungo, scientists implemented an interesting solution.

> One approach currently under study involves transplanting healthy coral into a bleached reef.

Here are some additional skeletal sentences based on sentences we found in published articles.

> Solutions to this problem are now widely discussed. One remedy is to. . . .

> One method to address this difficulty is to. . . .

> There are two possible ways of handling this problem. The first. . . . The second. . . .

> Several options are available to address this obstacle. However, the best one seems to be. . . .

> A radically different design/model of . . . can overcome this limitation.

> Recently, researchers have made significant progress in overcoming this difficulty by. . . .

The verb *solve* is a fairly common choice for introducing a solution, but a number of other verbs can be used as well. Indeed our own examples demonstrate variety in verb choice. We would like to further add that the examples are what we have referred to as skeletal phrases. In other words, these are phrases that you can adapt for your own writing, taking care that you add your own original content. For instance, in a text on fog harvesting, it is possible to write this sentence based on a skeletal phrase to introduce the solution.

> Recently, researchers have made significant progress in overcoming this difficulty by *introducing a simple fog harvesting system.*

One way to find skeletal phrases is to use Google Scholar to search for them. Rather than looking for journal articles, you can search for strings of language. For instance, you could do this search: "approach to * this problem" (note quotation marks are needed to search for the exact phrase; the * is a wild card that will reveal the language that appears between *approach* and *to this problem*). The results of this search would reveal these verbs that can complete the phrase: *overcome, solve, tackle,* and *address,* to name a few. You will also see possible grammar choices. In the example search, for instance, you will see both *approach to solving this problem* and *approach to solve this problem.* To determine which is most common in your field, you can also narrow your search by adding your area of study. If you are interested in robots, you can search for "approach to * this problem" robots.

We suggest that you exercise caution when searching for and using skeletal phrases. While skeletal phrases will help you with your academic phraseology, you do not want to borrow complete expressions of ideas, which could be considered plagiarism (see Unit Five).

TASK TWENTY

Write your own problem-solution text that includes both a process description and a definition, or write a review of the current state of knowledge in your field that raises a question about it and offers a possible or partial answer. Be sure to include the kind of detail that can convince readers of your claims.

Unit Four
Data Commentary

In many academic writing tasks, there comes a place where you need to discuss data. In fact, research has shown that in some fields such as Engineering, the ability to make a point or build an argument based on data is essential to successful writing (Wolfe, 2011). In many disciplines, the data is displayed in a table, graph, figure, or some other kind of non-verbal illustration. The data may come from a source, or it may be the outcome of your own work—that is, your results. (For more on writing up your results, see Unit Seven.) This data is likely incorporated in the main text, although in some cases it may be provided in an appendix. We have called data-focused writing subtasks *data commentaries*. The amount and level of specificity of commentary provided for a data set can vary considerably depending on the type of text being written (the genre). For instance, in published journal articles, some data commentaries may be as short as a single sentence and be very general. In a technical report, the commentary may be much longer.

Strength of Claim

Like many other aspects of academic writing, data commentaries are exercises in positioning yourself. There are, as a result, both dangers and opportunities. One danger is to simply repeat in words what the data has expressed in non-verbal form—in other words, to offer description rather than actual commentary or interpretation. An opposite danger is to read too much into the data and draw conclusions that are not well supported. The art of the commentary is for you to find the right strength of claim in discussing the data and then to order your statements in some appropriate way (perhaps in order of interest or relevance). This may involve moving in a general-specific direction (see Unit Two). To illustrate what we mean by finding the right strength of claim, we offer Task One.

TASK ONE

Work with a partner and decide whether the verb phrase choice results in a strong (S), weak (W), or neutral (N) statement. Some disagreement is reasonable. Can you think of other verbs or verb phrases that could complete the sentence? How would you evaluate the strength of claim for your alternatives?

Many studies have concluded that excessive credit growth _____ the global financial crisis.

_____ a. contributed to

_____ b. caused

_____ c. may have contributed to

_____ d. was probably a major cause of

_____ e. was one of the causes of

_____ f. might have been a factor in

As you can see, each of the options "fits" grammatically and each makes sense; however, only one may actually be the "right" choice in terms of what you know and think. Thus, your choice of verb can convey your stance or perspective and the extent to which you believe the explanation to be correct.

It is not easy to predict precisely what you might need to do in a data commentary, but some of the more common purposes are to

- highlight the results of research
- use the data to support a point or make an argument in your paper
- assess theory, common beliefs, or general practice in light of the given data

- compare and evaluate different data sets
- assess the reliability of the data in terms of the methodology that produced it
- discuss the implications of the data
- make recommendations

Typically, of course, a data commentary will include several of these elements.

TASK TWO

For this task, discuss these questions about students' internet activities with a partner and then look at some data.

1. What kinds of illegal or inappropriate activities do students engage in via the internet?

2. How common do you think these activities are among college students?

3. Which, if any, of the activities you identified should be tolerated or ignored?

4. Look at the data presented in Table 4 on page 142. What is your reaction? Is the data consistent with what you discussed in Questions 1 and 2? Does anything surprise you? After reviewing the data commentary on page 143, answer the questions on pages 143–144.

TABLE 4. University Student Respondents' Self-Reported Instances of Online Misbehavior during the Previous 12 Months (Data are the percentage of all student respondents, N = 1,222.)

		Once or Twice	A Few Times	More Than a Few Times	Overall Percentage
Misrepresentation of self	• Given false information about yourself to another person on the internet	34.0	12.0	5.0	51.0
	• Provided false information about your personal details on an online form	33.0	13.0	5.0	51.0
Unauthorized use of another's account	• Accessed someone else's email account without his or her knowledge	18.0	6.0	2.0	26.0
	• Used someone's credit details online without his or her knowledge	4.0	1.0	1.0	6.0
Plagiarism of an essay or assignment	• Copied a few sentences from a website into an essay or assignment without citing the source	39.0	16.0	5.0	60.0
	• Copied a few paragraphs from a website into an essay or assignment without citing the source	21.0	7.0	2.0	20.0
	• Copied a few pages from a website into an essay or assignment without citing the source	8.0	3.0	1.0	11.0
	• Copied a whole essay or assignment from a website without citing the source	2.0	1.0	0.6	4.0
	• Paid for an essay or assignment from a website	2.0	0.7	0.7	3.0
Unauthorized downloading of music or film	• Unauthorized downloading of music from the internet	18.0	22.0	36.0	76.0
	• Unauthorized downloading of film or video from the internet	18.0	16.0	19.0	53.0
Pornography use	• Viewed online pornography or pornagraphic pictures or films	17.0	12.0	11.0	40.0
	• Paid for online pornography or pornographic pictures or films	3.0	1.0	1.0	5.0

The commentary was written by a student enrolled in an academic writing course.

❶ Table 4 shows survey respondents' self-reported involvement in online misbehavior during the previous 12 months. ❷ According to the table, the most common online misbehavior is "unauthorized downloading of film and music." ❸ As can be seen, just over three out of four students in the study have downloaded music or film more than once a year. ❹ This very high percentage of misbehavior is especially alarming, since protection of intellectual property is a basic element for enriching the film and music industries.

❺ Another notable result is that viewing pornographic materials on the internet was reported by 40% of the respondents, although purchasing pornography was reported by only a small minority of these respondents. ❻ The least frequently reported misbehaviors were illegally using another person's email account or credit information, along with either completely copying homework from a website or buying an assignment from a source on the internet. ❼ It is worthwhile to note that these different forms of online misbehavior seem to be patterned according to the degree of the perceived seriousness of the bad behavior. ❽ Activities that are generally believed to be criminal (e.g., using someone's credit information) were less frequent than activities that, although unlawful, many do not view as criminal, such as downloading movies and music. ❾ Illegal downloading may have an economic cause, but other reasons might be important, as well. ❿ This problem will likely continue until reasons that students engage in this behavior are clearly identified.

5. What are the purposes of Sentences 1–3?

6. How is the commentary organized overall?

7. Which sentence contains the author's key point?

8. On pages 140–141 we listed seven common purposes for data commentaries. In which category (or categories) does this one fall?

9. To what aspect of the data does the author pay most attention? Why? Do you think this is enough? If not, what else should be discussed?

10. Where, if at all, do we get a sense of what the author thinks about the data and how committed the author is to the interpretations? How important is it that we know this? How important is the comment in Sentence 4, for instance?

11. Illegal downloading of music, film, and video was reported by 76% of the students. In Sentence 3, this is expressed as *just over three out of four*. What do you think about that reformulation and about these alternatives?

    a. about 75%   c. most
    b. as much as 76% of all   d. slightly more than 75%

12. Sentence 7 begins with *It is worthwhile to note that.* . . . Go to Google Scholar and search for "It is * to note that" to find other adjectives that could be used. (Be sure to use the quotation marks.) If you do not have access to the internet, try to list some possibilities on your own.

13. Which is more common: *it is worthwhile to note that* or *it is worth noting that*? How common is *it is worthwhile noting that*? If you have internet access, go to Google Scholar to compare the frequencies of each of the three expressions.

14. What are some of the features of this text that make it an example of written academic English? Look back to Unit One if you need help.

Structure of Data Commentary

Data commentaries usually have these elements in the following order.

1. location elements and/or summary statements
2. highlighting statements
3. discussions of implications, problems, exceptions, recommendations, or other interesting aspects of the data

Here is the data commentary from Task Two again, with these elements marked.

Location statement + indicative summary

❶ Table 4 shows survey respondents' self-reported involvement in online misbehavior during the previous 12 months. ❷ According to the table, the most common online misbehavior is "unauthorized downloading of film and music." ❸ As can be seen, just over three out of four students in the study have downloaded music or film more than once a year. ❹ This very high percentage of misbehavior is especially alarming, since protection of intellectual property is a basic element for enriching the film and music industries. ❺ Another notable result is that viewing pornographic materials on the internet was reported by 40% of the respondents, although purchasing pornography was reported by only a small minority of these respondents. ❻ The least frequently reported misbehaviors were illegally using another person's email account or credit information, along with either completely copying homework from a website or buying an assignment from a source on the internet. ❼ It is worthwhile to note that these different forms of online misbehavior seem to be patterned according to the degree of the perceived seriousness of the bad behavior. ❽ Activities that are generally believed to be criminal (e.g., using someone's credit information) were less frequent than activities that, although unlawful, many do not view as criminal, such as downloading movies and music. ❾ Illegal downloading may have an economic cause, but other reasons might be important, as well. ❿ This problem will likely continue until reasons that students engage in this behavior are clearly identified.

Highlighting statement in terms of a linking *as* clause

Interpretations and implications

TASK THREE

Table 5 provides some additional data on internet misbehavior. Work with your partner and consider what data you might highlight in a written commentary and why. How can you account for some of the differences in the groups?

TABLE 5. Respondent's Self-Reported Instances of Online Misbehavior during the Past 12 Months according to Background (Data are percentages.)

		Misrepresentation of Self	Unauthorized Use of Another's Account	Plagiarism of an Essay or Assignment	Unauthorized Downloading of Music or Film	Pornography Use
Gender	Male	66	24	65	85	79
	Female	59	29	59	72	14
Age	18	63	26	65	79	38
	19	61	28	60	75	38
	20	69	31	61	84	55
	>21	61	24	64	74	54
Perceived internet competence	Expert	70	30	65	85	48
	Non-expert	54	24	58	65	28
Access to internet	Private personal computer	63	27	62	79	40
	Shared public computer	66	29	64	70	40

From Selwyn, Neil, 2008, A Safe Haven for Misbehaving? An Investigation of Online Misbehavior Among University Students, *Social Science Computer Review, 26,* 446–465. Copyright Sage Publications. Used with permission.

We will now look at location elements and summaries in more detail.

Location Elements and Summaries

Many data commentary sections begin with a sentence containing a location element and a brief summary of what can be found in a visual display of information, as shown in these examples.

a. *Table 5 shows* the types of internet misbehavior common among university students.

b. *Table 6 provides* summary statistics for the variables used in the analysis.

c. *Figure 2 shows* a honeycomb solid oxide fuel cell (SOFC) unit with air cooling paths.

d. *Figure 1 plots* wealth as a function of age.

As you can see, location statements direct readers to view important information in a table, chart, graph, or other figure. Even though research indicates that readers often look at the visual information before reading, location statements are expected. They are considered to be a form of metadiscourse—sentences or phrases that help readers make their way through a text by revealing such things as organization, referring readers to relevant parts of a text, or establishing logical connections. Metadiscourse is a noticeable feature of academic writing, although its value and frequency of use varies from one writing culture to another.

While grammar checking tools may influence you to largely use active voice in your writing, the passive can also be used, as demonstrated here. In fact, in some published texts, the percentage of passive verbs has been found to be as high as 25 percent.

Summary + Location Element with Passive Voice

a. The types of internet misbehavior common among university students *are shown in Table 4.*

b. Summary statistics for the variables used in the analysis *are provided in Table 5.*

c. A honeycomb solid oxide fuel cell (SOFC) unit with air cooling paths *is shown in Figure 2.*

d. Wealth as a function of age *is plotted in Figure 1.*

We bring two points to your attention. First, note the consistent use of the present tense. This occurs because the author is talking about his or her present paper. Second, in English the active forms are just as appropriate as the passive versions. (However, in a number of languages it may not be natural to say that a graph or other inanimate object *reveals, gives,* or *suggests.*) Although switching between active and passive voice may seem to be a good stylistic strategy, a better strategy would be to choose active or passive on the basis of old-to-new information flow (see Unit One). Specifically, passive constructions can be used to place the old or familiar information in the subject position and the new information—that is, the location of the data at the end.

Notice that all the examples thus far provide general summaries of the data. We have been given no specific details or highlights. We do not know, for instance, what is significant in the SOFC design or at what age an individual might be the wealthiest or the poorest. Depending on what you are writing, you may want to focus more on some significant aspect of the data rather than merely generally pointing out what data is provided. This indication may be particularly important when you are using data to make a point. For instance, if you want to argue that students are likely to engage in misbehavior on the internet regardless of how they access it, you could write this sentence.

> Table 5 shows that students engage in misbehavior on the internet using both private and public computers.

If your point is that wealth increases slowly with age but decreases quickly after reaching a peak, you could write this sentence.

> Figure 1 reveals that wealth is accumulated slowly, but sharply declines after age 65.

Notice the use of *that* in the two sample sentences. Sentences containing *that* clauses do not easily go into the passive. (The flag indicates incorrect usage.)

> ⚑ That wealth sharply declines after age 65 is revealed in Figure 1.

While the passive version follows the rules of grammar, the sentence that results seems awkward in comparison to the version in the active voice. Thus, if you want to highlight some aspect of the data using a *that* clause, use the active.

These two ways of pointing the reader to the data are similar to a two-way classification often used to categorize journal article abstracts. *Indicative abstracts* merely indicate what kind of research has been done (i.e., they summarize); *informative abstracts* additionally give the main results and/or highlight something interesting about the data. The parallel, we believe, is close, and therefore we can describe location elements as either indicative or informative.

Language Focus: Verbs in Indicative and Informative Location Statements

There are appoximately a dozen verbs commonly used to make reference to non-verbal material. Some can be used with both types of location statement. *Show* is one such verb.

- *Indicative* statement that summarizes what kind of research was done

  Table 4 shows the types of internet misbehavior common among university students.

- *Informative* statement that highlights something interesting about the data

  Table 4 shows that illegal downloading of music or films is common among students.

Notice that the information after the *that* clause is given in a clause with a subject and a verb.

Some verbs can be used with only one type of location statement. *Provide*, for example, can only be used in an indicative location statement and cannot be used with a *that* clause. (The flag indicates incorrect usage.)

  Table 5 *provides* demographic information for the study participants.

  ⚑ Table 5 provides that most study participants were fairly competent internet users.

TASK FOUR

Decide whether each verb in the table can be used for an indicative (general summary) location statement, an informative statement (highlighting a specific aspect of the data), or both. Use the two sentences that follow the table to help you make your decision. Mark each box in the table with a Y for yes if the usage is possible and an N for No if it is not possible. The first two have been done as examples.

	Indicative	Informative
show	Y	Y
provide	Y	N
give		
present		
summarize		
illustrate		
reveal		
indicate		
display		
demonstrate		
suggest		

The table _____ the effect of social networking use on the duration of students' study time.

The table _____ that social networking has little, if any, effect on the duration of students' study time.

We looked at Ken Hyland's (2004) corpus of 80,000 words from 80 research articles in Biology, Physics, Electrical Engineering, Mechanical Engineering, Marketing, Applied Linguistics, Sociology, and Philosophy to determine which verbs are most frequently used in full sentences to refer to figures and tables (Hyland, 2004). Table 6 shows the results of our analysis. All the verbs were in the present tense.

TABLE 6. Active Verbs Following Reference to a Visual

	Reference to Figure	Reference to Table	Total
shows	31	15	46
presents	6	7	13
illustrates	7	3	10
summarizes	2	4	6
demonstrates	2	3	5
contains	0	5	5
provides	0	3	3
depicts	2	0	2
lists	0	2	2
reports	0	2	2
TOTAL			94

Hyland, 2004.

We then looked at verbs in the passive voice in references to figures and tables. The results are given in Table 7.

TABLE 7. Passive Verbs in Reference to a Visual

	Reference to Figure	Reference to Table	Total
shown in	21	23	44
illustrated in	29	5	34
presented in	2	10	12
given in	2	4	6
listed in	0	6	6
seen in	3	1	4
provided in	1	3	4
summarized in	1	3	4
seen from	3	0	3
TOTAL			117

Hyland, 2004.

Language Focus: Linking *as* Clauses

So far, we have used sentences in which the reference to non-verbal data is either the subject or the agent in the main clause. However, another common way to introduce informative statements is the linking *as* clause. Here are some examples.

> *As shown in Fig. 1 and Fig. 2*, the companies used in this survey varied significantly in geographical location, size, and method of operation.
>
> *As can be seen in Table 6*, the overall rate of recall, while low, also showed considerable variation.
>
> Shallow junction GM APDs, peripheral area test structures, and gate-controlled diodes, *as shown in Figs. 1(a), 1(b), and 1(c)*, were manufactured in p-type epitaxially grown bulk silicon using a conventional 1.5 μm CMOS process reported previously.
>
> *As can be seen in Figure 1*, the fully charged Lithium-ion battery supplies 4.2 volts.

These linking clauses (where *as* does not mean the same thing as *since* or *because*) are exceptional in English grammar. In the passive, these linking clauses have no subjects. Compare the following sentences.

> a. As it has been proved, the theory may have practical importance.
> b. As has been proved, the theory may have practical importance.

In Sentence a there is a causal relationship between the *as* clause and the main clause. Because the theory has been proved, it may have practical importance. In Sentence b the *as* clause serves to suggest that the practical importance of the theory (not just the theory) has been established. Although you may find examples that run contrary to this advice, remember not to use subjects in passive linking *as* clauses.

Finally, using prepositions with this type of linking statement can be tricky. Here are some of the main standard uses.

> *in*   As shown *in* Table 1 . . . .
> *by*   As predicted *by* the model . . . .
> *on*   As described *on* the previous page . . . .

TASK FIVE

Fill in the blank with an appropriate preposition.

1. As can be seen _____ Figure 4, earnings have decreased.

2. As predicted _____ the model, there is a strong positive relationship between water loss and gas uptake (Fig. 1).

3. As described _____ the previous section, there are two common types of abstracts.

4. As defined _____ the introduction, fraud is a form of intentional deception resulting in injury.

5. As reported _____ the previous literature, factors that affect electrode adhesion during the chlorination process are the average grain size and the pore density in the AgCl thin film.

6. As can be seen _____ a comparison of the two tables, peak oxygen uptake and exercise capacity are reliable predictors of quality of life.

7. As has been demonstrated previously _____ materials _____ this type, small cracks pose a serious problem.

8. As has been demonstrated _____ previous studies, organic polymer materials have advantages over inorganic substrates.

9. As shown _____ the line of best fit, there is no clear statistical relationship between fiscal costs and crisis length.

10. As noted _____ our discussion, prolonged exposure to morphine also produces apoptosis in cell culture.

TASK SIX

Look at two or three journal articles, preferably in your field of study and possibly those you used in Task Nine in Unit One, that present some data in visual form. How do the results in your tables compare with the information provided about data commentary so far? In which section or sections of the article did you find the commentary on the data? Complete the table.

Element	Yes or No?
Location Statements	
Full informative sentences	
Full indicative sentences	
As clauses	
Imperatives (e.g., *see Fig. 1*)	
Parenthetical phrases (*Fig. 1*)	
Present tense active	
Present tense passive	
Examples of possible useful language	
Verbs used in the location statements	
Language that softens or strengthens claims	

Now that you have done a bit of analysis, in this next task we ask you to add to a data commentary on the strategies of Japanese researchers writing in English.

TASK SEVEN

The following data commentary, which is based on Dr. Akiko Okamura's (2000) research on how Japanese researchers learn to write in English in their chosen field, is missing references to the non-verbal data given in Table 8. Expand the commentary by first starting with a location + summary statement and then by adding a suitable linking *as* clause. Review the material presented up to this point before you begin.

TABLE 8. Strategies Used by Japanese Scientists When Writing in English

Writing Strategy	Percentage
Think mainly in Japanese but write in English	61%
Think in Japanese and English but write in English	16%
Think in English and write in English	23%

Okamura, 2000.

Slightly more than three-fourths of the scientists surveyed adopted writing strategies that involved the use of their first language. Moreover, less than a quarter appear capable of writing directly in English. Overall, the figures would appear to suggest that most Japanese scientists have difficulties and frustrations when preparing papers for English-medium journals.

Highlighting Statements

The central sections of data commentaries consist of highlighting statements. Highlighting statements are points that can be supported by the details of the data. We have already seen some examples in the text that accompanies Task Two. Highlighting statements need good judgment. They are an opportunity to show your intelligence. In particular, they are an opportunity for you to demonstrate that

- you can spot trends or regularities in the data.
- you can separate more important findings from less important ones.
- you can make claims of appropriate strength.

Try to avoid

- simply repeating all the details in words.
- attempting to cover all the information.
- claiming more than is reasonable or defensible.

Language Focus: An Introduction to Qualifications and Strength of Claim

We said earlier that highlighting statements need good judgment. They also need good presentation of judgment. Thus, they have two requirements. One is the need to be cautious—and sometimes critical—about the data. As Skelton (1988) neatly observed, "It is important for students to learn to be confidently uncertain." The other requirement is to have the linguistic resources to express this caution. In this section, therefore, we deal with ways of qualifying or moderating a claim and indicating your stance toward your claims. Your stance or perspective is important in academic writing because it allows you to reveal not only *what you know*, but also *what you think*.

The way in which you reveal your stance contributes to author positioning. To reveal your stance, you can, for instance, indicate your attitude (for example, *I think*); soften or hedge your claim as in *it is likely that*; or employ boosters to strengthen your points such as *clearly there is a need to*. These stance markers are part of your textual or disciplinary *voice* (Hyland, 2008). Control of this voice is "central to building a convincing discourse" and integral to "texts that plausibly represent an external reality" (Hyland, 2008) and anticipate readers' reactions to those texts.

Although you might think that stance, and moderating your claims in particular, is important in only some fields, research shows that thoughtful, careful presentation of claims is characteristic of all fields—even those that are thought to deal with objective facts. Table 9 shows three types of stance markers identified in Hyland's corpus of 240 published research articles from eight disciplines.

TABLE 9. Stance Features by Discipline (per 1,000 words in journal articles)

Feature	Philosophy	Sociology	Applied Ling.	Marketing	Physics	Biology	Mech. Engin.	Elect. Engin.	Avg.
Hedges	18.5	14.7	18.0	20.0	9.6	13.6	8.2	9.6	14.5
Attitude Markers	8.9	7.0	8.6	6.9	3.9	2.9	5.6	5.5	6.4
Boosters	9.7	5.1	6.2	7.1	6.0	3.9	5.0	3.2	5.8
Stance	37.1	26.8	32.8	34.0	19.5	20.4	18.8	18.3	26.7

Adapted from Hyland, 2004.

TASK EIGHT

Discuss Table 9 with a partner. What is interesting or possibly relevant? List a few observations and be prepared to share these with your class.

Now let us look at Task Nine to see how two student writers attempted to present their claims in a manner that is suitable for a course paper.

TASK NINE

Read the data commentaries from MICUSP that were written by two different students, the first a doctoral student in Psychology and the second a graduate student in Operations Engineering. Underline the words or phrases that seem to express caution in making a claim. Circle language that boosts any claims.

A. ❶ There are a number of explanations for why musicians have superior cognitive abilities to non-musician controls. ❷ First, it is possible that only the more intellectually rigorous people continue with music training once they have been exposed to it. ❸ Practicing a musical instrument takes a tremendous amount of discipline. Individuals who are willing to work that hard may also work hard in academic settings, thus improving their cognitive abilities. ❹ Secondly, socio-economic class could be playing a role. ❺ In a study comparing scholastic aptitude among musicians and non-musicians, Phillips found a difference in the two groups, but once socio-economic class was taken into account the difference nearly disappeared (Phillips, 1976). ❻ It is possible that the differences between musicians and non-musicians is actually innate or caused by something not musically related in the environment.

MICUSP File PSY.G1.03.1

B. ❶ The overall size increase in many of the speedometer design parameters between speedometer set A to set B seems to have accounted for the overall lower average response times and lower average error and miss percentage rates. ❷ However, other design differences, such as location of the speedometer on the instrument display panel, did not have such influential effects on the data. ❸ Comparing speedometers 1 and 4 (speedometer on left side) to speedometers 2 and 3 (speedometer on right side) only one small pattern was seen. ❹ Speedometers 2 and 3 had, compared to their respective speedometer set, slightly lower average response times than the other speedometer in the set. ❺ Whether or not this small difference in average response time can be attributed to the location of the speedometers on the instrument display panel was not possible.

MICUSP File IOE.G0.02.1

Given the predominance of hedges in academic writing, in the next Language Focus we will examine some specific ways of moderating or qualifying a claim.

Language Focus: Specific Ways of Moderating or Qualifying a Claim

Likelihood

There are many ways of expressing your degree of commitment to your claims in written academic English. One simple way is to use a modal auxiliary (e.g., *may*, *might*, or *could*) as you saw in Task One of this unit. Notice how the claim changes in these sentences. Which one is the strongest? Which is the most cautious?

A. Word-of-mouth advertising influences a consumer's incentive to purchase a product.

B. Word-of-mouth advertising can influence a consumer's incentive to purchase a product.

C. Word-of-mouth advertising could influence a consumer's incentive to purchase a product.

D. Word-of-mouth advertising may influence a consumer's incentive to purchase a product.

E. Word-of-mouth advertising might influence a consumer's incentive to purchase a product.

In these examples, the phrases weaken in strength.

Stronger

A. It is clear that . . .

B. It is rather clear that . . .

C. It is very probable/highly likely that . . .

D. It is probable/likely that . . .

E. It is possible that . . .

F. It is unlikely that . . .

Weaker

} word-of-mouth advertising influences a consumer's incentive to purchase a product.

Stronger

A. There is a definite possibility that . . .

B. There is a strong possibility that . . .

C. There is a good possibility that . . .

D. There is a slight possibility that . . .

E. There is little possibility that . . .

Weaker

} word-of-mouth advertising influences a consumer's incentive to purchase a product.

Distance

Distance is another way of indicating your stance. This involves removing yourself from a strong—and possibly unjustified—claim. Notice how Sentence A leaves no room for doubt, which may be too strong.

A. Health education has a positive impact on a patient's quality of life.

B. Health education seems to have a positive impact on a patient's quality of life.

C. It seems that health education has a positive impact on a patient's quality of life.

D. It would appear that health education has a positive impact on a patient's quality of life.

An alternative strategy to distance yourself from the data is to attribute your point to someone else or to other studies, which can indicate that it is "soft."

Here are a few examples.

Based on the limited data available, . . .   the African
continent has
According to this preliminary study, . . .   relatively strong
wind power
Based on previous surveys, . . .   potential in parts
of the west,
According to some earlier studies, . . .   south, and east.

In the view of many scholars, . . .

Softening Generalizations

Writers sometimes want to make generalizations. These can be effectively used either to start developing a point for which support is later provided or drawing a conclusion from different pieces of information. Importantly, generalizations should be grounded in some reasonable evidence and stated cautiously so that they will be accepted by readers.

Three classic verbs for carefully stating a generalization are the verbs *appear (to)*, *seem (to)*, and *tend (to)*.

> Children living in poverty *appear to* do poorly in school.
>
> Children living in poverty *seem to* do poorly in school.
>
> Children living in poverty *tend to* do poorly in school.

If you remove *appear to, seem to,* or *tend to,* the result is a very strong claim that suggests all poor children will be unsuccessful.

> Children living in poverty do poorly in school.

By using *seem* or *tend,* you can avoid criticism from readers who may be aware of some poor children who are doing well.

Another way to make a generalization more acceptable is to qualify (limit) the subject.

> *Many* children living in poverty do poorly in school.
>
> A *majority of* children living in poverty do poorly in school.
>
> *Some* children living in poverty do poorly in school.
>
> *In most parts* of the world children living in poverty do poorly in school.

A third alternative is to add exceptions.

With the exception of

Apart from

Except for

} those enrolled in specialized programs, children living in poverty do poorly in school.

Weaker Verbs

Finally, claims can be reduced in strength by choosing a weaker verb. At the beginning of this unit, you compared these two claims.

> Many studies have concluded that excessive credit growth caused the global financial crisis. (stronger)

> Many studies have concluded that excessive credit growth contributed to the global financial crisis. (weaker)

As indicated at the beginning of the unit, your choice of verb can indicate your level of commitment to your claim.

Combined Qualifications

Sometimes several types of qualifications are combined in order to construct a defensible claim, as shown in this example. We start with a strong claim.

> When people have too many choices, they choose the safest one.

Now see what happens when the following qualifications are added.

> + *according to some recent research* (adding distance)

> + *in some cases* (weakening the generalization)

> + *tend to* (indicating likelihood)

So we now have this sentence.

> According to some recent research, in some cases when people have too many choices, they tend to choose the safest one.

This sentence is an example of the writer being "confidently uncertain," but perhaps it is overdone. One of the qualifying phrases could probably be omitted to avoid excessive qualification. Too much caution may result in your saying almost nothing, as in the following example from a journal in Anthropology.

> It could be concluded that some evidence seems to suggest that at least certain villagers might not have traded their pottery with others outside the community.

Examples of extremely, possibly overly cautious claims in the hard sciences can even be found.

> Studies have found that quantum entanglement may play a role in some types of magnetoreception with certain molecules, but more work is needed to explore this phenomenon.

In some cases, these overly hedged statements may be constructed in response to reviewer criticisms.

TASK TEN

Underline the verb that makes the weaker claim.

1. The results (indicate / establish) that there is a link between smoking and lung cancer.

2. The survey results (suggest / show) that the reuse of sentences or sections from one's previously published papers is a questionable practice.

3. The latest series of studies (question / challenge) the value of including consumer expectations in the assessment of service quality.

4. The results given in Figure 4 (validate / support) the second conclusion that certain bacteria can reduce arsenic (As) levels in groundwater.

5. Baseline conditions have been (assumed / shown) to be accurate at the time of the surveys.

6. Several studies have (identified / alluded to) the importance of cultural sensitivity as a precursor to culturally appropriate medical care.

7. Changes in ambient temperature may have (influenced / distorted) the test results.

8. Previous studies (failed / forgot) to consider the change in the fiber interface during the cracking process.

9. As shown in Figure 3, trade liberalization has (stimulated / encouraged) economic growth in developing countries, leading to rising incomes.

10. Figure 12 (depicts / clarifies) the relationship between these two systems.

TASK ELEVEN

Now, try to soften the claims in any four of the items. Make the sentences academically respectable and defensible.

1. Tall people have higher incomes than short people.

2. Economic sanctions are ineffective.

3. Alcohol causes brain damage in teenagers.

4. Passive smoking causes cancer.

5. Recycling is the best solution to the waste disposal problem.

6. Physical exercise prevents depression.

7. Deep tunnels are safer and less vulnerable to earthquake shaking than are shallow tunnels.

8. Private schools provide a better education than do public schools.

Organization

Data commentaries are usually ordered from general to specific. We saw this pattern, for example, in the short commentary on the Japanese scientists in Task Seven. Decisions about organization, however, become more complex with comparative data. Consider the following case: You are taking a graduate course in the social sciences. You have been studying differences in parental behavior with regard to their adolescent children. Your instructor suggests that, contrary to popular belief, American parents may be stricter with their teenage sons than they are with their daughters. You are given Table 10 on page 166, which is based on a survey conducted among suburban families in a midsize midwestern U.S. city, and asked to prepare a short commentary on the main findings.

TASK TWELVE

The information in this task contributed to a published study of how children begin to make choices regarding the time spent on doing homework and watching television, as well as deciding how to spend their money. Read the incomplete data commentaries based on Table 10 written by three students. The commentaries (on pages 166–167) include only the location statements and some highlighting statements. What are the differences among the three? Which do you think makes the best highlighting statement? Why?

TABLE 10. Decision-Making Patterns of U.S. Parents and Adolescents
(N = 6327, roughly similar numbers of boys and girls)

Adolescent Child Is Sole Decision-Maker	Total Sample (%)	Girls (%)	Boys (%)
Amount of allowance	2	2	3
Clothes	28	29	27
Spending	50	50	51
Friends	53	52	54
Curfew	2	2	3
Television	42	44	41
Religion	23	22	26
Parents Are Sole Decision-Makers			
Amount of allowance	91	91	92
Clothes	39	32	45
Spending	27	25	29
Friends	30	28	31
Curfew	88	88	88
Television	43	41	45
Religion	60	56	64

Based on Lundberg et al., 2009.

Student A

Table 10 shows who makes important decisions in key aspects of adolescents' lives. As can be seen, parents alone are responsible for the amount of allowance for 91% of girls and 92% of boys. Another category where parents exert a lot of control is curfew, as revealed by 88% of all adolescents. Most decisions about religion are also made by parents. In this category, however, there is a difference between boys and girls. Fifty-six percent of girls report that their parents decide matters of faith in contrast to 64% of boys. However, nearly one-fourth of the adolescents make decisions about religion on their own.

Student B

Table 10 shows the percentage of adolescents and parents who are solely responsible for important decisions in the lives of adolescents. As can be seen, decision-making patterns are very similar for both boys and girls for all types of decisions except one. Specifically, more boys than girls report parental involvement in clothing decisions. In this category, 45% of the boys reported sole parental decision making, but only 32% of girls did so.

Student C

Table 10 shows the decision-making patterns of parents and adolescents in relation to key aspects of adolescents' lives. As can be seen, overall, parents are similarly involved in decisions for both boys and girls, but the level of involvement differs depending on the type of decision. The percentage of sole parental decision making is highest for the amount of allowance, the time of curfew, and religion. The lowest percentages were reported for decisions regarding the child's friends and spending of money. Television viewing is the one area where similar percentages of children and their parents make decisions.

Language Focus: Comparisons

There is another kind of qualification that can be usefully employed in data commentary. We can illustrate this by looking again at the data on parental restrictions in Table 10. We have already said that it may not be a good idea to simply repeat the data in words. Therefore, it may not be a good strategy to make a series of statements like this example.

Fifty-six percent of girls report that their parents decide matters of faith in contrast to 64% of boys.

A series of such statements seems to imply that the reader is unable to read the numbers. Instead we might opt for comparative statements like the following.

Fewer girls than boys reported that their parents decide matters of faith.

More boys than girls reported that their parents decide matters of faith.

Not as many boys reported that their parents decide matters of faith.

One problem here is the vagueness of *more* or *fewer*. How much, for example, is "more"—2%, 10%, or 50%? We could more exactly write this.

Eight percent more boys than girls reported . . . .

Look at the information in Table 11 about cell phone use while riding a bicycle.

TABLE 11. Bicycle Commuters' Perception of Danger while Using Mobile Phones

	Men n = 1000	%	Women n = 1000	%	p value*
Not at all	51	5.1	18	1.8	<0.001
Slight	158	15.8	73	7.3	
Moderate	426	42.6	469	46.9	
Quite a bit	248	24.8	333	33.3	
Extreme	117	11.7	107	10.7	

Based on Ichikawa and Nakahara, 2008.

In a data commentary, it would be possible to make these observations.

a. More than twice as many men as women reported . . . .

b. A smaller percentage of women reported . . . .

c. Nearly three times as many men reported . . . .

d. Nearly the same number of men and women . . . .

These observations are also possible.

e. The percentage of men who thought there was only a slight risk was over twice that of women

f. The percentage of men who thought there was only a slight risk was over two times higher than that of women

g. The percentage of women who thought there was quite a bit of risk exceeded that of men.

TASK THIRTEEN

Write a full data commentary for Table 10. Begin with a location element and summary. Create whatever highlighting statements you want. In Task Eleven, Students A, B, and C offered no cautious explanations of the results. When you write your commentary, be sure to do so. Review the two Language Focus sections on qualifications and strength of claim (pages 156–157 and 159–163).

TASK FOURTEEN

Examine Table 12 on page 170 and study the commentary. You should be able to analyze its organization by now.

❶ Table 12 shows the median number of years to complete a doctoral program for both U.S. and international students (indicated by temporary visa status). ❷ As can be seen, U.S. students in most fields on average complete doctoral programs in less time than international students. ❸ The difference in median years to completion ranges from a relatively low 0.4 years in the humanities to a high of one year in the life sciences. ❹ The consistent difference in time to degree is not fully understood at present. ❺ However, one key factor may be the students' relationships with their advisors. ❻ Advisors typically expect their advisees to work independently, an expectation that might run contrary to the expectations of international student advisees, who may expect their advisors to give explicit input with regard to how to navigate their way through the doctoral program. ❼ Expectations that are "unmet, unclear, or unarticulated" (Barnes, 2010) could influence the length of time it takes to earn a doctorate.

TABLE 12. Median Years to Doctorate for Selected Doctoral Programs in the United States

Time to Degree and Demographic Characteristics	All Fields		Life Sciences[a]		Physical Sciences[b]		Social Sciences[c]		Engineering		Education		Humanities		Other Non-Science & Engineering Fields	
	Median	Number	Median	Number	Median	Number	Median	Number	Median	Number	Median	Number	Median	Number	Median	Number
Years since entering graduate school	7.7	44,667	7.0	10,321	6.7	7,594	7.7	6,958	6.9	7,013	12.3	5,811	9.5	4,403	9.7	2,567
All doctorate recipients[d,e]																
Sex																
Male	7.6	23,810	7.0	4,668	6.7	5,345	7.9	2,907	6.9	5,510	12.6	1,932	9.6	2,121	9.7	1,327
Female	8.0	20,847	7.0	5,651	6.5	2,246	7.7	4,049	6.7	1,501	12.3	3,879	9.5	2,281	9.9	1,240
Citizenship																
U.S. citizen/ permanent resident	7.7	30,800	6.7	7,434	6.2	4,246	7.7	5,335	6.3	3,043	12.8	5,276	9.7	3,726	10.7	1,740
Temporary visa holder	7.7	13,689	7.7	2,847	7.3	3,309	8.2	1,598	7.3	3,941	9.0	515	9.3	660	8.7	819

[a] Includes agricultural sciences/natural resources, biological/biomedical sciences, and health sciences.
[b] Includes mathematics and computer and information sciences.
[c] Includes psychology.
[d] Includes those of unknown citizenship.
[e] Includes only cases with a valid year of entry into graduate school.

From NSF/NIH/USED/USDA/NEH/NASA, 2009 Survey of Earned Doctorates.

Here are the instructor's comments on the commentary. The
instructor is a professor in Comparative Higher Education. Mark
the comments as reasonable (R) or unreasonable (U) and discuss
your choices with a partner. How would you edit the passage to
reflect your reactions? There are no absolutely right or wrong
answers.

_____ 1. I am curious about your focus on the fact
that international students take longer to finish their
PhDs. This seems a bit negative. You could just as
easily focus on the fact that there is not a lot of
difference.

_____ 2. What do you think about the data on education? The
numbers for education look really different from the
others. I think you should address this.

_____ 3. It is strange that you do not mention the English
language factor. At least at first sight, this would
seem to suggest that this would matter a lot.

_____ 4. The median of almost 8 years from entering
a PhD program to completing the PhD seems really
long. What factors could be contributing to this? This
seems a lot longer than what is typical for our
program. Most programs here say the PhD program is
about 5 years.

_____ 5. What are you suggesting with your point about
advisors? Are you saying that international students
have more difficulty than domestic students? Do you
have any concrete evidence?

Concluding a Commentary

Concluding a commentary requires some original thinking. In fact, you may recall that the conclusion of the commentary on internet misbehavior did not merely stop, but offered the author's view that misbehavior will persist.

> ⑩ This problem will likely continue until reasons that students engage in this behavior are clearly identified.

The discussion of time to degree also concluded with some speculation about the reasons for differences in time to PhD completion.

> ⑦ Expectations that are "unmet, unclear, or unarticulated" (Barnes, 2010) could influence the length of time it takes to earn a doctorate.

One of the challenges in writing the conclusion is believing that you have something that is worth saying and that it reasonably follows from the data. In this regard, research has shown that strong writers engage in some reasonable speculation about the meaning of their findings, while weak writers avoid doing so, often due to concerns about being wrong (Wolfe, 2011). Thus, to position yourself as knowledgeable and capable, you may want to consider including some of these elements in your conclusion.

- explanations and/or implications of the data (usually required)
- explanation of the reasoning process that led to the conclusions (if appropriate)
- unexpected results or unsatisfactory data (if necessary)
- possible further research or possible future predictions (if appropriate)

TASK FIFTEEN

Work with a small group and discuss how to revise the draft data commentary for Figure 8. Then re-write it. The grammar of the commentary is fine. However, you may want to think about the points discussed in the commentary, the reference to the figure, phrases that can link the discussion to the figure itself, and the strength of the conclusion.

FIGURE 8. Survival Time in Water of Different Temperatures When
Wearing Different Types of Clothing

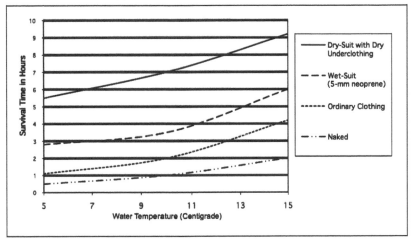

Based on Noakes, 2000.

The figure shows how long people can survive in water when they
wear different kinds of clothing that have different levels of insula-
tion. Clothing has an influence on how long a person can survive.
The effect of clothing is greater at warmer temperatures. A person
wearing no clothing in cold water can survive only less than one
hour.

The data you are working with may not always be perfect. In other words, it
could contain some anomalies, or there may be discrepancies between the
actual findings and the expected ones. Additionally, there may be obvious
limitations in the study for which the data was collected. If any of these
problems or limitations exist, usually the best strategy is to make a comment
about them. Try to explain why these unexpected results or errors occurred.
Think back to Sam in Unit One. As you may recall, Sam was faced with a
problem concerning the validity of his data. By bringing the problem out in
the open, Sam was able to present himself as a perceptive and intelligent
scholar.

---

⑤ Language Focus: Dealing with Unexpected Outcomes or "Problems"

If your data is not quite what you expected, your first reaction might be to ignore the data that does not fit. Instead you should try to find a way to discuss the data. In fact, such a discussion can help you position yourself as knowledgeable, if you are able to offer a brief explanation and perhaps suggest what work could be done in the future to overcome problems with your data. The verb phrases in these example sentences may be helpful as you discuss imperfect data.

> The difference between expected and obtained results *may be due to* fluctuations in the power supply.
>
> This discrepancy *can be attributed to* the small sample size.
>
> The anomaly in the observations *can probably be accounted for by* a defect in the camera.
>
> The lack of statistical significance *is probably a consequence of* weaknesses in the experimental design.
>
> The problem with dating this archaeological site *would seem to stem from* the limited amount of organic material available.

Now notice how *due to* is used in these sentences. Only the first three uses are definitely correct.

1. The error may be due to improper installation of the program.
2. The error may be due to the fact that the program was not properly installed.
3. The error may be due to the program not being properly installed.
4. ℔ The error may be due to the program was not properly installed.
5. ℔ The error may be due to not properly installing the program.

Sentence 4 is not well formed, while Sentence 5 is doubtful. While *due to* can sometimes be followed by an *-ing* clause, Sentence 5 is problematic because of the lack of a clear agent. Notice that in the correct statements the verb phrase is followed by a noun phrase. If necessary, as in Sentence 2, a noun phrase like *the fact that* could be added, even though *due to the fact that* is considered awkward by some instructors. Nevertheless, sometimes this is the only solution.

TASK SIXTEEN

Read an extended version of the commentary on the Japanese scientists from Task Seven. Label each sentence according to its function and list the qualifying words or phrases in the chart. The first one has been done for you.

❶ Slightly more than three-fourths of the scientists surveyed adopted writing strategies that involved the use of their first language. ❷ Moreover, less than a quarter appear capable of writing directly in English. ❸ Overall, the figures would appear to suggest that most Japanese scientists have difficulties and frustrations when preparing papers for English-medium journals. ❹ Given the well-known differences between scientific English and scientific Japanese (Okamura, 2002), the heavy reliance on Japanese is somewhat unexpected. ❺ This phenomenon probably reflects a lack of confidence in English. ❻ Nevertheless, all the findings need to be treated with some caution since they are based on what scientists said they did, rather than on direct observations of their writing. ❼ Case studies of actual writing practices would be one possible direction for further research.

Sentence	Purpose	Qualifying Words or Phrases
1.	highlighting statement	slightly
2.		
3.		
4.		
5.		
6.		
7.		

Now that you have analyzed a data commentary text in terms of the purpose of each sentence and the qualifying words or phrases, you are ready to write your own commentary of data that can be interpreted in several ways.

TASK SEVENTEEN

Imagine you are a teaching assistant for an introductory Biology course with a total enrollment of 150. Exams are usually given in the evening to avoid losing valuable class time. Because some students have evening commitments, a make-up (alternative) exam is always given. The professor has noticed a big discrepancy between the scores of the last regular exam and those of the make-up exam. Because you administered the last make-up exam, you have been asked to offer an explanation. You have prepared the data in Table 13. Write a data commentary either as a report or an email message to your professor.

TABLE 13. A Comparison of the Regular and the Make-Up Exam

	Regular Exam	Make-Up Exam
Average score (points out of 100)	86	72
Time administered	Wednesday, 7:00 PM	Friday, 4:00 PM
Difficulty of questions	average	average
Number of students	125	25
Proctor	professor	teaching assistant
Two sample questions and answers discussed right before the exam	yes	no, considered unnecessary
Room temperature	about 20°C	about 28°C

Dealing with Graphs

So far we have primarily focused on tables. Discussions of graphs essentially follow the same principles as those for tables, with one major difference. Much of the vocabulary used to comment on graphs is quite different.

TASK EIGHTEEN

Look at the graph in Figure 9 and the data commentary on page 178 that was written by one of our students. We have omitted certain words and phrases. Can you complete the passage? Work with a partner.

FIGURE 9. Comparison of the Actual CO_2 Levels with the Model Predictions

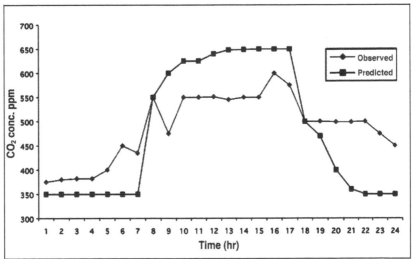

The observed and predicted CO_2 levels for 24 hours in a commercial building ❶ _____ in Figure 9. The actual CO_2 concentrations were ❷ _____ directly from sites in the building by the CO_2 Trapping Method. The predicted concentrations were calculated by using one of the available indoor air quality models. In this case the "fully stirred and conservative reactor with internal source model" ❸ _____ since it was assumed that the air was completely replaced and mixed with fresh air every hour, and there was no degradation.

❹ _____ shows that the predicted CO_2 concentrations increase sharply after 8 AM and ❺ _____ steeply after 6 PM. This is because the CO_2 levels were ❻ _____ to be dependent on the number of people in the building since people produce CO_2 as a result of respiration. However, the model overestimates the CO_2 levels during the occupancy periods (8 AM–5 PM) and ❼ _____. The lower CO_2 levels found in the occupancy period ❽ _____ several factors such as the presence of plants, which generate oxygen, while using CO_2.

❾ _____, the predicted levels are lower than the ❿ _____ during the vacancy period because the model assumed that nobody was in the building after 6 PM and that the air was fully mixed. In fact, there might be overtime workers in the building after 6 PM or the ventilation rate ⓫ _____ during the vacant period. Although the "fully stirred and conservative reactor with internal source model" tends to overestimate or underestimate ⓬ _____ occupancy, overall, it performs well with a coefficient of 0.9 ($r = 0.9$).

Jiyoung Lee, minor editing

Jiyoung has produced an excellent draft of a data commentary. But, look at the last paragraph again. What changes would you suggest? Do you have any suggestions for changes in tense usage?

One feature of Jiyoung's data commentary in Task Eighteen is that she made little explicit reference to the lines on her graph, as many writers do when dealing with historical or technical data. As you know, graph lines have a special terminology. In fact, they have somewhat different terminologies depending on the discipline.

TASK NINETEEN

Choose a term from the list on page 180 that you think best describes the graph in **Figure 10** at each of the given ages.

FIGURE 10. Sense of Humor as Character Strength for Different Ages

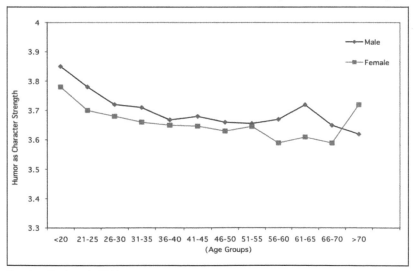

Based on Ruch et al., 2010.

downward trend	peak	low point	sharp rise
steep fall	rise	level off	fall off
remain steady	spike	increase	decline

1. Humor as character strength ages 61–65 for males:

   _____

2. Humor as character strength ages 26–45 for females:

   _____

3. Humor as character strength ages 65–70 for males:

   _____

4. Humor as character strength ages 60–65 for females:

   _____

5. Humor as character strength ages 20–50 for males:

   _____

Now look at this graph from the physical sciences in Figure 11 and choose a term from the list that best describes each letter. Some terms may be used more than once.

FIGURE 11. Hard Sciences Graph

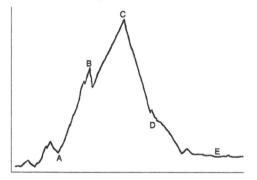

minimum	local dip/local minimum	local maximum
spike	maximum/peak	level off
kink	linear increase	

A. _____   D. _____

B. _____   E. _____

C. _____

In what way are the terms for the physical sciences different?

Dealing with Chronological Data

The graph in Figure 12 has a time dimension. Such data often presents writers of data commentary with an organizational problem. On the one hand, writers want to follow the general-specific rule. On the other, they may want to respect the chronological order, that is, start with the earliest and finish with the latest. Usually, it works best to try to combine both strategies.

Figure 12 provides data on hand temperature for two different kinds of soccer goalkeeping gloves, which are very important for goalkeepers. The two sets of gloves were made of normal foam material (NFM) and phase control material (PCM), the latter being designed to change its physical state from solid to liquid to gas over a range of temperatures.

FIGURE 12. Changes in Mean Hand Temperature for PCM and NFM Glove Conditions during Exercise

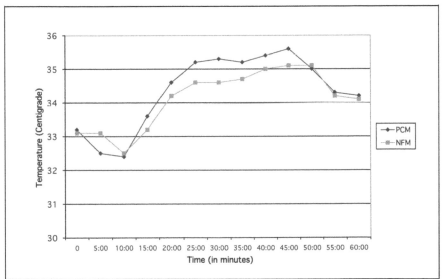

Based on data from Purvis and Cable, 2000.

TASK TWENTY

The sentences in this commentary expand on the information given in Figure 12 on page 181. They are not in the correct order. Rearrange them in an appropriate order. Place 1 in front of the first sentence, 2 before the second, and so on. Work with a partner.

—— a. Hand temperatures for PCM were consistently higher during the 45-minute exercise period, reaching a maximum temperature of just under 36°.

—— b. As can be seen, after an initial decrease, hand temperature increased in each condition.

—— c. However, the increase in temperature was more pronounced for the PCM condition.

—— d. The PCM gloves were designed to maintain a steady and comfortable hand temperature.

—— e. Figure 12 displays the absolute skin temperature of the hand during exercise for both the PCM and NFM conditions.

—— f. When exercise stopped at 45 minutes, hand temperatures for the two conditions fell at approximately the same rate.

—— g. Thus, the PCM glove performance was inferior to that of traditional NFM and would not necessarily lead to enhanced goalkeeper performance.

—— h. An overall increase in temperature is inevitable since goalkeeping gloves of any kind prevent heat loss and evaporation, leading to discomfort and a negative effect on performance.

—— i. However, as can be seen, the PCM gloves did not perform as intended.

What can you conclude about how this data commentary is organized?

🌀 Language Focus: Prepositions of Time

The commentary in Task Twenty made few references to specific points at a particular time. However, it would have been possible to do so by including one or two sentences like these.

> *From* the 10th to the 45th minute, hand temperature increased.
>
> *During* the first ten minutes, hand temperature dropped.
>
> Hand temperature fluctuated *throughout* the period.
>
> Hand temperature remained over 35°C *from* the 25th to the 50th minute for the PCM condition.
>
> Hand temperature remained under 34°C *until* the 20th minute for the PCM condition.
>
> The highest temperature occurred *in* the 45th minute for the PCM condition.
>
> *In* the last ten minutes, hand temperature decreased for both conditions.
>
> *After* 50 minutes had passed, hand temperature began to decrease.
>
> *At* time 0, hand temperature for both gloves was 33°C.

TASK TWENTY-ONE

Write a suitable data commentary for Table 14 (page 184) or Figure 13 (page 185). You do not need to use both data sets. Find current data to supplement the information if you can. Can you speculate about the future? If you are interested in countries or regions other than those given here, go to the source of this data (www.scimagojr.com/index.php) and make some other selections. Alternatively, if you are familiar with H factors, explain for a new scholar how they are calculated, using information from the table.

TABLE 14. Country Rankings for Publications in *Elsevier Journals* 1996–2010

Country	Citable Documents	Citations	Self-Citations	Citations per Document	H Index
1 United States	4,530,542	87,296,701	40,680,446	19.08	1,139
2 China	1,508,308	5,614,294	2,948,990	5.17	279
3 United Kingdom	1,277,760	21,030,171	5,139,059	16.39	689
4 Japan	1,315,158	14,341,252	4,411,776	11.08	527
5 Germany	1,212,919	17,576,464	4,712,414	14.86	607
6 France	885,310	12,168,898	2,880,568	14.21	554
7 Canada	678,129	10,375,245	2,086,045	16.49	536
8 Italy	652,700	8,407,658	2,004,523	13.59	477
9 Spain	486,926	5,498,629	1,438,981	12.26	377
10 Australia	431,908	5,940,125	1,299,736	14.98	413
11 India	437,455	2,590,791	891,790	6.62	227
12 Russian Federation	439,232	2,121,202	649,236	4.86	262
13 Netherlands	371,845	6,628,024	1,157,260	18.78	465
14 South Korea	365,246	2,710,566	636,127	9.12	258
15 Brazil	273,053	1,970,704	636,353	8.91	239
16 Switzerland	265,772	5,123,829	736,533	20.49	466
17 Sweden	267,358	4,657,464	801,285	17.95	410
18 Taiwan	264,035	1,957,112	496,308	8.86	209
19 Poland	231,790	1,553,359	428,883	7.32	232
20 Belgium	203,276	3,064,642	479,902	16.04	360
21 Turkey	190,023	1,110,749	317,389	6.93	158
22 Israel	163,727	2,484,606	383,457	15.58	340
23 Austria	139,976	1,969,446	292,996	15.02	310
24 Denmark	140,234	2,563,344	392,209	19.14	338
25 Finland	148.239	2.277.054	392.301	16.64	318
26 Greece	134.246	1.227.591	234.462	10.55	216
27 Hong Kong	124.183	1.347.442	221.574	11.97	238
28 Mexico	120.830	926.074	206.334	8.92	193
29 Norway	116.118	1.618.371	275.923	15.63	277
30 Czech Republic	117.453	861.365	215.673	8.26	195
31 Iran	115.044	434.990	179.227	7.20	101
32 Singapore	104.747	988.263	146.276	11.02	209
33 New Zealand	94.462	1.209.745	203.690	13.91	238
34 Portugal	95.994	873.105	183.305	11.35	191
35 Argentina	90.135	814.586	185.945	9.85	183

The H index is a reflection of both the number of publications and the number of citations per publication.

FIGURE 13. Papers Published with Authors from More than
One Country

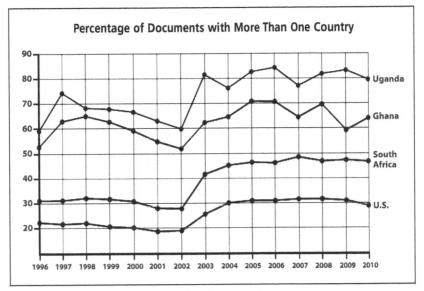

SCImago. (2007). SJR — SCImago Journal & Country Rank. Retrieved from www.scimagojr.com.

TASK TWENTY-TWO

If you have some data that you have gathered from your own research, write a data commentary about it. Alternatively, gather some data from your classmates on some aspect of their university experience that you think would be of interest. You could focus on topics such as housing and transportation, free time activities, their use of Skype or other forms of computer-mediated communication to stay in touch with others, their awareness of support services on campus, or any other suitable topic. Put together a very short questionnaire that is easy to distribute, complete, and analyze. A Likert-type questionnaire (in which choices are *strongly disagree, disagree, neither agree nor disagree, agree,* or *strongly agree*) would be a good choice. Keep it simple. Here is an example of a questionnaire on food preferences put together in one of our writing courses. The questionnaire was designed after the students had read an article entitled "The Use of Food Attitudes and Behaviors in Determination of the Personality Characteristic of Openness: A Pilot Study," which examined whether individual food attitudes and preferences were related to the personality characteristic of "openness" and willingness to experience new things.

1. Are you a graduate or undergraduate student?

   _____

2. Which country did you grow up in? _____

What is your reaction to the following? Circle one response.

3. I mostly eat food from my own culture that I am familiar with.

   strongly   *disagree*   *neither agree*   *agree*   *strongly*
   disagree   *nor disagree*   *agree*

4. It's fun to try new foods that I have never had before.

| strongly disagree | disagree | neither agree nor disagree | agree | strongly agree |

5. If offered something new, I would eat it only after I had asked what it was.

| strongly disagree | disagree | neither agree nor disagree | agree | strongly agree |

6. I think I am an adventurous person.

| strongly disagree | disagree | neither agree nor disagree | agree | strongly agree |

Comments or explanations

_____

_____

Unit Five
Writing Summaries

Of all the writing tasks we have discussed so far, summary writing may well be the one you are most familiar with. We make summaries of many different things, including meetings, lectures, and readings. Our summaries may be quite elaborate, or they may only involve one or two key phrases, depending on our purpose for writing them. These summaries of what others have written or said may be for our own personal use. Most often we use this material for future reference. In an academic setting especially, summaries can form an essential part of our preparation for an exam, a class discussion, a research paper, a thesis, or a dissertation. In these situations, we are free to concentrate on what we think is important or interesting about the source.

In the first half of this textbook, you could successfully complete most of the writing tasks by relying either on information that you already possessed or on a small amount of information from a source. In the second half, we will pay more attention to writing that heavily relies on the use of sources. Unit Five deals with summary writing. Unit Six expands our discussion of summary writing to the writing of critiques of or critical responses to source material, including book reviews. Finally, in the last two units, we move on to writing sections of an entire research paper.

Summary writing may be part of a more public communication (such as a published research article) and an integral part of other work that you may do. For example, your advisor may ask you to summarize some recent literature that could be useful for your research group. Instructors may ask you to write a literature review or critique articles. You may need to write a major research paper at key points in your degree program or write a proposal. At the very least you will need to summarize some published work to support claims in your papers and to build a foundation for your research. In each of these cases, you use the work of others to add credibility to your claims and you have an opportunity to "display" your understanding of the work in your field. Look back at the reality television text that starts on page 56. By summarizing relevant portions of this text, you can support your view as to whether reality TV programs are similar to or different from traditional documentaries.

Considerations before Writing a Summary

It is not likely that you will be assigned to produce a simple summary of a published paper or book unless you are writing an annotated bibliography. Instead, it is more likely that you will need to write a summary as part of some other writing task. These summaries can be extremely challenging to write. A good summary has three principal requirements.

1. It should be focused on the aspects of the source text or texts that are relevant for your purpose.

2. It should represent the source material in an accurate fashion.

3. It should condense the source material and be presented in your own words. Summaries that consist of directly copied portions of the original rarely succeed. Such a summary may suggest that you can find potentially important information but will likely fail to reveal the extent to which you have understood it. In addition, you may be plagiarizing (see pages 196–197).

Notice that we have not said anything about the length of a summary, which will often be determined by your purpose. Sometimes instructors will ask for a one-page summary of an article (or maybe a two-page summary of a book) as part of a critique assignment. They may also ask for a paragraph-length abstract (see Unit Eight) or even a mini-summary of one to two sentences (as is typical of annotated bibliographies). Regardless of the type of text, to do a good job, you must first thoroughly understand the source material you are working with. So, here are some preliminary steps in writing a summary.

1. Skim the text, noticing and noting the subheadings. If there are no subheadings, try to divide the text into sections.

2. If you have been assigned the text, consider why. Determine what type of text you are dealing with—that is, the genre of the source text (e.g., a research paper) or perhaps the organization (problem-solution or general-specific). This can help you identify important information and focus your reading strategies.

3. Read the text, highlighting important information or taking notes.

4. In your own words, list the points of each relevant section. Try to write a one-sentence summary of each.

5. List the key support points for the main topic, and include minor details if necessary.

6. Make sure your notes reflect the strength of the claims or conclusions.

7. Write your reactions or thoughts about the sections you have identified as important. (Keep in mind that information from sources should support, but not become or be offered instead of, your own interpretation and explanation.)

8. Go through the process again. Read the text several times if necessary, making changes to your notes as appropriate.

TASK ONE

Let's say you have been asked to write a paper in Public Health that examines the consumption of energy drinks such as Red Bull, Lipovitan-D, and Cobra. You come across this article and want to use it to support your claim that these drinks are potentially harmful and should be closely regulated. Underline the information you might borrow to support your perspective. Be prepared to discuss your choices.

Caffeinated Energy Drinks—A Growing Problem
Reissig, C. J., Strain, E. C., and Griffiths, R. R. (2009).
Drug and Alcohol Dependence, 99, 1–10.

❶ In 2006, annual worldwide energy drink consumption increased 17% from the previous year to 906 million gallons, with Thailand leading the world in energy drink consumption per person, but the U.S. leading the world in total volume sales (Zenith International, 2007). ❷ Although "energy drinks" first appeared in Europe and Asia in the 1960s, the introduction of "Red Bull" in Austria in 1987 and in the U.S. in 1997 sparked the more recent trend toward aggressive marketing of high caffeine content "energy drinks." ❸ Since its inception, the energy drink market has grown exponentially, with nearly 500 new brands launched worldwide in 2006

(Johnson, 2006), and 200 new brands launched in the U.S. in the 12-month period ending July 2007 (Packaged Facts, 2007). ❹ From 2002 to 2006, the average annual growth rate in energy drink sales was 55% (Packaged Facts, 2007) (Fig. 1). ❺ The total U.S. retail market value for energy drinks (from all sources) was estimated to be $5.4 billion in 2006 and has shown a similar annual growth rate over this same period (47%) (Packaged Facts, 2007).

❻ These drinks vary widely in both caffeine content (ranging from 50 to 505 mg per can or bottle) and caffeine concentration (ranging from 2.5 to 171 mg per fluid ounce) (Table 1). ❼ For comparison, the caffeine content of a 6 oz cup of brewed coffee varies from 77 to 150 mg (Griffiths et al., 2003). ❽ The main active ingredient in energy drinks is caffeine, although other substances such as taurine, riboflavin, pyridoxine, nicotinamide, other B vitamins, and various herbal derivatives are also present (Aranda and Morlock, 2006). ❾ The acute and long-term effects resulting from excessive and chronic consumption of these additives alone and in combination with caffeine are not fully known. ❿ Although the full impact of the rise in popularity of energy drinks has yet to be realized, the potential for adverse health consequences should be considered and may be cause for preemptive regulatory action.

Figure 1. Energy Drink Sales in the U.S. 2002–2006

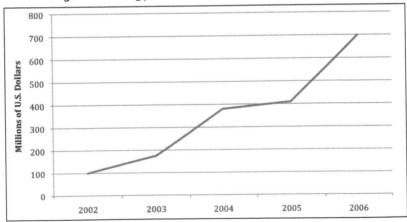

Fig. 1. Data are based on scanner data from over 32,000 stores such as supermarkets, drug stores, and discount merchandisers other than Wal-Mart. Data are from retailers with $2 million or more in annual sales but exclude: clubstores/warehouse clubs, convenience stores, dollar/variety stores, food service, vending, concession sales and specialty channels/retailers of all types (e.g., gourmet/specialty food stores, hardware/home improvements stores, military exchanges). (Based on data from Packaged Facts, 2007.)

Table 1. Caffeine in Energy Drinks (United States)

	Ounces per Bottle or Can	Caffeine Concentration (mg/oz)	Total Caffeine (mg)
Top selling energy drinks*			
Red Bull	8.3	9.6	80.0
Monster	16.0	10.0	160.0
Rockstar	16.0	10.0	160.0
Amp	8.4	8.9	75.0
Tab Energy	10.5	9.1	95.0
Higher caffeine energy drinks**			
Wired X505	24.0	21.0	505.0
Fixx	20.0	25.0	500.0
BooKoo Energy	24.0	15.0	360.0
SPIKE Shooter	8.4	35.7	300.0
Cocaine Energy Drink	8.4	33.3	280.0
Lower caffeine energy drinks**			
Bomba Energy	8.4	8.9	75.0
HiBall Energy	10.0	7.5	75.0
Vitamin Water (Energy Citrus)	20.0	2.5	50.0
High concentration energy drinks**			
RedLine Power Rush	2.5	140.0	350.0
Ammo	1.0	171.0	171.0
Powershot	1.0	100.0	100.0
Fuel Cell	2.0	90.0	180.0
Classic soft drinks			
Coca-Cola Classic	12.0	2.9	34.5
Pepsi Cola	12.0	3.2	38.0
Dr Pepper	12.0	3.4	41.0
Mountain Dew	12.0	4.5	54.0

* Top selling energy drinks in the U.S. 2006, listed sequentially as a percentage of market share (based on data from Packaged Facts, 2007).
** Examples of energy drinks drawn from the hundreds of energy drink products currently marketed in the U.S., listed sequentially on total caffeine content.

Data on drink volume and caffeine content were obtained from the manufacturer via product label, website, or personal communication with manufacturer representatives. The one exception was that the caffeine content for BooKoo Energy was obtained from the energyfiend website (Energyfiend website, 2008).

Here are two other possible writing scenarios that are very different from the original task.

1. You are working on a course project focused on product development for a beverage company, and you have been asked to propose ideas for a new beverage. You think that the company should create an energy drink. Would you choose the same information as you did at the beginning of the task (see page 190)?

2. You have been asked to write a recommendation about including energy drinks in campus vending machines. Would your selections from the source text change?

Underlying the three hypothetical scenarios in Task One are yes-no questions that can be answered using information from the text. For instance, in the case of public health, the question is broadly, "Are energy drinks a possible public health problem?" If your answer is yes, you will choose information consistent with that perspective. Note that by considering an underlying yes or no question, you need to take a stance. What might be the yes-no questions underlying the other two scenarios? What is your stance?

In this next task we would like you to take a look at some attempts at using the energy drink text to support the claim that energy drink use may be a growing health concern. But first, we need to make a few comments. Whenever possible, you should directly cite original sources, rather than cite a citation (indirect citation). If you wanted to use the information on the number of energy drinks introduced to the market, you should find and read the Johnson (2006) paper. As a scholar, it is better to check the original source to make sure that the information you saw elsewhere is accurate. If the source is not accessible but you want to use information from it, then you need to make it clear that this is what you have done by citing both sources. The data in the report prepared by Packaged Facts, a market research company, is not easily accessed and so it would be reasonable to use the cited information from it.

This citation suggests that you have read the report yourself, which would be misleading.

> Research by Packaged Facts (2007) has shown . . .

To indicate that you are citing a citation, this would be appropriate.

> Research conducted by Packaged Facts (as cited in Reissig et al., 2009) has shown that . . . .

Note that this citation clearly attributes the data to Packaged Facts and not to Reissig et al.

TASK TWO

Which of these five texts seems best as a general background paragraph for a paper arguing that energy drinks are a potential public health problem? Explain your choice.

1. In the U.S., 200 new energy drink brands were launched in the 12-month period ending July 2007 (Packaged Facts, 2007). From 2002 to 2006, the average annual growth rate in energy drink sales was 55% (Packaged Facts, 2007) (Fig. 1). In 2006, the total U.S. retail market value for energy drinks (from all sources) was approximately $5.4 billion and has shown a similar annual growth rate over this same period (47%) (Packaged Facts, 2007). These drinks vary widely in both caffeine content (ranging from 50 to 505 mg per can or bottle) and caffeine concentration (ranging from 2.5 to 171 mg per fluid ounce).

2. According to Packaged Facts (as cited in Reissig et al., 2009), between 2006 and 2007 hundreds of energy drink brands were introduced into the U.S. market. This was likely a result of producers recognizing energy drinks as a very profitable product with growth potential. In fact, the average annual growth rate in energy drink sales was 55% (Packaged Facts, 2007) (Fig. 1). Research by Packaged Facts (as cited in Reissig et al., 2009) shows that the total U.S. retail market value for energy drinks (from all sources) was estimated to be $5.4 billion in 2006 and has shown a similar annual growth rate over this same period

(47%). These drinks vary widely in both caffeine content (ranging from 50 to 505 mg per can or bottle) and caffeine concentration (ranging from 2.5 to 171 mg per fluid ounce). Since the long-term effects of these high levels of caffeine are not known, there is a chance that consumption of these drinks may be harmful.

3. In 2002, sales of energy drinks in the United States were just over $100 million. By 2006, however, this figure was $700 million. Although this tremendous growth is welcome news for producers and retailers, it is unclear what the long-term health consequences may be (Reissig et al., 2009). This uncertainty may even encourage higher levels of consumption, leading to possible health issues.

4. Hundreds of new energy drink brands have been introduced into the market over the past decade (Johnson, 2006). Along with this growth, sales have also dramatically increased, reaching a market value of billions of dollars in the U.S. alone. Clearly, the demand for caffeine, which varies widely in these drinks, is insatiable and a public health crisis is about to emerge.

5. Energy drink consumption is rapidly growing, which is a source of concern among health professionals (Reissig et al., 2009). Specifically, researchers do not know what the long- and short-terms effects of caffeine and other additives in these drinks may be (Reissig, 2009). Thus, we may soon be facing a public health crisis.

Now use information from the Reissig et al. text to respond to the question of whether energy drinks pose a public health problem.

At this point, we want to draw your attention to an issue that has been receiving increasing attention within and outside academia, specifically using your own words when you borrow information from the work of others as you write your papers.

Some Notes on Plagiarism

Plagiarism is best defined as a deliberate activity—the conscious copying from the work of others. The concept of plagiarism has become an integral part of North American and Western European countries. It is based on a number of assumptions that may not hold true in all cultures. One is a rather romantic assumption that the writer is an original, individual, creative artist. Another is that original ideas and expressions are the acknowledged property of their creators (as is the case with a patent for an invention). Yet another is that it is a sign of disrespect—rather than respect—to copy without acknowledgment from the works of published authorities. This even includes the use of images and figures that you have downloaded from the internet, but for which you give no source.

Of course, borrowing the words and phrases of others can be a useful language learning strategy. Certainly you would not be plagiarizing if you borrowed items that are frequently used in academic English (skeletal phrases) or that are common knowledge, such as these examples.

Paris is the capital of France.

An increase in demand often leads to an increase in price.

The results from this experiment seem to suggest that . . . .

These results are statistically significant.

Indeed, if you can never use standard phraseology and expressions of your field or academia in general, it would be difficult to improve your writing. The key is knowing the difference between language used by most writers to present their own perspectives and new ideas and language that expresses someone else's unique content and ideas. For instance, let's look at a text that we provided in Unit Two.

❶ The increasing popularity of electric vehicles (EVs) and plug-in hybrid electric vehicles (PHEVs) is attributed to the savings in fuel costs compared to conventional internal combustion engine (ICE) vehicles. ❷ EVs and PHEVs save energy due to the employment of reverse regenerating braking during the deceleration cycle. ❸ This energy is typically stored in batteries and ultracapacitors (UCs). ❹ The incorporation of on-board energy storage systems (ESS) and generation in PHEVs has been facilitated and dictated by the market demands for enhanced performance and range.

In this text, we believe there is language in Sentence 1 that you can borrow.

> ❶ The increasing popularity of _____ is attributed to
> _____.

So, you might write this new sentence for a completely different topic.

> ❶ The increasing popularity of Voice over Internet Protocol
> (VoIP) can be attributed to its low cost.

In Sentence 4, we think it would be fine to use this language. Can you complete the sentence using information from your field? We offer an example to get you started.

> ❹ The incorporation of _____ in _____ has been
> facilitated by _____.
>
> The incorporation of corpus data in academic writing courses
> has been facilitated by the availability of large corpora on the
> internet.

It would not, however, be acceptable to take the original sentences in their entirety and use them in your own text—unless you placed quotation marks around them. Copying sentences without quotation marks amounts to passing off someone else's work as your own.

You should also be aware that you should not borrow "famous" phrases without at least putting them in quotation marks. Here, for example is a famous quotation by Louis Pasteur, which was originally in French.

> Chance favors the prepared mind.

If you wanted to use this phrase, you should recognize its special status. We would encourage you to borrow standard phraseology of your field and skeletal phrases when appropriate, but not special expressions such as the Pasteur quote (unless these are placed in quotation marks).

TASK THREE

Here are some approaches to writing, beginning with a plagiarizing approach and ending with an acceptable quoting technique. Where does plagiarism stop? Draw a line between the last approach that would be considered plagiarism and the first approach that would produce acceptable original work.

1. Copying a paragraph as it is from the source without any acknowledgment.

2. Copying a paragraph making only small changes, such as replacing a few verbs or adjectives with synonyms.

3. Cutting and pasting a paragraph by using the sentences of the original but leaving one or two out, or by putting one or two sentences in a different order.

4. Composing a paragraph by taking short standard phrases from a number of sources and putting them together with some words of your own.

5. Paraphrasing a paragraph by rewriting with substantial changes in language and organization, amount of detail, and examples.

6. Quoting a paragraph by placing it in block format with the source cited.

University plagiarism policies are readily available on the internet. We recommend that you find and read through the plagiarism policy of your institution and become familiar with it, even if you do not agree with all of it.

Let's now look more closely at the summary writing process by working with a text from Mechanical Engineering.

TASK FOUR

Students in one of our writing courses were given a section of a research paper on a driver support system and asked to respond to this question: Is there a need for a shift in the focus of research on car safety systems? With this question in mind, read the passage, and then underline the information that you would include in your response. Can you tell how the text is organized?

Design of a Haptic Gas Pedal for Active Car-Following Support

Mulder, M., Abbink, D. A.,
van Paassen, M. M., and Mulder, M. (2011).
IEEE Transactions on Intelligent Transportation Systems, 12, 268–279.

❶ The fact that the motor vehicle fatality rate per 100 million vehicle miles has gone down from 5.1 to 1.4 [2] since the 1960s is most certainly the result of improved driver safety regulations, higher driver training standards, better road design, and advancements in car-safety systems. ❷ From the early seatbelts and anti-crash bodies to airbags and side impact protection systems, car manufacturers have come up with a broad range of passive safety improvements that significantly reduce the severity of driver, passenger, and pedestrian or cyclist injury when involved in a traffic accident.

❸ However, with the increased importance of the car as a personal means of transportation, nondriving–related devices, such as car stereos, mobile phones, and, more recently, navigation systems, divert drivers' attention increasingly more away from the primary sources of information necessary for safe operation of the vehicle: the road and other road users. ❹ With traffic accident statistics attributing driver inattention as one of the major causes of traffic accidents [3–5], this increase of in-vehicle devices is worrisome at least—if not dangerous.

❺ To bridge the gap between the gain in improved passive safety and the increasing development and use of nondriving–related in-vehicle devices, research on car safety systems is directed more towards systems that actively support drivers in their driving task. ❻ Ultimately, active support systems aim to prevent drivers from getting into accidents. ❼ This is a radically different approach compared with that of passive safety systems, which help lessen the impact of driving accidents but do nothing to contribute to preventing drivers from getting into an accident.

❽ The goal of this paper is to present the design of an active haptic* support system for car-following. ❾ The intended application range of the proposed system is limited to speeds of approximately 80 km/h and higher (minimum highway speeds). ❿ The system is intended to provide continuous car-following support within a wide range of car-following situations—not only in critical situations. ⓫ The intensity of the support is, therefore, continuously adapted to the car-following situation.

If you recall, we said that it is important to read and take notes on the text that you will summarize. To inform your understanding and guide your choice of important information from the text, you could use these questions.

Questions	Answer
What is the issue or problem addressed in the publication?	
Why is this important?	
What was done to address or solve it?	
How does the solution or treatment work?	
Who did it?	
What about the research is different/ innovative/advantageous?	

Note that the questions are simply a starting point. You can devise your own questions when you summarize parts of papers from your own field.

---

*having to do with the sense of touch.

In answering the questions, you may have extracted this information, which you could then use to discuss whether there is a need to change the focus of vehicle safety research.

- The number of accidents and the severity of injuries have decreased because of better safety.
- Drivers these days have a lot of technology that is accessible, but not necessarily needed, to operate a vehicle.
- Technology distracts drivers.
- Distraction is a major cause of accidents.
- There is an interest in preventing accidents and not just in protecting drivers.
- Accidents can be prevented if driver support systems are developed and installed.

In the next step, these elements can be strung together to form the basis of a response to the question. Of course, special care has to be taken to ensure a logical flow of ideas. Here is a draft written by one of our students in response to the question posed in Task Four.

❶ Since the 1960s the motor vehicle fatality rate per 100 million vehicle miles has gone down from 5.1 to 1.4. ❷ This improvement is the result of improvements in driver safety regulations, higher driver training standards, better road design, and advancements in car-safety systems. ❸ Important advances in car safety include seatbelts, anticrash bodies, airbags, and side impact protection systems (Mulder et al., 2011). ❹ All of these are systems that have no influence on a driving situation until an accident occurs. ❺ Because they are idle until needed they are known as passive safety systems.

❻ Passive systems are important, but may not be enough to protect today's drivers, whose vehicles now contain nondriving–related devices, such as car stereos, mobile phones, and, more recently, navigation systems, that can divert their attention increasingly more away from the primary sources of information necessary for safe operation of the vehicle: the road and other road users (Mulder et al., 2011). ❼ Thus, to continue the improvement in driving safety, there is a need for a shift in the focus of research on car safety systems that take into account driver distraction.

❽ Rather than focusing on protecting drivers in an accident, research should be directed more towards systems that actively support drivers in their driving task so that they do not get into accidents in the first place. ❾ This is a radical change from the focus on passive safety systems, which do nothing to help prevent drivers from getting into an accident (Mulder et al., 2011).

This is perhaps a reasonable beginning. The writer has retained the important parts of the text. However, this summary has some weaknesses.

1. For the most part, too much of the text is written in the words of the original, although no whole sections were borrowed. It may very well be an example of plagiarism—work copied from a source without proper attribution. Notice, for instance, that much of Sentence 1 is very close to the beginning of the source and throughout several stretches of language from the source have been copied.

2. The draft does not display a high level of understanding of the source passage. While it does show that the writer can pull out important information, it may not convince the reader that the summary writer understands the issues and need for research.

Overall, although this response is a reasonable draft, it needs more work before it would be fully acceptable as a written assignment. Now, let us consider how the summary could be improved. One obvious approach would be to paraphrase the sentences of the original.

Paraphrasing

A paraphrase is a restatement (in your own words) of the ideas in the original. Good paraphrasing can demonstrate that you have understood the text you have read and can avoid plagiarizing. The most common strategy used to accomplish this involves replacing words in the source with synonyms and perhaps changing the grammar. Look again at Sentence 3 from the text on new car safety systems.

. . . nondriving–related devices, such as car stereos, mobile phones, and, more recently, navigation systems, divert drivers' attention increasingly more away from the primary sources of information necessary for safe operation of the vehicle: the road and other road users.

If you want to use this information but write it in your own words, you could begin by identifying the important information in the sentence and the relationships between points. You then might think about language to establish relationships, as demonstrated here.

Important points

- There are a lot of devices in cars that have nothing to do with operating a vehicle.
- These devices can distract drivers.
- Drivers are so distracted that they may not pay attention to the road and other drivers.

Important relationships

- cause and effect

Linking phrases and expressions that can connect the two points

- *because*
- *therefore*
- *as a result*

Verbs that might establish other relationships

- *is due to*
- *caused by*
- *can be attributed to*
- *leading to*

Next you might consider **possible synonyms** for the source vocabulary and changing the part of speech (nouns to verbs, for instance).

- *such as* → *like, including*
- *more recently* → *lately?*
- *devices* → *technology*
- *divert* → *distract, sidetrack, take away, diversion*
- *non-driving* → *?*
- *primary sources* → *main inputs?*
- *necessary* → *needed, required*
- *safe* → *secure?*

Other considerations

- Is this always true? Should the claim be softened?

Finally, you are ready to try your own paraphrase.

TASK FIVE

Re-write the excerpt at the bottom of page 202 using *because* and *lead to*, changing the vocabulary and grammar as necessary. Here are two examples using *due to*.

<u>Example</u>: *due to*

Safe driving practices may be compromised *due to* the presence of technology in cars that is not directly related to vehicle operation including cell phones, music players, and GPS.

Drivers today may fail to concentrate on the road and other drivers *due to* the presence of technology such as cell phones, music players, GPS, and other technology that is unrelated to driving.

1. Use *because*

_____

_____

_____

2. Use *lead to*

_____

_____

_____

3. Write two paraphrases of this short text. Before writing, break
    the task into important points, relationships, linking phrases and
    connectors, and synonyms.

> Passive safety systems help lessen the impact of driving
> accidents. They do nothing to contribute to preventing
> drivers from getting into an accident.

Important points

_____

_____

Relationship between the points

_____

Linking phrases or expressions to connect the points

_____

Possible synonyms

_____

_____

Paraphrase 1

_____

_____

_____

Paraphrase 2

_____

_____

_____

As the task suggests, paraphrasing is hard work, particularly when it
comes to vocabulary.

Careful Use of Synonyms

When using synonyms, you need to be careful about your choices. Not all synonyms work equally well in all contexts. Take this example, for instance.

> The system is intended to provide continuous car-following support within a wide range of car-following situations—not only in critical situations.

If you follow a simple synonym substitution process, you may produce something like this.

> In many kinds of car-following situations—not only in grave situations—the system is planned to present persistent car-following support.

The rearrangement of the ideas is good and is an important strategy for paraphrasing. However, *grave* and *critical* are not quite similar enough in this context. Perhaps *dangerous* would be a better choice here. In addition, *present persistent car-following support* does not work so well because the collocation (simply put, words that tend to go together) is awkward. *Offer* might be a better choice.

If you need to check whether the words you want to use go together, you can search the internet, ideally Google Scholar. To conduct your search, place the expression of interest in quotation marks and, if you think it would be helpful, use a wild card indicated by an asterisk (*) in the expression so that you can capture variations of the expression. For instance, we did this search on Google Scholar. To narrow hits to your field of study, include a relevant term outside the quotation marks.

> "the system is * to * support"

We found these interesting possibilities.

The system	is designed	to provide	support
	is configured	to deliver	
	is built		
	is intended		
	is expected		
	is developed		
	is able		
	is placed		

We even found many instances of useful modification and split infinitives.

The system	is designed	to fully	support
	is configured	to directly	
	is built	to unobtrusively	
	is intended	to optionally	
	is expected		
	is developed		
	is able		
	is placed		

So, we can write something like this.

The system is configured to provide ongoing car-following support in many types of situations, not only those that are identified as dangerous.

Note that the language has been substantially changed, although the sense of the original is fully maintained. A paraphrase approach to summarizing can be somewhat successful, but if you do this sentence by sentence for a longer stretch of text, you run the risk of not demonstrating your full understanding of the passage. You might miss an opportunity to highlight key points. Another possible danger is that the resulting summary may not be original enough and could be considered plagiarism by some.

If you (understandably) feel that your paraphrasing ability is not strong, you can copy some material and place it in quotation marks; however, a better but more difficult strategy would be to carefully consider the elements you have identified as important, put the original away, and write what you have understood. This may allow you to condense the ideas in the source even further.

To sum up, when you write a formal summary of someone else's ideas, you should keep in mind the following guidelines.

1. Always try to use your own words.

2. Include enough support and detail so that your message is clear.

3. Do not try to paraphrase specialized vocabulary or technical terms.

4. Make sure the summary reads smoothly. Focus on old-to-new information flow; use transition devices where necessary; and provide supporting detail. You do not want a collection of sentences that does not flow.

5. If it is impossible to use your own words, then quote the material. Remember, however, that too much quoting will not likely result in a successful paper. Information from sources should *support, but not replace,* your own ideas, interpretations, and explanations.

TASK SIX

Here is a second draft of the response to whether there is a need for a shift in the focus of research on car safety systems. Read it and answer the questions on page 209.

❶ Over the past five decades there has been a dramatic improvement in the risks associated with driving. ❷ During this time, deaths resulting from driving accidents have decreased nearly fourfold (Mulder et al., 2011). ❸ Much of this improvement has to do with appropriate safety regulations and equipment in vehicles designed to protect drivers and their passengers (e.g., safety belts, air bags, and other passive safety mechanisms) (Mulder et al., 2011). ❹ This improvement, however, may begin to diminish as drivers face new risks related to the availability of technology that is not needed for vehicle operation, but does reduce drivers' attention to their task. ❺ This, of course, includes a variety of devices such as music systems, mobile phones, and even GPS, all of which, but particularly mobile phones, have been shown to have an impact on safe driving.

⑥ While previous safety measures were targeted at protection and have been highly successful, it seems now that driver distraction needs to be addressed if the gains in safety are to be maintained or enhanced. ⑦ Thus, there is a need to shift the focus of safety research to help drivers themselves be more aware of their surroundings during the operation of their vehicles. ⑧ For instance, drivers may not be aware that they are following a car too closely and be unable to stop safely. ⑨ If a car-following alert system (Mulder et al., 2011) could be devised to warn drivers of the potential danger, accidents could be prevented.

1. Does the response answer the question?

2. Does the response capture good supportive information from the source? Does the source information serve as support or does it seem to be the focus?

3. To what extent has the author of the draft used his/her own words?

4. How well has the draft author revealed his/her understanding of the problem and solution?

5. Can you identify any instances of evaluation and where the author has incorporated some ideas not found in the source? Are these appropriate?

6. If you were to revise the draft, what would you do?

7. Write your own response to the question using the source text.

Since many of the summaries you write will be woven into your own original text, it is very important to identify at least the source author, depending on your field of study.

Note that when your citation style requires the use of author names, you need to provide the family name. First names only are not used in in-text citations since this makes it difficult for your reader to know to whom you might be referring. One of our students chose to identify the source of the vehicle safety text in this way.

> According to Mark and his co-authors, car safety research should be directed at preventing accidents.

This is obviously a first attempt because a reader unfamiliar with the source will reasonably assume that Mark is the family name and may then look in the reference list to find the article. Mark happens to be the first name of the first author of the car safety article and the in-text citation would be confusing. Also, since there is more than one author in our example, this needs to be acknowledged. We propose the following revision.

> According to Mulder et al. (2011), car safety research should be directed at preventing accidents.

Generally, family names alone are sufficient, but occasionally, you may see citations that include both first and last names of a single author. One reason to do this is to distinguish two authors with the same family name. Another reason has to do with requirements of certain styles such as MLA that may prescribe the use of an author's full name the first time that author is cited. Finally, another reason, for which we can offer only anecdotal evidence, is to acknowledge an author's status in the field. Well-known figures in certain fields are frequently referred to by both first and last names. Take, for example, these sentences.

Physics
These relations arise from the energy conservation consideration originally proposed by Albert Einstein.

Economics
According to John Maynard Keynes, "There is, clearly, no absolute standard of 'liquidity.'"

Anthropology
Other possible models include those of the Kibbutz as explained by Bettleheim (1969) and Kaffman (1972) or the Samoan Village as described by Margaret Mead (1961).

Language Focus: Identifying the Source

Most summaries will have a sentence near the beginning that contains two elements: the source and a main idea. Notice the use of the present tense in many of the examples.

According to Fairchild (2011), _____.
(main idea)

Ho and Neidell's 2009 paper on fluoridation discusses _____.
(main idea)

Bernstein (2004) states that _____.
claims   (main idea)
argues
maintains

Barinaga (2004) suggests that _____.
asserts   (main idea)
hypothesizes
states
concludes

Lamport [1] proposed _____.
demonstrated
found
identified

_____ was first reported in [13].
proposed
identified
given

You may cite your source material following APA (American Psychological Association), MLA (Modern Language Association), IEEE (Institute of Electrical and Electronics Engineers), or another style, depending on your field of study. The APA and MLA systems refer to a source similarly, by author and date. The following citations are in APA style.

> Reissig et al. (2009) questioned whether energy drinks are safe.

> The safety of energy drinks has not yet been established (Reissig et al., 2009).

> In their study of energy drinks, Reissig et al. (2009) suggested that energy drinks may not be entirely safe. They also indicated that more research is needed.

How does the citation in the second sentence differ from those in the other two sentences?

For a thorough discussion of APA and MLA styles, see *Publication Manual of the American Psychological Association* and *MLA Handbook for Writers of Research Papers*. In Engineering and some other fields, it may be more common to use reference numbers.

> Photorefractive crystals may be useful in the development of high-speed electrical signals.[1]

Always check the style guides in your discipline to learn more about proper documentation. Members of a field expect writers to be familiar with their disciplinary practices.

There is a range of reporting verbs that you may use when referring to your source material. In fact, a study by Ken Hyland (1999) identified more than 400 different reporting verbs; however, nearly 50 percent of these were used only one time in his corpus of 80 research articles. A much smaller number of verbs tend to predominate. In Table 15 we show the most frequently used reporting verbs from a variety of disciplines, with the most frequent on the left and the sixth most frequent on the far right. As you can see, there are some disciplinary differences.

TABLE 15. High-Frequency Reporting Verbs

Discipline	Verbs and Frequency					
	Rank					
	1	2	3	4	5	6
Harder Sciences						
Biology	describe	find	report	show	suggest	observe
Physics	develop	report	study	find	expand	
Electrical Engineering	propose	use	describe	show	publish	develop
Mechanical Engineering	describe	show	report	discuss	give	develop
Epidemiology	find	describe	suggest	report	examine	show
Nursing	find	suggest	report	identify	indicate	show
Medicine	show	report	demonstrate	observe	find	suggest
Softer Sciences						
Marketing	suggest	argue	find	demonstrate	propose	show
Applied linguistics	suggest	argue	show	explain	find	point out
Psychology	find	show	suggest	report	demonstrate	focus
Sociology	argue	suggest	describe	note	analyze	discuss
Education	find	suggest	note	report	demonstrate	provide
Philosophy	say	suggest	argue	claim	point out	think

Data for Biology, Physics, Electrical Engineering, Mechanical Engineering, Applied Linguistics, and Sociology from Hyland, K. Academic attribution: Citation and the construction of disciplinary knowledge, *Applied Linguistics* 20 (1999): 341–367. Other data thanks to Carson Maynard.

TASK SEVEN

If you have not done so already, find at least five, but preferably more, well-written published research papers that are typical of papers in your area of study. It does not matter whether these are seminal papers or where the research was conducted. We simply want you to have a small data set (a corpus) that you can analyze to gain some insights into the important characteristics of published work in your discipline. Choose 2 to 5 papers from your collection (or more) and underline all the reporting verbs. If your field is represented in Table 15, do your results match with those in the table? If your field is not represented, is there one field that is close to yours in its use of reporting verbs?

A variety of reporting verbs can be used in summary writing to reveal your personal stance toward the source material. Notice how the reporting verbs in the following examples could allow the writer of the summary to convey his or her attitude.

> Campbell (2010) *presumes* that the findings will be representative of the whole population. . . .

> The authors *speculate* that people who scrap their old cars will immediately buy another, new(er) car.

Notice also how the addition of an adverb (in mid-position, of course) can even more clearly reveal your stance, which you may want to do when writing to critique.

> The authors *incorrectly assume* that patients will always take the medicine that has been prescribed.

TASK EIGHT

Some reporting verbs are less objective than others. Can you identify which verbs in the table seem to be objective and which verbs have the potential to be evaluative? The first one has been done for you.

	Objective	Evaluative
describe	X	
recommend		
claim		
assume		
contend		
propose		
theorize		
support		
examine		

In formal academic English, many reporting verbs are followed by a *that* clause containing both a subject and a verb. Can you identify the verbs in the table that are not followed by *that*? List them.

That clauses have a variety of functions. In the following sentence, the *that* clause is the direct object of the verb *state*.

> Benfield and Howard (2000) state that many medical journals are now published in English because of a desire to attract greater readership and to attract better, more international manuscripts.

In spoken English, *that* in clauses that function as direct objects is often omitted, as in the next example. Notice also that in the spoken English alternative, the choice of the verb *said* is less formal.

> Benfield and Howard (2000) said a lot of medical journals are published in English now because they want to attract greater readership and to attract better, more international manuscripts.

You may have wondered why we have not said anything about the verb *mention* to refer to your source. If you were to use *mention* instead of one of the other verbs suggested, you would greatly change the importance of the information that follows.

> Benfield and Howard (2000) mention that many medical journals are now published in English because of a desire to attract greater readership and to attract better, more international manuscripts.

Mention is used for information that was most likely given without detail or support. The example sentence using *mention* makes it seem as if the reason journals are now published in English is a minor point in the article. We suggest that you avoid using *mention* in summaries, unless the point is truly a minor one. A better choice here would be *note*.

TASK NINE

Here are some citation statements that students wrote in a discussion of the benefits of caffeinated energy drinks using the passage in Task One of this unit. Which, if any, would you prefer to have written? Why? Edit the weaker sentences.

1. Author Chad Reissig and colleagues state that how caffeine content in energy drinks may be hazardous to our health.

2. "Caffeinated Energy Drinks—A Growing Problem" by Reissig et al. claims that the caffeine and other components in energy drinks consumed may be a health hazard.

3. According to "Caffeinated Energy Drinks—A Growing Problem," Chad Reissig and colleagues suggest that research is needed to understand the effect of caffeine and other components in energy drinks.

4. Reissig et al. mention that energy drink consumption is growing rapidly.

5. Reissig and colleagues said in their article energy drinks might be harmful.

 Language Focus: Summary Reminder Phrases

In a longer summary, you may want to remind your reader that you are summarizing:

> The author goes on to say that . . . .
>
> The article further states that . . . .
>
> [Authors' surnames here] also state/maintain/argue that . . . .
>
> [Authors' surnames here] also believe that . . . .
>
> [Authors' surnames here] conclude that . . . .
>
> In the second half of the paper, [author's surname here] presents . . . .

In fact, if your summary is quite long, you may want to mention the source author's name at different points in your summary—the beginning, the middle, and/or the end. When you mention the author in the middle or end of the summary, be sure to use the surname only.

> Reissig et al. go on to describe . . . .
> The author further argues that . . . .

Some of the following sentence connectors may be useful in introducing additional information.

additionally	*also*	*further*
in addition to	*furthermore*	*moreover*

TASK TEN

Look back at the student text in Task Six on pages 208–209. Would you insert a reminder phrase? If so, where? Now read these summary reminder sentences written by our students. Which, if any, of these would you prefer to have written? Try to improve the weaker sentences.

1. Reissig et al. (2009) finally say that we need more research.

2. In addition, the article also discusses the caffeine levels.

3. In Reissig et al.'s (2009) article, they also point out that no one knows the long-term effects of caffeine and the other components.

4. Reissig and colleagues (2009) conclude that current research is insufficient.

5. Reissig and others (2009) conclude about the current risks that exist.

Sometimes you may want to capture only the main idea(s) of a source. In this case, you might choose some specific information or you may recast the source material so that it is more general than in its original form.

TASK ELEVEN

Read "Improving the Environment in Urban Areas" and try to determine the text-type. Then read the texts that follow. Decide which you think is most successful at supporting the point that urban planners can have a positive effect on the environment. Write one or two sentences after each text, explaining what you like or dislike. Then discuss each with a partner.

Improving the Environment in Urban Areas:
The Role of Urban Planners

❶ Recently, increasingly significant problems regarding urban sprawl, greenhouse gas emissions from vehicles, and the loss of open, green areas have become the focus of urban planners. ❷ To address some of these concerns, many countries, especially developed countries, have devised technology to control harmful vehicle emissions. ❸ However, as these countries already have an abundance of vehicles that continues to grow in number, the efficacy of these measures is diminished. ❹ Since cars and other vehicles create more air pollution than any other human activity, the most effective means to reduce pollution is to shift the reliance on automobiles towards other modes of transportation. ❺ One way to achieve this goal is for urban planners to focus on transit oriented development (TOD). ❻ TOD generally refers to higher-density urban development that places pedestrians in the center so that they have easy access to environmentally friendly travel modes such as light rail. ❼ TOD land use strategies, for instance, encourage construction of public transit stations and stops in convenient locations near homes and entertainment that will promote their use. ❽ In addition to a reduction in vehicle use, TOD can have other energy and environmental benefits in terms of housing development and workplace efficiency improvements. ❾ TOD requires less land than does standard development, which can lead to preservation of farmland and green areas as well as lower energy use. ⑩ Specifically, suburban TOD dwelling units and offices may be more energy efficient because they are smaller than those in standard suburban spaces. ⑪ TOD dwellings also have shared walls as in the case of townhouses and may consist of multi-family buildings and multi-story offices. ⑫ Because they have fewer exposed surfaces and therefore less exterior heat loss, such structures are typically more energy efficient than individual single-family dwellings or one-story buildings.

Yasufumi Iseki, some editing

1. According to Yasufumi Iseki, TOD is a form of urban planning that can effectively protect the environment.

2. Iseki maintains that cars and other vehicles create more pollution than any other activity; thus, decreasing the number of vehicles is the most effective way to improve the environment in urban areas. Another way to decrease pollution is to design smaller, more environmentally friendly dwellings. These improvements may be possible by implementing a form of strategic development of public transit known as transit oriented development (TOD).

3. Iseki states that the number of cars and other vehicles in urban areas needs to be reduced to improve the urban environment. This reduction could be achieved through transit oriented development (TOD).

4. Iseki claims that urban planning can play a role in improving urban environments by prompting a shift away from heavy vehicle use. Although this will be difficult to achieve because of the overabundance of vehicles in developed countries, it is worth pursuing.

5. According to Iseki, transit oriented development (TOD) can help solve environmental problems such as urban air pollution by providing city dwellers transportation that is convenient and by encouraging the design of smaller, more energy efficient dwellings.

TASK TWELVE

Think of a topic in which you have some interest and then find an article on that topic. Create a yes-no question that could be answered using the information from the article. If you need some examples, review the yes-no questions in Task One on page 193.

Syntheses of More than One Source

Writing tasks that require you to deal with more than one source are common in many graduate courses. They can be assignments on their own, part of a longer paper, or a response to an examination question. Such summaries can be more challenging to write than simple summaries because they require you to analyze and use information from two or more sources that may overlap, slightly differ, or contradict each other. When working with multiple sources, you often need to infer and make explicit the relationships among them. In doing so, you can reveal your understanding of a line of inquiry in your field together with the accepted knowledge and the debates.

TASK THIRTEEN

The following are questions from the fields of Neurobiology, Economics, and Epidemiology. How would you approach each of these tasks? What do you think are the instructor's expectations?

1. What do Alkon and Farley believe the role of serotonin to be in memory? In what ways do they fundamentally differ? How are they similar? Is one perspective more comprehensive than the other?

2. How do Winder & Gori and Agran view the political implications of recent evidence regarding occupational cancers?

3. Relate Kohl and Jaworski's recent article "Market Orientation: The Construct, Research Propositions, and Managerial Implications" to product and service quality. Consider the perspectives of Juran, Feigenbaum, Deming, and Crosby. What common themes emerge, and how do they differ?

4. Recent studies have examined the suitability of various agriculturally derived fuel oils as alternatives to petroleum products. Straight Vegetable Oil (SVO) studies in particular have generated interest because of the potential benefits of SVO as a possible replacement for Diesel #2 in some engines. One common problem is that most SVO has a much higher viscosity than diesel. Discuss the nature of this problem and the current approaches to dealing with it. Is there one approach that looks more promising than the others?

5. Construct a similar task for your own field of study, based on the question you created in Task Twelve. How would you plan to answer it? Be prepared to explain your task and plan in class.

TASK FOURTEEN

Students in an Acoustics course were asked to write a paper on unpleasant sounds, one section of which was required to discuss why certain sounds are considered highly unpleasant. This, of course, required the use of previous studies. Read this first draft of the section and mark the instructor comments on pages 222–223 as reasonable (R) or unreasonable (U). If you are unsure, indicate this with a question mark (?).

1. ❶ In 1986 Halpern, Blake, and Hillenbrand investigated how people respond to different terrible sounds. ❷ In one experiment, listeners rated the unpleasantness of different sounds. ❸ Participants generally agreed that the worst sound was that of a garden tool scraped on a piece of slate shaped into a roofing tile, which sounds similar to fingernails scraped on a traditional blackboard. ❹ The researchers found that the negative reaction to the sound could mainly be found in a band of 2–4 kHz.

❺ Also in 1986, Blake did a study of a scraping noise, comparing its sound wave with that of monkey warning cries. ❻ The waveforms of the two were quite similar. ❼ Because of this similarity, Blake concluded that humans react negatively to scraping noises because they still have some innate reaction mechanism from their ancient ancestors. ❽ In other words, humans still have the same response mechanism as monkeys who hear a warning cry.

❾ McDermott and Hauser in 2004 explored reactions of humans and a type of monkey known as a tamarin to scraping sounds and screeching, respectively. ❿ They also examined their reactions to some white noise. ⓫ The humans clearly preferred white noise to scraping, while the tamarins reacted to this noise as negatively as they did to screeching.

⓬ In 2008 Cox conducted an experiment of scraping sounds in which participants had both audio and visual inputs. ⓭ The goal was to determine whether the sound and visualizing how it feels to make the sound were in some way related. ⓮ Cox found that the sound of scraping fingernails on a blackboard was perceived as much worse when participants were shown a picture of a hand on a blackboard. ⓯ He concluded that visualizing the making of the sound, a process that is unpleasant, is a significant factor in the perception of unpleasantness.

Instructor Comments

I think you have a good start here, but I think you can do more to explain where the current thinking is on the issue.

_____ 1. You have discussed three studies only. Are there others that you could include?

_____ 2. The discussion deals with the studies in chronological order. I don't find this to be a particularly useful strategy because you don't make any connections among the studies.

_____ 3. Overall, I am not sure what your point is. You seem to be discussing the past work only because you know you are supposed to talk about what others have done. But discussing what others have done should not stand in place of making a point. Do you have a point to make?

___ 4. *I am not getting a sense that you understand where the field stands as to why certain sounds are considered really unpleasant. Can you revise to reflect your understanding?*

___ 5. *What is the upshot of McDermott and Hauser's study? What is the larger implication?*

___ 6. *Does the study by Cox mean that the frequency of a sound is not a factor? Can you comment on this?*

Now read this second draft and discuss with a partner how it differs from the previous one. Has the author positioned herself as knowledgeable and capable? Explain your conclusion.

2. ❶ The acoustic environment contains many sounds that are considered extremely unpleasant. ❷ To understand why these sounds are characterized in this way a small number of studies have been carried out. ❸ Interestingly, all of these have investigated scraping sounds and within this category the sound of fingernails scraped on a blackboard has been of considerable interest (Halpern, Blake, and Hillenbrand, 1986; Blake, 1986; McDermott and Hauser, 2004; Cox, 2008). ❹ Studies of scraping sounds have shown that the negative reaction to the sound could mainly be found in a band of 2–4 kHz (Halpern, Blake and Hillenbrand, 1986; Kumar et al., 2008). ❺ This differs from very early research suggesting that high frequencies create the unpleasant quality of this and other scraping sounds (Boyd, 1959; Ely, 1975). ❻ Other research has looked beyond frequency, seeking to understand whether there might be some vestigial reasons for the perceived unpleasantness and using data collected from monkeys (Blake, 1986; McDermott and Hauser, 2004). ❼ For instance, Blake (1986) compared scraping sound waves with those of monkey warning cries and found that the waveforms of the two were quite similar. ❽ Because of this similarity, Blake concluded that humans react negatively to scraping noises because they still have some innate reaction

mechanism from their ancient ancestors. ⑨ In other words, humans still have the same response mechanism as monkeys who hear a warning cry. ⑩ In related research, McDermott and Hauser (2004) explored reactions of humans and a type of monkey known as a tamarin to blackboard scraping sounds and screeching, respectively, as well as their reactions to some white noise. ⑪ Both humans and tamarins had similar reactions to the unpleasant sounds. ⑫ However, they differed considerably in their perceptions of white noise. ⑬ While humans clearly preferred white noise to blackboard scraping, the tamarins reacted to this noise as negatively as they did to screeching. ⑭ These findings call into question Blake's theory that primates, both human and non-human, have the same underlying mechanism for reacting to sounds.

⑮ Unlike studies exploring a biological basis for perceptions of sound, Cox proposed that humans may find certain sounds highly unpleasant when they can visualize creating those sounds. ⑯ Cox found that the sound of fingernails scraping on a blackboard was perceived as much worse when participants were shown a picture of a hand on a blackboard. ⑰ He concluded that the visualization of and possible tactile association with making a sound, particularly one that is unpleasant, are significant factors in the perception of the degree of unpleasantness. ⑱ Thus, the frequency of a sound may be somewhat less important than previously thought. ⑲ Given the small number of studies, however, it remains unclear why certain sounds, particularly scraping sounds, are almost universally perceived as extremely unpleasant, suggesting the need for more research.

As you noticed, the first text in Task Fourteen, while accurate in terms of content, fails to highlight the similarities and/or differences among the different studies. As such, it is difficult to see what point is being developed. The author has missed the opportunity to reveal a broader understanding, causing the reader more work to find the important information on his or her own. In the second text, the writer has revealed an ability to see connections, overlapping views, and important differences in the research. This is accomplished because the author has organized the discussion in terms of the topics addressed, rather than according to the studies at hand. It is difficult enough deciding what information to include in a summary of one article, but when working with two or more sources, clearly your job becomes even more complicated.

If you are writing a comparative summary or a discussion of two or more texts, to begin you may want to set up a chart, table, diagram, or even spreadsheet that includes your articles and the key points they address. Once you have all of your key information before you, you may have an easier time "eyeballing" the literature, making connections, and, most importantly, finding enough common threads. In short, you may be able to "see things that have not quite been seen before" and display this understanding to your reader (Feak and Swales, 2009).

When working with multiple sources you may find it useful to incorporate some common language of comparison and contrast.

Language Focus: Showing Similarities and Differences

To Show Similarity

Similarly,	According to Macey (2011), the average four-year-old in the U.S. watches approximately four hours of TV each day. Similarly, those in Australia view about 3.5 hours of TV daily (Smuda, 2010).
Similar to	Similar to Kim (2008), Macey (2011) found that the average four-year-old in the U.S. watches four hours of TV each day (Smuda, 2010).
Likewise, . . .	Macey (2011) found that the average four-year-old in the U.S. watches four hours of TV each day. Likewise, in Australia four-year-olds watch several hours of TV daily.
As in X, in Y . . .	As in Australia, the average four-year-old in the U.S. watches more than three hours of TV each day (Macey, 2011).

Like X, Y . . .	Like in the U.S., the average four-year-old in Australia watches several hours of TV daily.
the same . . .	According to Macey (2011), the average four-year-old in the U.S. watches approximately four hours of TV each day. Four-year-olds in Australia view about the same number hours of TV daily (Smuda, 2010).
as well	Macey (2011) interviewed 250 parents of young children. Kim (2010) interviewed a similar number of parents as well.

To Show Contrast

In contrast, . . .	In contrast to Nigerians, 28% of whom have internet access, Liberians have very limited opportunities to connect to the internet.
Unlike X, Y . . .	Unlike Indonesians who have limited access to the internet, the majority of Japanese have easy access.
In contrast to . . .	In contrast to the U.K. where internet access is widespread, less than 10 percent of the population in India can connect to the internet.
On the other hand, . . .	In developed countries internet access is viewed as a necessity. In most African countries, on the other hand, it is a luxury.
. . . ; however, . . . *. . . . However, . . .*	Overall, just over 30% of the world's population has internet access; however, only 11% of Africans have this same opportunity.
, but . . .	Nearly 45% of the Turkish population can easily access the internet, but in nearby Syria this is possible for only 20% of the population.
Whereas . . . , . . . *. . . , whereas . . .*	Whereas 16% of Argentinians have internet access, only 8% of Columbians do.
While . . . , . . . *. . . , while . . .*	While 87% of South Koreans consider themselves to be frequent internet users, 50% of Brazilians do so (Lee, 2011).

Other Expressions of Similarity and Contrast

To Show Similarity

to be similar to	The conclusion that emerges from this study is
to resemble	similar to that in Lee et al. (2010).
to be comparable to	
to correspond to	

To Show Contrast

to differ from	The conclusion in this study differs from that
to contrast with	in Barber et al. (2011).
to be different from	

Take a look at the second discussion in Task Fourteen. Find the devices used by the author to highlight similarity or difference.

TASK FIFTEEN

Review and respond to the task you created for yourself in Task Thirteen (Item 5). Alternatively, come up with a yes-no question on a topic in your field that you are interested in exploring. Find three or four published journal articles that you can use to respond to your question. Using the articles you have chosen, write up your response to your question. Note that your response may in fact resemble a brief literature review. For a more in-depth exploration of writing literature reviews, you may want to consult *Telling a Research Story: Writing a Literature Review*, which is published by the University of Michigan Press (Feak and Swales, 2009).

Unit Six
Writing Critiques

In this unit, we extend the work begun in Unit Five to the writing of critiques. *Critique* is a French word that means "a critical assessment" (positive, negative, or a mixture of both). Some common types of critique that you may be familiar with are film reviews in the popular press or book reviews in journals. Critiques may have various structures, but the simplest is a short summary followed by an evaluation. This unit will concentrate on the evaluation portion.

In our experience, critique assignments are employed somewhat variously in U.S. graduate programs. Certain instructors—from a wide range of programs—use them on a regular basis; certain others almost never do. In some fields, critiques are a regular part of take-home examinations; in other fields, they rarely are. Instructors may assign critiques

1. to ensure that students actually do reading assignments.
2. to assess the students' understanding.
3. to help students develop habits of analytical reading.
4. to train students to integrate lecture material and the assigned reading with other readings they have done, especially by making comparisons.
5. to give students a better sense of the scholarly expectations in their chosen field.

The first four purposes are similar to those we have already seen for summaries. The fifth is somewhat different. Summaries focus on an accurate recasting of some content of an original source. Critiques require that students also learn to express their evaluative comments within their field's accepted standards of judgment. It is important that critiques be "fair and reasonable." Part of being "fair" means that criteria that are reasonable in one field should not necessarily be applied to another field where they might be unreasonable. For example, in terms of how precise a measurement needs to be, psychology is not comparable to physics. Or, in terms of the expected size of a sample group, the standards for research on language teaching methodology are not the same as those for efforts to measure elementary school reading ability. The question of how "fair" criticism varies from one field to another is an issue that we will return to later.

We should also note at this stage that different fields are likely to impose different emphases on critiques. In the humanities, attention may focus on how "interesting" the arguments are; in the social sciences, on the methodology; and in the sciences and Engineering, on the results and what they might (or might not) imply for the real world. The final point we want to make is that we have restricted this unit to the critiquing of written work. We know that students are sometimes asked to write critiques of other things: paintings, music, films, famous buildings, and so on. Critiques of works of art require special training and special writing conventions that lie beyond the scope of this book.

TASK ONE

Discuss with a partner the kinds critiques of written texts that are common in your field. What are some of the main challenges junior scholars face when evaluating the written work of others?

Critique	Challenges

Book Reviews

In your discussion of Task One, you might have mentioned book reviews, a common critique assignment in the social sciences and humanities. In some fields, such as Sociology, students may be asked to critique books as often as every two weeks. This can be particularly hard for students who may not be fast readers. Although you may not need to review books as part of your degree program, book reviews can still help you gain an awareness of evaluative language as well as scholarly expectations and values of your field. Thus, we will begin our discussion of critique writing by taking a look at this genre, focusing only on academic book reviews as opposed to more general book reviews that might appear elsewhere.

Academic book reviews have been an important part of academia beginning in the 1700s (Salager-Meyer et al., 2007). Although early book reviews were once largely uncritical discussions of the content, they have evolved into a highly evaluative and conventionally structured genre, which plays a major role in the softer sciences and a somewhat less important role in the sciences.

TASK TWO

Discuss with a partner whether you agree (A), disagree (D), or are unsure (?).

_____ 1. Published academic book reviews are usually strongly negative.

_____ 2. Book reviews should start with a summary of the book.

_____ 3. The judgments expressed in a published book review could have career consequences.

_____ 4. Published book reviews may be somewhat threatening for the author of the book being reviewed.

_____ 5. Book reviews can be a good first publication for a graduate student or junior faculty member trying to build a publication record.

_____ 6. Members of your field regularly read book reviews.

_____ 7. Published book reviews may not only discuss issues of content, but other issues such as price or quality of production.

_____ 8. On occasion reviewers use the book under review as a springboard for their own points of view.

_____ 9. Book reviews may be written in a less formal style.

_____10. Book reviews generally do not contain references to previous literature.

Unlike book reviews written for a class assignment, published book reviews can be a "direct, public, and often critical encounter with a text and therefore its author, who must be considered as a primary audience for the review" (Hyland, 2004). Therefore, book reviewers must exercise some discretion when writing for publication. In addition, book reviewers should very carefully consider the broader journal audience, purpose, and strategy so as to display familiarity with the field, expertise, and intelligence. If the book review is for a course, your audience may be easily identified; in that case, your purpose and strategy will need to take into account the course content.

The writers of book reviews have a certain freedom in the content and organization of their reviews, because, in the end, they are expressions of their own perspective or position. Even so, most book reviews provide an overview of the content of the book under review, either by chapter or larger section; general and specific evaluation; a discussion of the relevance of the book to the field; and an endorsement (despite shortcomings). In her investigation of 60 published book reviews in Economics, Chemistry, and Linguistics, Motta-Roth (1998) proposed a schematic description of the elements in book reviews, which we have adapted and shown on page 232.

General Aim		Specifically Accomplishing that Aim

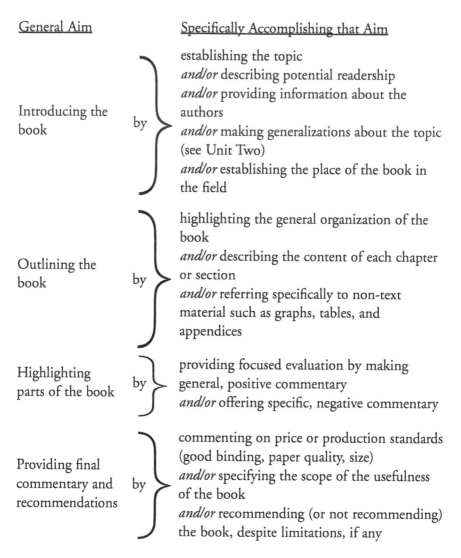

Introducing the book — by — establishing the topic
and/or describing potential readership
and/or providing information about the authors
and/or making generalizations about the topic (see Unit Two)
and/or establishing the place of the book in the field

Outlining the book — by — highlighting the general organization of the book
and/or describing the content of each chapter or section
and/or referring specifically to non-text material such as graphs, tables, and appendices

Highlighting parts of the book — by — providing focused evaluation by making general, positive commentary
and/or offering specific, negative commentary

Providing final commentary and recommendations — by — commenting on price or production standards (good binding, paper quality, size)
and/or specifying the scope of the usefulness of the book
and/or recommending (or not recommending) the book, despite limitations, if any

This, of course, is not an exhaustive list of things "to do" in a book review but, rather, a suggestion of the aspects of a book that you can address. Typical topics for praise and criticism are the degree of originality, coherence of an argument, readability/style, extent or relevance of references, and even the author of the book under review (Hyland, 2004).

TASK THREE

Think about a book review that you might write (or have already written) for a class assignment. Are your aims the same as those identified by Motta-Roth? Why or why not? Alternatively, look at a book review from your own field. Compare the writer's aims to those of Motta-Roth.

To examine book reviews in more detail, we first will examine published reviews and some related research, after which we turn our attention to book reviews as course assignments.

TASK FOUR

Read this book review published in the journal *Library & Information Science Research*, and discuss the questions on pages 235–236 with a partner. The book being reviewed deals with the value and evaluation of research.

The Critical Assessment of Research:
Traditional and New Methods of Evaluation

Bailin, Alan, and Grafstein, Ann. Oxford: Chandos Publishing, 2010.
121 pp. $95.00 (pbk). ISBN: 978-1-84334-543-5.

❶ At just 99 pages, *The Critical Assessment of Research* fits well within a series of works that are targeted at the "busy information professional." ❷ The text is tightly structured around the main theme of research assessment, scaffolded with a clear introduction and useful concluding summaries at the end of each chapter. ❸ In short, it discusses a number of strategies that non-specialists can deploy when considering the value of research output that reaches beyond their domain of expertise. ❹ The focus falls on standard means of evaluating research output that will be familiar to active researchers, but perhaps not so well-understood by information professionals for whom research is not a part of their everyday role. ❺ Another obvious target audience for the book is students.

❻ The authors pay particular attention to the range of issues that can affect the validity of research output and the means of identifying when these are at play. ❼ These include the initial source of funding for any project, the role of that source in setting up ideological biases in the work to be completed, and the influence of this on the interpretation of findings and on the findings per se. ❽ The theoretical models that underpin the research domain and dominance of particular paradigms are also examined as lenses that can distort the research process and its outcomes. ❾ Here reference is made to how studies are designed, for example, in terms of determination of research questions, the hypotheses investigated, and the field of study. ❿ Choices for the dissemination of research findings also merit coverage, as do the economic and ideological systems that determine what is published. ⓫ Taking these factors together, the reader is reminded of the power of context in all research endeavors.

⓬ The real strength of the book is how the authors succeed in illustrating the main points made in the text with a series of interesting and engaging case studies. ⓭ These are drawn from a range of disciplines in the hard sciences, social sciences, and arts and humanities. ⓮ A general readership will be familiar with many of the cases cited, such as the Enron scandal and the debate over the long-term effects of hormone replacement therapy. ⓯ The recent case studies sit nicely alongside classic tales of the influence of external factors on the reporting of research by early scientists, such as Galileo's withdrawal of suggestions that the planets revolve around the sun following accusations of heresy. ⓰ In a teaching environment, these case studies would form the good basis for classroom discussions which, most likely, would lead into broader debates around the impact of research on aspects of our lives in general, such as our health and financial well-being.

⑰ If any criticism were to be leveled at the book it would be to note that its coverage of traditional methods of evaluation is much stronger than coverage of the new. ⑱ Related to this point, it is a pity that more attention is not paid to research output and social media, especially in the light of the discussion of how and why new research domains emerge in new publication fora.

⑲ This book arms its readers with the right questions, for instance when they need to assess the value of the research of others, particularly when mediated by print and broadcast media. ⑳ In this short text they learn how economic, political, or social self-interest may motivate the misreporting of findings into spin or, at the other end of the scale, fraudulent claims that can have devastating impacts on people's lives and their livelihoods.

Hazel Hall
Edinburgh Napier University
Library and Information Science 33, (2011), 256–257.
Copyright Elsevier. Used with permission.

1. Does the review give the impression of being fair? Why or why not?

2. How serious do the cited weaknesses seem to be? How important do you think it is to cite weaknesses in what is by and large a good book? Is anything gained by doing so? (Consider "positioning," which was described in Unit One.)

3. The review consists of five short paragraphs. Explain the purpose of each. Use Motta-Roth's scheme, if possible.

4. Hyland (2004) concludes that praise is global but criticism is specific. Does this hold true for the review here?

5. Which of the sentences contain positive evaluation and which contain negative evaluation? Where do the criticisms appear? In the beginning, middle, end, or throughout? Does the author use different parts of speech in her evaluative comments?

6. What tenses are used in the review?

7. Has the author attempted to soften any of her negative evaluative comments? (See the discussion in Unit Four on strength of claim.)

8. In Sentence 17, the author writes, *If any criticism were to be leveled at the book it would be to note that. . . .* This is an unreal conditional statement. Why do you think the author chose to introduce her criticism in this way?

9. How would you explain the use of *would* in Sentence 16?

10. The author does not use *I*, but instead focuses on an imagined reader (see Sentence 11) or readership (Sentence 14). What is the effect of this focus on readers? Could she have used *I*? Why or why not?

As with most written genres, there are disciplinary differences in published book reviews. Notable among these is the focus of the evaluative commentary. For instance, in Biology and Sociology, book reviewers tend to discuss such aspects as style, clarity, diagrams, and references—as if these are observable data (Tse and Hyland, 2006) and evidence to be scrutinized. In these fields, there is less of a tendency to create an argument for or against an opinion. In Philosophy, however, reviewers are more likely to extend their evaluation beyond the surface observations and to deal with the issues presented, thus creating an argument. These disciplinary differences in emphasis give rise to differences in stylistic choices, such as those having to do with how authors state their claims in an effort to persuade readers. Apart from disciplinary differences, you will also see that many book reviewers may adopt a somewhat more conversational and engaging style.

TASK FIVE

Read this book review and underline any aspects that you think might be informal or not typical in a traditional research paper in your field. Discuss the questions on page 239. Do you think this review is typical of book reviews in Physics and Engineering? Why or why not?

Quantum Field Theory in a Nutshell (2nd edn)

Zee, Anthony. Princeton: Princeton University Press, 2010. 576 pp. US $65, UK £44.95 (cloth) ISBN: 978-0-691-14034-6.

❶ Anthony Zee is not only a leading theoretical physicist but also an author of popular books on both physics and non-physics topics. ❷ I recommend especially 'Swallowing Clouds,' on Chinese cooking and its folklore. ❸ Thus, it is not surprising that his textbook has a unique flavor. ❹ Derivations end, not with 'QED' but with exclamation points. ❺ At the end of one argument, we read 'Vive Cauchy!'; in another 'the theorem practically exudes generality.' ❻ This is quantum field theory taught at the knee of an eccentric uncle; one who loves the grandeur of his subject, has a keen eye for a slick argument, and is eager to share his repertoire of anecdotes about Feynman, Fermi, and all of his heroes.

❼ A one-page section entitled 'Electric Charge' illustrates the depth and tone of the book. ❽ In the previous section, Zee has computed the Feynman diagram responsible for vacuum polarization, in which a photon converts briefly to a virtual electron-positron pair. ❾ In the first paragraph, he evaluates this expression, giving a concrete formula for the momentum-dependence of the electric charge, an important effect of quantum field theory. ❿ Next, he dismisses other possible diagrams that could affect the value of the electric charge. ⓫ Most authors would give an explicit argument that these diagrams cancel, but for Zee it is more important to make the point that this result is expected and, from the right point of view, obvious. ⓬ Finally, he discusses the implications for the relative size of the charges of the electron and the proton. ⓭ If the magnitudes of charges are affected by interactions, and the proton has strong interactions but the electron does not, can it make sense that the charges of the proton and the electron are exactly equal and opposite? ⑭ The answer is yes, and also that this was the real point of the whole derivation.

⑮ The book takes on the full range of topics covered in typical graduate course in quantum field theory, and many additional topics: magnetic monopoles, solitons and topology, and applications to condensed matter systems including the Peierls instability and the quantum Hall fluid. ⑯ It is a large amount of territory to cover in a single volume. ⑰ Few derivations are more than one page long. ⑱ Those that fit in that space are very smooth, but others are too abbreviated to be fully comprehensible. ⑲ The prose that accompanies the derivations, though, is always enticing. ⑳ Zee misses no opportunity to point out that an argument he gives opens the door to some deeper subject that he encourages the reader to explore. ㉑ I do warn students that it is easy to learn from this book how to talk quantum field theory without understanding it. ㉒ To avoid this pitfall, it is important (as Zee emphasizes) to fill in the steps of his arguments with hard calculation.

㉓ One topic from which Zee does not restrain himself is the quantum theory of gravity. ㉔ In the first hundred pages we find a 'concise introduction to curved spacetime' that includes a very pretty derivation of the Christoffel symbol from the geodesic equation. ㉕ Toward the end of the book, there is a set of chapters devoted to the quantization of the gravitational field. ㉖ The structure of the graviton propagator is worked out carefully. ㉗ The van Dam-Veltman discontinuity between massless and massive spin 2 exchange is explained clearly. ㉘ But after this Zee runs out of steam in presenting fully worked arguments. ㉙ Still, there is room for more prose on connections to the great mysteries of the subject: the ultraviolet behavior, the cosmological constant, and the unification of forces. ㉚ A new chapter added to the second edition discusses 'Is Einstein Gravity the Square of Yang-Mills Theory?' and suggests an affirmative answer, based on brand-new developments in perturbative quantum field theory.

③ Quantum field theory is a large subject that still has not reached its definitive form. ③ As such, there is room for many textbooks of complementary character. ③ Zee states frankly, "It is not the purpose of this book to teach you to calculate cross sections for a living." ③ Students can use other books to dot the i's. ③ This one can help them love the subject and race to its frontier.

Michael E. Peskin
Stanford University
Classical and Quantum Gravity, 28, (2011), 089003.
Copyright IOP Publishing, Ltd. Used with permission.

1. What is your reaction to this book review? Do you think it is objective?

2. Is there any language in the review that you think might be useful in the writing of a book review in your field?

3. If you were a student in Physics or Engineering, would you buy this book?

Language Focus: Stating Opinions

As we discussed in Unit Four, authors need to exercise good judgment when interpreting data and giving an opinion. The same is true when you are evaluating the scholarship of others in a published book review. Carefully chosen language can contribute to the reader's willingness to accept your claims. Recall that opinions can be softened (hedged); they can also be strengthened (boosted), as shown here.

Scientists and industrialists disagree about the health hazards of dioxins, the latter stating that the risks are exaggerated.

Hedged   Scientists and industrialists disagree about the health hazards of dioxins, the latter stating that the risks *may be exaggerated.*

Boosted   Scientists and industrialists disagree about the health hazards of dioxins, the latter stating that the risks *are clearly exaggerated.*

Boosters and hedges are common in book reviews and other evaluative genre as are other features such as markers of attitudes and engagement and self-mentions (Tse and Hyland, 2006). Authors can indicate their attitudes toward a proposition or idea by indicating surprise, disbelief, understanding, or "interestingness," as shown in these examples.

> *It is surprising that* a relatively small amount of doping (say 10% F doping for O) does not preserve the magnetic ordering.

> With such vague and circular notions, *it is hard to accept* the author's later conclusions.

> *I understand that* web development is a broad field and it is impossible to cover everything in one single book.

> *It is interesting to note that*, at least to my knowledge, no such comprehensive book has ever been published.

Authors may also attempt to establish a connection with their readers and bring them into the text through the use of engagement markers. Engagement markers can take a variety of forms including personal pronouns (e.g., *we* and *you*), questions, commands, or directly addressing *the reader* or *readers*. Here are some examples.

> If *you* are an experienced dc motor engineer, *you may* enjoy reading Chapter 6.

> When *you* are looking for a reference work in econometrics that will be on *your* "frequently used" bookshelf for the next years to come, please *take* another pick.

> The overlaps are not necessarily repetitions, but represent variations on a theme. *Take for example* the idea of "primary resistance" in Africa, which Mazrui returns to in a number of different meanings.

> *How are we to* place Sachs's prescriptions for ending world poverty into the development economics literature?

> *Readers* may be pleasantly surprised to note that the case examples, provided throughout the text, begin within the very first chapter.

Finally, critical book reviewers insert themselves into their texts with some frequency. For instance, D'Angelo (2008) found an abundance of self-mentions in book reviews in Applied Linguistics, Law, Economics, and Medicine. Tse and Hyland (2006) also found frequent self-mentions in Philosophy and Biology, but fewer in Sociology. Self-mentions are not unexpected, if we consider that a book review is the outcome of a request for a personal opinion about a book.

> *I think that* the discussion about institutions, cluster policies, and relations that bridge and connect clusters with external agents deserves more attention.

> *It seems to me* that the book is more or less an overview of the authors' research plus other examples that are methodologically close to it.

> *In my opinion* this book is the most comprehensive book written to date on the subject of corona from overhead transmission systems.

Table 16 shows the variation in the use of engagement markers, hedges, attitude markers, boosters, and self-mentions in three disciplines. As you can see, the differences do not appear to be as great as one might expect, suggesting some uniformity in book reviewing practices.

TABLE 16. Some Stylistic Features of Book Reviews in Philosophy, Sociology, and Biology per 1,000 words

Category	Philosophy	Sociology	Biology
Engagement markers	16.1	6.2	9.7
Hedges	11.2	9.4	8.4
Attitude markers	8.5	8.4	9.5
Boosters	8.5	6.7	6.8
Self-mentions	3.4	1.2	3.3
TOTAL	47.7	31.9	37.7

Tse and Hyland, 2006.

TASK SIX

Find a published book review in a journal from your field. Bring it to class and be prepared to discuss such features as organization (as compared to that proposed by Motta-Roth), style, the nature of the praise and criticism, boosters, hedges, attitude markers, engagement markers, self-mentions, and evaluative language.

Language Focus: Evaluative Language

As you have seen in the sample texts, writing a good review requires an awareness of evaluative language. According to Hyland's 2004 study of 160 book reviews from eight disciplines (Cell Biology, Electrical Engineering, Mechanical Engineering, Physics, Marketing, Applied Linguistics, Philosophy, and Sociology), some evaluative terms cut across several disciplines, while others have preferred status in one or two. Here is a summary of his findings.

Frequently used evaluative adjectives in all disciplines: *useful, important, interesting*

Frequently used evaluative nouns in the "soft" fields: *clarity, accessibility*

Frequently used evaluative adjectives in the hard sciences: *detailed, up-to-date*

On a more specific level, philosophers and applied linguists often described books as *detailed*, while philosophers and marketing specialists praised books for being *insightful* and *significant*. Books in Engineering were commended for being *comprehensive* and *practical*. Of course, not all evaluation is positive. For all fields the most common negative adjective was *difficult*. In the softer fields, books were criticized for being *inconsistent, restricted,* and *misleading*.

In our discussion so far, we have examined issues of content, organization, opinion giving, and evaluative language. Although there is more to be said on each of these topics and we will return to some later in the unit, at this point we believe you have sufficient background to attempt your own short book review. You have had experience in summary writing. You are familiar with the role and place of qualifications or hedges. In addition, you have a better sense of your instructor as your audience and are learning to present yourself in your writing as a junior member of your chosen discipline.

TASK SEVEN

It is important to be fair when you critique. In this next task, examine some praise and criticisms of earlier editions of *Academic Writing for Graduate Students*. Consider which comments constitute praise, criticism, or neither. Discuss whether you think they are reasonable (R) or unreasonable (U) with a partner.

____ 1. "Students who already have a good enough command of the written language often lack the time and patience to work systematically through a textbook of this kind." (Breeze, 2005)

____ 2. "Some teachers may question the wisdom of encouraging novices to begin the research paper at the Methods section [although other ESP specialists besides Swales and Feak, e.g., Jacoby, Leech and Holton (1995) do encourage the "Methods first" composing sequence]." (Belcher, 1995)

____ 3. "It is surprising that the book does not begin with a more intellectually compelling perspective of academic writing such as MacDonald's view of academic writing as a vehicle for constructing knowledge claims." (Belcher, 1995)

____ 4. "The book does not offer specific guidance for students in all fields." (Chambers, 2008, personal communication)

____ 5. "No book can offer everything a student needs; thus teachers should expect to deviate from and supplement it, as the Commentary recommends, and most of all to 'negotiate the syllabus.'" (Reinhart, personal communication)

____ 6. "The book is aimed at classrooms with students from different backgrounds who can then benefit from discussions of how academic writing conventions differ across disciplines." (Conway, unpublished manuscript)

____ 7. "Each chapter focuses on the various types of writing that one finds in some upper-level undergraduate classes and most graduate classes." (Smith, 2008)

____ 8. "I think the section on book reviews is good, but how many students actually have to write book reviews? The book covers so many topics that students actually need, so why spend time on a genre students do not need to produce?" (Anonymous reviewer, 2012)

_____ 9. "An additional strength is that the text approaches academic writing as needing to be effective, sophisticated, and clear, rather than focusing on the 'right' or 'wrong' way to express ideas in writing." (Smith, 2008)

_____ 10. "There are many sample texts from many fields ranging from Engineering to Psychology. This, however, could be a drawback since students may have difficulty understanding them." (Anonymous reviewer, 2010)

Book Reviews for Course Assignments

Much of what we have said about published book reviews so far, of course, would apply to the writing of a book review for a class. However, there will be some differences, some of which we would like you to consider in the next task.

TASK EIGHT

Discuss with a partner whether these statements should apply to a book review that you write for a course. Mark the statements as agree (A), disagree (D), or unsure (?).

_____ 1. My review should provide some evidence that I can situate the book within ongoing discussions or debates or theoretical lineages in my field.

_____ 2. My review should reveal that I can relate the focus of the book to the course material.

_____ 3. My review should demonstrate that I can evaluate using criteria and language appropriate for my field.

_____ 4. I should provide a summary of the book and of each chapter before beginning my evaluation.

_____ 5. I should recommend whether others should read the book.

_____ 6. I should write something about the author and take into account his or her status in the field.

_____ 7. I should consider the date of publication and how this shapes my evaluation.

_____ 8. I should discuss concepts that are surprising or different from what I have learned in my course.

_____ 9. My review should identify the book I am reviewing and not assume that my readers (i.e., the professor or grader) have read it.

_____ 10. (a consideration of your own) _____

_____

This next task features a book review written by a student that appears in MICUSP.

TASK NINE

This review was written by a student in the interdisciplinary field of Natural Resources. After reading it, answer the questions on page 248.

The World Bank and IMF: Broken but Worth Fixing

❶ "But for millions of people globalization has not worked. ❷ Many have actually been made worse off" (Stiglitz, 248). ❸ In *Globalization and its Discontents*, Stiglitz challenges the World Bank and the IMF, questioning their motives and their successes. ❹ As a Nobel Prize winner and former chief economist of the World Bank, he shines a credible light on the institutions. ❺ This makes his arguments powerful and enlightened. ❻ He offers insightful suggestions on improving the organizations, so people everywhere can enjoy the attainable benefits globalization offers. ❼ The World Bank and IMF started after WWII with different missions. ❽ Currently they have similarities and differences, strengths and weaknesses, explained logically by Stiglitz so the reader can synthesize an opinion of their value today. ❾ While the pair exhibit severe deficiencies, their power for good, though largely unrealized, makes them necessary, once improved, in today's world.

⑩ The World Bank opened after WWII to rebuild Europe, and the IMF to provide global financial stability. ⑪ With Europe's recovery from the war, the institutions turned to developing nations. ⑫ Today, Stiglitz says that "one (the World Bank) is devoted to eradicating poverty, the other (the IMF) to maintaining global stability" (23). ⑬ Both organizations ultimately answer to the western powers: the USA and the European Union. ⑭ As a result, the World Bank and IMF see the developing world through an industrialized lens. ⑮ Stiglitz repeatedly notes that though the duo intends to do good, they fall short because of their ties to the western governments and financial communities. ⑯ The author differentiates the two, writing that the IMF acts less transparently than the World Bank, and with an unflinching adherence to the Washington Consensus policies of the 1980s. ⑰ The sincere nature of the World Bank, in its mission to alleviate poverty, puts it ahead of the stubborn IMF in Stiglitz's view. ⑱ Both fall short in helping developing nations cope with globalization, but the World Bank less so.

⑲ "The problem is that the institutions have come to reflect the mind-sets of those to whom they are accountable" (216). ⑳ From this statement stem the problems with the World Bank and the IMF. ㉑ The World Bank's programs of education, community development, and infrastructural improvement point to its commitment to help the poorest countries. ㉒ In the end though, the head of the bank receives his/her appointment from the president of the U.S., which puts its goals ahead of those of the developing nations. ㉓ Until that organization focuses on poverty alleviation above all, it will continue to face scrutiny and fail in its service. ㉔ The more opaque IMF more forcefully imposes its will on the countries with which it works. ㉕ They receive money with many strings attached. ㉖ These conditions do not make sense, as seen repeatedly with the former Soviet nations and East Asian countries. ㉗ When compared to success stories like China, which avoided the IMF, one wonders who it actually wants to aid. ㉘ Until it reforms its ways away from disproved Washington Consensus policies, the IMF will hurt developing nations it ostensibly aims to help. ㉙ Should the two organizations and the industrialized countries backing them fail to devote themselves to the developing world, they will increasingly face backlash and suffer from a lack of credibility.

㉚ The World Bank and the IMF have great potential; they provide the framework necessary to humanely bring globalization to the world. ㉛ Developing nations need the projects brought by the World Bank, and the stability supposedly provided by the IMF. ㉜ The U.S., the EU, and the other countries controlling the two need to loosen their grip. ㉝ If the pair would operate in a more egalitarian way, they would do a better job. ㉞ This means opening governance to developing nations, granting them votes and a deserved say in any matter which affects them. ㉟ The United Nations provides a good model overall, which the two could emulate. ㊱ The World Bank's development strategies should come from within countries. ㊲ The IMF should restructure its policies and economic models to reflect reality, not what works in a perfect world. ㊳ While we should not eliminate the two organizations, fundamental changes must occur to ease globalization's pains.

㊴ Stiglitz brings a strong perspective to the globalization debate, and makes valid points about the World Bank and the IMF's failings. ㊵ They possess the power to lift people and nations from poverty, but currently they lack the leadership, independence, and policies to do so. ㊶ The western powers which control them must recognize that they should support each country's unique strategy for dealing with and benefiting from globalization. ㊷ If they fall short, one can hardly blame those hardest hit for pushing back unpredictably and violently against the two institutions and their western controllers, which have backed them into a corner.

MICUSP File NRE.G0.02.1

1. Which of the ideas presented in the statements given in Task Eight (pages 244–245) are reflected in the review?

2. The author used several quotes. Where in the paragraph are they placed? What is the connection between the quotes and the other information in the paragraph?

3. Underline the evaluative language. How strongly are the opinions stated? Do you notice any instances of hedging? Do the language choices contribute to author positioning?

4. How easy is it to distinguish what Stiglitz is saying from what the student is saying?

5. Would you have given the review a top score?

6. What do you think about beginning the text with the word *but*?

Evaluating a Published Article

Graduate students in the United States (and elsewhere) are often expected and encouraged to evaluate journal articles, sometimes as part of a journal club run by an instructor or advisor. While the word *critique* may not be used, students are asked to analyze, examine, or investigate, with the underlying assumption that students will do these activities with a critical eye. Writing an article critique may be somewhat easier than writing a book review, since an article usually centers around a narrow research question or problem. However, as with book reviews, they can still be particularly challenging to write because they require you to take on an "unfamiliar persona"—that of an authority of some kind (Dobson and Feak, 2001). Another similarity to book reviews is that what you choose to examine will largely depend on your discipline. In a field such as History, you might evaluate conclusions by critiquing the evidence used to support those conclusions. In Sociology, on the other hand, you may focus on the theoretical model employed in a study and the impact the model has on the conclusions. In Psychology, your critique may center on the instrument used to collect data, while in Engineering, you may notice that conclusions or explanations in a paper are not well supported and thus require further testing or more evidence. In writing a critique, it may help to know something about the author of the text, which can help you understand the perspective of the paper and perhaps the reason the article was chosen for evaluation.

Having worked with many students on critique assignments, we have noticed that the articles students are asked to review often have a weakness that can be identified by reflecting on the course readings and lectures. For instance, if a course has emphasized the importance of a well-articulated plan for data collection, such as employing triangulation, the paper assigned for critique may lack such a plan. Thus, it is a good idea to consider what has been highlighted in your course and review the article with these highlights in mind.

If no evaluation criteria have been provided, then it is also important to have some general questions in mind to guide your thinking as you read and to form the foundation for critical inquiry (Dobson and Feak, 2001). We offer a few questions for you to consider as you read an article.

1. Who is the audience?

2. What is the purpose of the article?

3. What research questions or hypotheses are being addressed in the article? Are the questions relevant? (Stating the research questions or hypotheses as yes or no questions will help you identify the focus of a paper as well as evaluate the evidence and conclusions. In our experience, a question such as *Does herbal tea cause tooth decay* can be more useful in guiding your thinking than can a simple statement establishing the topic, as with *This paper is about herbal tea and tooth decay.*)

4. What conclusions does the author draw from the research? (Hint: Does the author answer yes or no to the research questions?)

5. What kind of evidence was collected to explore the research questions? Is there any evidence that could or should have been collected and included but was not? How good is the evidence? How well does the evidence support the conclusions?

6. Are the author's conclusions valid or plausible based on the evidence? Why or why not? How do the conclusions relate to what you have been learning in class? Are they consistent or inconsistent?

7. Are there any important assumptions underlying the article? How do these influence the conclusions?

8. Are the charts, tables, and figures clear? Do they contribute to or detract from the article?

9. Does the research make an original contribution to the field? Why or why not?

10. If the evaluation is focused on a published article, why was the article chosen? Is the research consistent with material, best practices, and perspectives presented in class?

TASK TEN

Read this excerpt from a short communication entitled "The Increasing Dominance of Teams in Production of Knowledge" and analyze it using the questions provided on pages 249–250. Discuss your responses with a partner. Note that the definition of self-citation used in the paper is

> . . . any citation where a common name exists in the authorship of both the cited and the citing papers. All citations were removed in which a citing and cited author's first initial and last name matched. This method can also eliminate citations where the authors are different people, but share the same name.

Also note that when figures or tables are designated with an S, they can be found in online supplemental materials. For this paper, the supplement contains Figs. S1 to S5, Tables S1 to S4, and References. Finally, if you want to know more about short communications, go to Unit Seven.

The Increasing Dominance of Teams in Production of Knowledge

Wuchty, S., Jones, B. F., and Uzzi, B. (18 May 2007). *Science, 316*(5827), 1036–1038.

Abstract

We have used 19.9 million papers over 5 decades and 2.1 million patents to demonstrate that teams increasingly dominate solo authors in the production of knowledge. Research is increasingly done in teams across nearly all fields. Teams typically produce more frequently cited research than individuals do, and this advantage has been increasing over time. Teams now also produce the exceptionally high-impact research, even where that distinction was once the domain of solo authors. These results are detailed for sciences and engineering, social sciences, arts and humanities, and patents, suggesting that the process of knowledge creation has fundamentally changed.

[First page omitted]

For science and engineering, social sciences, and patents, there has been a substantial shift toward collective research. In the sciences, team size has grown steadily each year and nearly doubled, from 1.9 to 3.5 authors per paper, over 45 years.

Shifts toward teamwork in science and engineering have been suggested to follow from the increasing scale, complexity, and costs of big science. Surprisingly then, we find an equally strong trend toward teamwork in the social sciences, where these drivers are much less notable. Although social scientists in 1955 wrote 17.5% of their papers in teams, by 2000 they wrote 51.5% of their papers in teams, an increase similar to that in sciences and engineering. Mean team size has also grown each year. On average, today's social sciences papers are written in pairs, with a continuing, positive trend toward larger teams. Unlike the other areas of research, single authors still produce over 90% of the papers in the arts and humanities. Nevertheless, there is a positive trend toward teams in arts and humanities (P < 0.001). Lastly, patents also show a rising dominance of teams. Although these data are on a shorter time scale (1975–2000), there was a similar annualized increase in the propensity for teamwork. Average team size has risen from 1.7 to 2.3 inventors per patent, with the positive trend toward larger teams continuing.

The generality of the shift to teamwork is captured in Table 1. In sciences and engineering, 99.4% of the 171 subfields have seen increased teamwork. Meanwhile, 100% of the 54 subfields in the

Table 1. Patterns by Subfield

	N_{fields}	Increasing Team Size		RTI >1 (with self-citations)		RTI >1 (with no self-citations)	
		N_{fields}	%	N_{fields}	%	N_{fields}	%
Science and engineering	171	170	99.4	167	97.7	159	92.4
Social sciences	54	54	100.0	54	100.0	51	94.4
Arts and humanities	27	24	88.9	23	85.2	18	66.7
Patents	36	36	100	32	88.9	—	—

For the three broad ISI categories and for patents, we counted the number (N) and percentage (%) of subfields that show (i) larger team sizes in the last 5 years compared to the first 5 years and (ii) RTI measures larger than 1 in the last 5 years. We show RTI measures both with and without self-citations removed in calculating the citations received. Dash entries indicate data not applicable.

social sciences, 88.9% of the 27 subfields in the humanities, and 100% of the 36 subfields in patenting have seen increased teamwork.

Trends for individual fields are presented in Table S1. In the sciences, areas like medicine, biology, and physics have seen at least a doubling in mean team size over the 45-year period. Surprisingly, even mathematics, long thought the domain of the loner scientist and least dependent of the hard sciences on lab scale and capital-intensive equipment, showed a marked increase in the fraction of work done in teams, from 19% to 57%, with mean team size rising from 1.22 to 1.84. In the social sciences, psychology, economics, and political science show enormous shifts toward teamwork, sometimes doubling or tripling the propensity for teamwork. With regard to average team size, psychology, the closest of the social sciences to a lab science, has the highest growth (75.1%), whereas political science has the lowest (16.6%). As reflected in Fig. 1A, the humanities show lower growth rates in the fraction of publications done in teams, yet a tendency toward increased teamwork is still observed. All areas of patents showed a positive change in both the fraction of papers done by teams and the team size, with only small variations across the areas of patenting, suggesting that the

Figure 1. The Growth of Teams

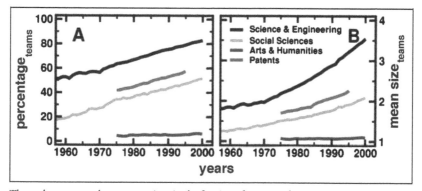

These plots present changes over time in the fraction of papers and patents written in teams (A) and in mean team size (B). Each line represents the arithmetic average taken over all subfields in each year.

conditions favoring teamwork in patenting are largely similar across subfields.

Our measure of impact was the number of citations each paper and patent receives, which has been shown to correlate with research quality (15–17) and is frequently used in promotion and funding reviews (18). Highly cited work was defined as receiving more than the mean number of citations for a given field and year (19). Teams produced more highly cited work in each broad area of research and at each point in time.

To explore the relationship between teamwork and impact in more detail, we defined the relative team impact (RTI) for a given time period and field. RTI is the mean number of citations received by team-authored work divided by the mean number of citations received by solo-authored work. A RTI greater than 1 indicates that teams produce more highly cited papers than solo authors and vice versa for RTI less than 1. When RTI is equal to 1, there is no difference in citation rates for team- and solo-authored papers. In our data set, the average RTI was greater than 1 at all points in time and in all broad research areas: sciences and engineering, social sciences, humanities, and patents. In other words, there is a broad tendency for teams to produce more highly cited work than individual authors. Further, RTI is rising with time. For example, in sciences and engineering, team-authored papers received 1.7 times as many citations as solo-authored papers in 1955 but 2.1 times the citations by 2000. Similar upward trends in relative team impact appear in sciences and engineering, social science, and arts and humanities and more weakly in patents, although the trend is still upward (20). During the early periods, solo authors received substantially more citations on average than teams in many subfields, especially within sciences and engineering (Fig. 2E) and social sciences (Fig. 2F).

Figure 2. The Relative Impact of Teams

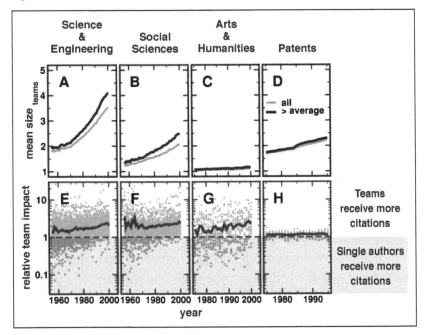

(A to D) Mean team size comparing all papers and patents with those that received more citations than average in the relevant subfield. (E to H) The RTI, which is the mean number of citations received by team-authored work divided by the mean number of citations received by solo-authored work. A ratio of 1 indicates that team- and solo-authored work have equivalent impact on average. Each point represents the RTI for a given subfield and year, whereas the black lines present the arithmetic average in a given year.

By the end of the period, however, there are almost no subfields in sciences and engineering and social sciences in which solo authors typically receive more citations than teams. Table S1 details RTIs for major individual research areas, indicating that teams currently have a nearly universal impact advantage. In a minority of cases, RTIs declined with time (e.g., −34.4% in mathematics and

−25.7% in education), although even here teams currently have a large advantage in citations received (e.g., 67% more average citations in mathematics and 105% in education).

The citation advantage of teams has also been increasing with time when teams of fixed size are compared with solo authors. In science and engineering, for example, papers with two authors received 1.30 times more citations than solo authors in the 1950s but 1.74 times more citations in the 1990s. In general, this pattern prevails for comparisons between teams of any fixed size versus solo authors (Table S4).

A possible challenge to the validity of these observations is the presence of self-citations, given that teams have opportunities to self-cite their work more frequently than a single author. To address this, we reran the analysis with all self-citations removed from the data set (21). We found that removing self-citations can produce modest decreases in the RTI measure in some fields; for example, RTIs fell from 3.10 to 2.87 in medicine and 2.30 to 2.13 in biology (Table S1). Thus, removing self-citations can reduce the RTI by 5 to 10%, but the relative citation advantage of teams remains essentially intact.

Because the progress of knowledge may be driven by a small number of key insights (22), we further test whether the most extraordinary concepts, results, and technologies are the province of solitary scientists or teams. Pooling all papers and patents within the four research areas, we calculated the frequency distribution of citations to solo-authored and team-authored work, comparing the first 5 years and last 5 years of our data. If these distributions overlap in their right-hand tails, then a solo-authored paper or patent is just as likely as a team-authored paper or patent to be extraordinarily highly cited.

Our results show that teams now dominate the top of the citation distribution in all four research domains (Fig. 3, A to D). In the early years, a solo author in science and engineering or the social sciences was more likely than a team to receive no citations, but a solo author was also more likely to garner the highest number of citations, that is, to have a paper that was singularly influential.

However, by the most recent period, a team-authored paper has a higher probability of being extremely highly cited. For example, a team-authored paper in science and engineering is currently 6.3 times more likely than a solo- authored paper to receive at least 1000 citations. Lastly, in arts and humanities and in patents, individuals were never more likely than teams to produce more-influential work. These patterns also hold when self-citations are removed (Fig. S5).

Figure 3. Exceptional Research

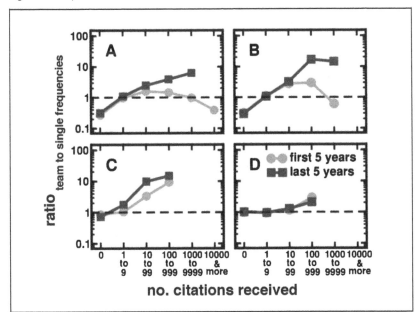

Pooling all publications and patents within the four research categories, we calculated frequency distributions of citations received. Separate distributions are calculated for single authors and for teams, and the ratio is plotted. A ratio greater than 1 indicates that a team-authored paper had a higher probability of producing the given range of citations than a solo-authored paper. Ratios are compared for the early period (first 5 years of available data) and late period (last 5 years of available data) for each research category, sciences and engineering (A), social sciences (B), arts and humanities (C), and patents (D).

[Last page omitted]

While it is possible to evaluate an article without reference to other published work or course material, your evaluation may be improved if you consider the ideas or findings of others. To demonstrate, we now turn to Task Eleven.

TASK ELEVEN

Now that you have read and analyzed the article on team and individual production of knowledge, consider the following opinions on the topic. As you read, mark each as reasonable (R) or unreasonable (U). If you are unsure, indicate this with a question mark (?). To what extent, if any, do some of these claims influence your opinion of the article? Is your opinion now more or less favorable?

_____ 1. "Beyond individual interests and motivation of individual scientists, teamwork and scientific collaboration is one of the characteristics of 'big science' (Price, 1966). Of course, in inter- and cross-disciplinary areas, where scientists from different fields are jointly doing research, intensive collaboration is expected (see Glänzel et al., 2003)." (Glänzel et al., 2009)

_____ 2. Cronin (2003) argues that in many science disciplines fraud and honorific authorship have become a matter of concern.

_____ 3. "Suppressed, fraud, honorific, hyper-authorship or even 'mandatory' authorship, e.g., of supervisors', questions the possibility of fixing the degree of the individual co-authors' contribution to the paper (Cronin, 2001), and may raise the question: Co-authorship—who's contributing?" (Glänzel, 2008)

_____ 4. Research by Persson et al. (2004) revealed that the increase in the number of co-authors on papers is outpacing the growth in the number of publications indexed in the Science Citation Index (SCI) database. This expansion in co-authorship indicates that the network of collaboration is becoming more concentrated and co-authorship is gradually becoming more intense.

_____ 5. "Research co-operation is certainly a necessary and positive phenomenon in the era of 'big science' but the notion of collaboration as a recipe for guaranteed success remains a myth." (Glänzel, 2008)

_____ 6. "Collectivisation is typically associated with big-science projects and hence with big, expensive apparatus. Here the danger is that the team, or the apparatus, takes over priority (socially as well as epistemically) from the individual scientist." (Kragh, 2001)

_____ 7. "When average productivity is plotted against mean cooperativeness, field specific patterns can usually be observed: Productivity increases first with co-operativeness until a field specific threshold is reached; beyond this level, correlation turns negative. This threshold value ranges depending on subject peculiarities from 1–2 in mathematics, over 3–4 in chemistry, to 5–6 co-authors in neurosciences and biomedical research." (Glänzel and Schubert, 2004)

_____ 8. "The fact that a paper is less frequently cited or even still uncited several years after publication provides information about its reception but does not reveal anything about its quality or the standing of its author(s). Uncited papers by Nobel Prize winners may just serve as an example." (Glänzel, 2008)

_____ 9. Self-citation has little impact on how important a paper is. (Glänzel, 2008)

TASK TWELVE

We want you to start thinking about what you could write in a critique of the excerpt from "The Increasing Dominance of Teams in the Production of Knowledge." List three or four evaluative comments that you could make about the article. Discuss them with a partner. Keep in mind that you are not being asked to give your *opinion* on whether teamwork does in fact lead to better research and higher-quality papers. Focus on the article and the quality of the research, using your responses from Tasks Ten and Eleven as a guide.

In a critique, you may want to express criticism by saying what the author should have done but did not do. Here is one example of this.

> This was a well-written review of current information, but the connection between nutrient stress, secondary compounds, and herbivory rates in wetland plants *could have received* greater coverage.

For the text on team or individual scholarship, you could make this observation.

> The paper would have been somewhat more relevant, if the authors had used a better measure to determine authorship.

Language Focus: Unreal Conditionals

Here are two additional examples of unreal conditional statements.

This article *would have been* more persuasive *if* the author *had related* the findings to previous work on the topic.

It *would have been* better *if* the authors *had given* their main findings in the form of a table.

Past Unreal Conditionals

Notice the structure of these conditionals:

noun phrase	modal + *have*	past participle	comparative expression	*if*	noun phrase	*had*	past participle	adverbial or complement
The images	would have	been	more informative	if	they	had	been	in color.
The resolution of the gel material	might have	changed		if	substantial Joule heating	had	occurred.	
The damage assessment	would have	been	more accurate	if	it	had	been done	immediately after the earthquake.

These conditionals refer to an unreal situation in the past. Past unreal conditionals are common in critiques because the texts being critiqued have already been put into final form—either published or turned in. There is no opportunity to revise the text in light of the criticism because the time frame is closed. Since these conditionals express something that is impossible or contrary to fact, linguists and philosophers often call them *counterfactuals.* In a critique, the *if* clause in the past unreal conditional often occurs second. Why is this so?

Present Unreal Conditionals

Present unreal conditionals, on the other hand, describe a hypothetical situation in the present. In these, the simple past tense forms are used. In a consultation with your writing instructor, you may have heard a sentence such as this.

Your paper *would be* stronger if you *included* some additional information.

In this example, it seems that there may still be a possibility for revisions or improvements. However, in the case of a published paper, sentences such as this may appear in a literature review.

It *would have been* helpful if the authors *had provided* information about the patients who were screened, but not included in the study.

These types of sentences are sometimes called *contrary to fact* or *hypothetical conditionals*. In the second sentence, we can assume no possibility for revision exists.

TASK THIRTEEN

Consider these situations and comment on how they might have turned out differently. Use an unreal conditional. The first one has been done for you.

1. A bad presentation

   My presentation would have been better if I had spent less

   time on basic concepts.

2. A bad grade on an examination or paper

   _____

   _____

3. A missed deadline

   _____

   _____

4. An unsuccessful meeting with an advisor or a committee

   _____

   _____

5. A rejected paper or conference proposal

   _____

   _____

Now notice the italicized verb forms in these sample sentences.

The author *should have provided* more data about her sample.

Although this is an interesting and important paper, the authors *could have given* more attention to the fact that their model of consumer choice is based entirely on U.S. data.

Notice that *should* expresses a strongly negative comment, while *could* is less strong. *Should have* is a criticism, *could have* is more a suggestion, and *might have* is a weak suggestion. The use of *could* and *might* in unreal conditionals also reminds us that it is important to make your points with an appropriate amount of strength. Criticisms that are too strong and lack support will not help you position yourself, nor will evaluative comments that are expressed in too weak a manner.

Language Focus: Evaluative Language Revisited

As you already know, the different parts of speech can be used for evaluation.

Nouns:	*success*	*failure*
Verbs:	*succeed*	*fail*
Adjectives:	*successful*	*unsuccessful*
Adverbs:	*successfully*	*unsuccessfully*

For instance, you could write variations of these two claims.

Verbs

The article *succeeds in* demonstrating how bio-gas has improved daily life in Nepal.

The article *fails* to serve teachers who clearly need to make much more complex judgments about their students than the four stage model implies.

Adverbs

The article *successfully* demonstrates how bio-gas has improved daily life in Nepal.

Early papers *unsuccessfully* attempted to use cross-section distributions of accident counts to distinguish between true and spurious state dependence.

Adjectives

> The protocol described in the paper is *successful* at accurately tracking randomly moving targets over a wide range of speed.

> The article is *unsuccessful* at convincing readers of the benefits of new taxes on all-electric vehicles to compensate for short-falls in the federal highway budget.

Note the difference in the strength of claim in these two versions.

> Early papers *unsuccessfully* attempted to use cross-section distributions of accident counts to distinguish between true and spurious state dependence.

> Early papers *failed* to use cross-section distributions of accident counts to distinguish between true and spurious state dependence.

Sometimes, we can make contrasting pairs of adjectives. The pairing of a positive and a negative can certainly soften the criticism.

> In this *ambitious, but flawed* study, the authors attempt to show that domesticated animals are in some way just as responsible as automobiles for our current CO_2 imbalance.

> In this *flawed, but ambitious* study, the authors attempt to show that domesticated animals are in some way just as responsible as automobiles for our current CO_2 imbalance.

Notice how the emphasis changes depending on the information you place first. Can you create three other suitable combinations?

In addition to pairing adjectives, you can also make other pairings using other linking words and phrases, especially those used to express adversativity (see Unit One).

> *Although* the author suggests that journal articles written in languages other than English may have limited impact, he fails to recognize that they may be important at the regional level.

> The author suggests that journal articles written in languages other than English may have limited impact; *however,* he fails to recognize that they may be important at the regional level.

> *Despite* the many interesting citations in support of his view, the citations are dated and are not likely meaningful today.

TASK FOURTEEN

Rate the adjectives using the scale. Use the sample sentence to guide your decision.

++ very positive + positive 0 neutral/ambiguous – negative – – very negative

> In this _____ study, the authors attempt to show that domesticated animals are in some way just as responsible as automobiles for our current CO_2 imbalance.

____ unusual	____ limited	____ ambitious	____ modest
____ small	____ restricted	____ important	____ flawed
____ useful	____ significant	____ innovative	____ interesting
____ careful	____ competent	____ impressive	____ elegant
____ simple	____ traditional	____ complex	____ small scale
____ exploratory	____ remarkable	____ preliminary	____ unsatisfactory

Evaluative Adjectives across Disciplines

Classes composed of students from several disciplines do not always agree about these adjectives listed in Task Fourteen. This is fully understandable. Take the case of the *simple/complex* contrast. Students in the sciences and medicine, for example, think of *simple* as a positive and *complex* as a negative. For such students, *simple* equals "well planned" or "clearly designed," and *complex* equals "confused" or "messy." In contrast, social scientists equate *simple* with "unsophisticated" and *complex* with "sophisticated."

In an interesting study (note the evaluative adjective!), Becher (1987) surveyed adjectives of praise and blame among historians, sociologists, and physicists in Britain and the United States. He found considerable differences among the three groups. Although the preferences listed in Table 17 only indicate general tendencies, they are quite revealing.

TABLE 17. Adjectives of Praise and Blame among Historians, Sociologists, and Physicists in Britain and the United States

	Good Work	Average Work	Poor Work
Humanities	scholarly original	sound	thin
Social sciences	perceptive rigorous	scholarly	anecdotal
Physics	elegant economical	accurate	sloppy

Becher, 1987. Copyright Taylor & Francis. Used with permission.

List some typical evaluative adjectives (both good and bad) used in your field. What about *neat* or *kludgy*, for example?

Critical Reading

The discussion so far has strongly pointed to the need to engage in critical reading combined with critical thinking about both what is given in a text and what is not. Also important is your evaluation of how the text delivers its message. Critical reading is more than simply reading carefully. As we have pointed out, your reading should allow you to evaluate other work by making inferences and interpretations. This involves taking into account what you already know, have read, or perhaps have recently learned in a course. By synthesizing all of these elements you can reveal not only *what you know*, but also *what you think* about published work in relation to some reasonable criteria.

As you read critically and formulate your evaluation, it is also important to be fair. After all, being seen as fair and reasonable is part of graduate student positioning. For example, it may not be fair to criticize the teamwork article for not looking at whether the teams consisted of mostly men or women. For one, the paper was clear about its focus on the broader issue of teams and, for another, trying to determine gender on the basis of author name would likely be extremely difficult, if not impossible, in some instances. This is not to say that team characteristics are not worthy of investigation; it would, in fact, be reasonable to suggest this as a way to extend this line of inquiry.

To be fair in your evaluation also keep in mind the genre you are dealing with. Our expectations for a conference abstract are, of course, different from those for a research paper and should again be different for a short communication. In a short communication, such as the teamwork article, authors cannot be expected to provide all the background information readers might require to have a complete understanding of the issue. We would, however, expect a full article to provide significantly more detail.

TASK FIFTEEN

Here are some comments on the teamwork excerpt that were made by some of our students. Discuss the comments and consider whether they would contribute to a fair critique and to author positioning. Mark the points that you think would be worthwhile to include in a critique with a check mark (✓). Remember that even if a comment is fair, it may not be worth including in a critique.

_____ 1. The number of articles included in the study seems large enough to support the conclusions.

_____ 2. The article is written in a style that is easy to follow.

_____ 3. We do not know where the patent data comes from. It might only be the U.S. patents.

_____ 4. There is a lot of information in the supplement that we cannot easily see. The supplement information should be in the article.

_____ 5. The definition of self-citation does not seem quite right. Maybe the way this is defined influences the results.

_____ 6. I think the figures are hard to read.

_____ 7. The authors looked only at the Institute for Scientific Information (ISI) Web of Science database and patent records, so they might have missed a lot of work that is not recorded in these two places.

_____ 8. The research seems to have been carefully done.

_____ 9. I do not understand why the authors looked at humanities or, I should really say, the arts. Do artists or creative writers work in teams to produce published work?

_____ 10. I think the authors should have looked at the country of origin of the papers to see whether the impact of teams is stronger in one part of the world or another.

Do you have any other criticisms of the teamwork article that you consider fair and reasonable? Work in a group to come up with at least two more. Be prepared to offer them to the class.

While negative criticism is to be expected, thinking only negatively is probably ill-advised. After all, instructors rarely choose articles for critiquing because they think they are worthless. Further, you do not want to give the impression that you are only a "hatchet" person—someone who is unable to find anything positive and does nothing but criticize. If you do offer a largely negative critique, consider offering something positive with the negative.

The authors	provide	a small	piece of research on	an interesting	topic.

However, the study	suffers from	a number of limitations.
	exhibits	several weaknesses.
	can be criticized on	several counts
	raises	as many questions as it answers.

To be fair, negative criticism of a short communication (see Unit Seven), should perhaps be qualified (see Unit Four). Here is an example.

However, _at least in its current form_, the study _apparently_ suffers from a number of limitations.

TASK SIXTEEN

Write a draft of your own critique of the teamwork excerpt in Task Ten.

Language Focus: Beginning the Critique

Most likely you will begin your evaluation of an article with a summary. After the summary, you then need to make a transition into your analysis. Finding just the right sentence to begin your critique can indeed be a challenge. We read through several commentaries (critiques) published in *Behavioral and Brain Sciences*, one of the growing number of journals that publishes expert responses to manuscripts. We found some very interesting opening sentences, which we have transformed into skeletal sentences for you.

> [Authors' names] present a plausible case that . . . Less adequate is their discussion of . . . .
>
> [Authors' names] take on the difficult task of . . . . Unfortunately, . . .
>
> [Authors' names] present an important discussion of . . . . Although we may not agree on all the issues raised in the article, we praise the authors for . . . .
>
> The article by [author name] is an ambitious feat of synthesis, encompassing diverse theories of . . . . This effort, however, is not fully successful.
>
> [Authors' names] have written an important and timely article on . . . . Despite its many strengths there are a number of small, but important, weaknesses.
>
> [Authors' names] present a compelling argument for . . . ; however, . . .
>
> While the authors' position that . . . is attractive, there are a number of weaknesses in this concept.

Published commentaries (also referred to as *reactions, comments, responses,* or *discussions*) can be extremely interesting, as they often highlight key debates within your field. Do you know of a journal in your field that publishes them? If you can find and examine such a journal, you will see the large difference in style between the research article and the commentary.

Language Focus: Inversions

You already know that English usually requires an inverted word order for questions. You also probably know that a different word order is required if a "negative" word is used to open a sentence.

> *Not only has the author* presented some valuable new information, he has also presented it in a very clear and coherent manner.

> *In no case do the authors* provide any statistical information about their results.

Notice how the auxiliary verb precedes the subject, as in a question. Now look at this statement, first inverted, and then in normal word order.

> *Particularly prominent were* functional strategies . . . .

> *Functional strategies . . . were* particularly prominent.

This kind of inversion, even with simple adjectives or participles, is quite common in poetry (*Broken was the sword of the king*). However, in academic English, it only occurs with expressions that are emphatic (e.g., *particularly*) or comparative (e.g., *even more*). The inversion is a strong highlighting device and should only be used for special emphasis, as when we want to single out one result/fault/problem/virtue from many others.

TASK SEVENTEEN

Complete the following inversions.

Example: Particularly interesting

> Particularly interesting was the way in which Cheng introduced sociological ideas about the influence of older scientists on younger scientists.

1. Especially notable _____

2. Much less expected _____.

3. Especially noteworthy _____.

4. Of greater concern _____.

TASK EIGHTEEN

Write a critique of a paper from your own field. Consider beginning with a brief summary. Make sure that there is a good fit between your summary and critique.

Reaction Papers

Throughout this book, we have placed strong emphasis on academic style. We will continue to do so in Units Seven and Eight. However, in this section of Unit Six we would like to introduce you to a kind of critique that permits—and encourages—a more personal and informal style of writing: reaction or response papers. Reaction papers may be more common in the U.S. than elsewhere.

Reaction papers encourage students to draw on their own experiences, feelings, and ideas as well as to make methodological and analytic comments in relation to, for instance, a talk or a written text. When writing these papers students sometimes consider these questions.

- What was the text or the talk about?
- Who wrote the text or gave the talk?
- What was the main message of the text or the talk?
- How do you feel about what you read or heard?
- What impressions did the text or talk have on you?
- What do you agree or disagree with?
- How does what you read or heard relate to the course in which the reaction paper was assigned?
- Can you identify with or do you see yourself in what you read or heard?

International students can often have an advantage here because they can incorporate observations and experiences that reflect their own special backgrounds, although this genre may be completely new to them and be particularly challenging to write. Often, the comments in a reaction paper will open instructors' eyes to new thoughts and ideas on a topic.

TASK NINETEEN

Read these two short student reactions to the teamwork text given in Task Ten and answer the questions on page 273. We have numbered independent clauses as sentences for ease of discussion. Consider which of the two reaction papers you would prefer to have written and which would likely appeal to an instructor.

A.

Personal Reaction: "The Increasing Dominance of Teams in Production of Knowledge"

❶ The article "The Increasing Dominance of Teams in Production of Knowledge" discusses the impact of teams, as opposed to individuals, on the production of research today. **❷** A team of researchers themselves, the writers convey the idea that unless one is the next Einstein, Kant, or Newton, one's individual genius is not on par with a combined effort. **❸** From my experience, this can be true; **❹** for example, if I am schooled in syntax and my partner in semantics, our exploration of the interface of the two will be significantly improved by our coordination.

❺ However, as a leader, a perfectionist, and a person who focuses best alone, I have found that coordination of effort can have its drawbacks. **❻** When working in teams, I often find myself doing all of the work, having to redo all of the work, or spending so much time getting others to do their work that our output is worse than if I had done it myself. **❼** And while I have had my share of successful team efforts, I have always found it difficult to decide how my team should go about it; **❽** if each person is assigned one portion, one runs the risk of losing potential ingenuity in a team member's portion and missing something fundamental about one's own. **❾** And if everyone does the same thing and then reconvenes, it is often the case that the most dominant personality, rather than the most competent work, survives.

⑩ Although the research shows that teams are exponentially being cited more than individuals, I would argue that in some cases, two heads are not better than one, but rather double the work.

Kohlee Kennedy

B.

Response: Group Work

❶ Personally, I find that in linguistics, the classic approach of "armchair linguistics" is often applied to my work in that I rarely work in groups. ❷ However, when I do find a class or assignment where teamwork is required, it is often time that is not fulfilling. ❸ Most of the time is spent on organizing when the team will meet, who will do what; ❹ and more than likely, one or more members will not pull their weight and will drag the overall performance of the group dynamic down. ❺ For instance, I had a group project my freshman year of college that involved a brief presentation and a paper for a psychology course. ❻ My teammates, while claiming to be good students, did practically none of the work, and the work that they did was subpar. ❼ This forced me to do most of the work myself, which was incredibly frustrating, and it gave me a skewed view of working with others on a project.

❽ Nevertheless, according to Wuchty et al. (2011), teamwork produces higher quality work, as made evident from the number of citations coming from groups vs. citations from individual authors. ❾ While teamwork may be beneficial, in these settings, these are researchers who have established rapport with each other and have similar educational backgrounds. ⑩ In contrast, the group work settings that I often work in are with students from different majors and who are strictly classmates. ⑪ These two factors may contribute to my personal bias against group work, but I can understand the benefits of several people working towards a research or practical goal.

Patrick Kelley

1. Make a list of all the personal expressions used in the reaction papers.

2. How would you say the reactions are organized? Are they similar to a problem-solution or general-specific text?

3. In which sentence(s) do the authors make use of their own experiences? Are these personal experiences effective?

4. The writers of these reaction papers do not offer an overall positive reaction to teamwork, focusing instead on the drawbacks. Do you think they have adequately explained their perspectives?

5. Do the reactions make good use of the teamwork article? Why or why not?

6. Were any of the authors' comments interesting to you? Which one(s)?

7. Where would you place the writing style of each text on a continuum from highly informal to highly formal? Does the style seem appropriate?

8. Which of the two papers has the better title? Why?

9. Is one of the reactions stronger than the other? How did you decide this?

10. Compare one or both of the reaction papers to the critique you wrote for Task Sixteen. In what significant ways do the papers differ?

Language Focus: Non-Standard Quotation Marks (Scare Quotes)

The standard uses of quotation marks indicate

- the exact written words of other writers
- quoted speech
- unusual technical terms
- linguistic examples (as in *"quote" is a five-letter word*)

In addition, there are other uses of quotation marks that are not standard; these are commonly called *scare quotes,* and they function similarly to the way "air quotes" or "finger quotes" are used by speakers to show they are not to be understood literally. Scare quotes consist of two main types. First, there are "distancing" scare quotes that often have a so-called function, as in this example.

> . . . (in some countries) dishonest superintendents sometimes take a new teacher's first paycheck as "payment" for having helped the teacher secure his or her position

MICUSP File EDU.G2.01.1

Here, of course, it is not really a payment, but more of a bribe or kickback.

Given the distancing effect, you can see that scare quotes may be very useful in writing a critique, particularly when you may question an author's opinion.

> The author argues that we are all, in some sense, "screened" from reality.

The second type of scare quote has to do with *stylistic* matters; here the writer wants the reader to recognize that the writer knows that a word or phrase does not necessarily conform to expectations of academic style. Here is an example from another MICUSP paper from Education. Obviously, the use of *"cool"* is not a typical adjective in academic writing.

> Learning about what causes the large and dangerous flashes of lightning they see during thunderstorms will be "cool" and engaging.

MICUSP File EDU.G0.06.3

Several manuals advise students not to use scare quotes, but, in fact, they are used quite often and largely successfully in the MICUSP data. Scare quotes of the first type can show sophistication about disciplinary concepts and, those of the second type, sophistication about academic language. However, there is a great deal of disciplinary variation here. Scare quotes are most common in Sociology, presumably because writers want to show that they can be distanced and careful about "troubled" concepts such as *class* or *culture* (*troubled* is itself a scare quote). They are also frequent in History, Linguistics, and English but rare in fields like Civil Engineering, Mechanical Engineering, and Nursing. The MICUSP data also shows that the use of scare quotes among student writers slowly increases from the final undergraduate year to the third year of graduate school. Finally, our study of the MICUSP data reveals that compared to their native speaker counterparts, non-native speakers are somewhat less likely to employ scare quotes.

You can find several sample texts in this volume that make use of scare quotes; one text with many such uses is the Unit Two text about reality TV (pages 56–58). You will also notice that on occasion they appear in this textbook.

Our advice on the use of scare quotes is that, if you are working in a humanities or social science field, certainly use scare quotes in moderation. However, do not overuse them. In the "hard" sciences (another scare quote), they are infrequent.

TASK TWENTY

Choose one of these tasks. Write a short reaction to a paper in your field or to an oral presentation you have attended. Alternatively, write a paper that reacts to Unit Six. You may want to consider some of the questions offered earlier in this section or focus on something else.

A Few Thoughts on Manuscript Reviews for a Journal

You may at some point be asked to review a manuscript that has been submitted for publication. Journals generally provide you with guidelines for evaluating the manuscript. In your first few reviews, you may want to adhere to the guidelines, but as you gain more experience, you should also have confidence in your ability and develop your own reviewing style. In the guidelines of one journal with which John and Chris are very familiar, reviewers are asked to consider such things as the level of interest others in the field might have, the originality of the manuscript, the author's familiarity with the field, the appropriateness of the methodology and statistical analyses, the appropriateness of the conclusions, and writing style. Regardless of the quality of the article that you are reviewing, as with all other forms of critique, it is important to be fair and to suggest improvements that could actually be made. For instance, if a study is a secondary analysis of data collected for another purpose, it may not be fair to suggest that the authors collect additional data. Your job is not to find as much fault as possible with a manuscript, but to offer feedback that could either improve a manuscript that is potentially publishable or respectfully explains your opinion why it is not. Reviews that are disrespectful can discourage novice scholars and frustrate those who have experience. We suggest that you consider yourself as being in the role of a peer advisor engaged in a written dialogue with the author, albeit a dialogue that may be one-sided if you do not recommend the manuscript for publication. If you happen to be on the receiving end of a manuscript for review, you may want to consult *Navigating Academia,* which is published by the University of Michigan Press (Swales and Feak, 2011).

Unit Seven

Constructing a Research Paper I

Units Seven and Eight consolidate many of the aspects of academic writing that have been stressed in earlier units. However, they also break new ground and differ from the previous units in one important way. At this stage, we think that you may be carrying out research of some kind. The purpose of these units, therefore, is to help prepare you with writing up your own research.

TASK ONE

If you have not done so already, find 5–10 well-written published research papers that are typical of papers in your area of study. It does not matter whether these are seminal papers or where the research was conducted. We simply want you to have a small data set (a corpus) that you can analyze to gain some insights into the important characteristics of published work in your discipline.

Before we delve into the writing of research papers (RPs) and work with your corpus, we need to narrow our focus here somewhat. This narrowing is necessary because we want to draw your attention to types of journal publications other than the traditional empirical research paper, not all of which we have the space to deal with in this book.

Types of Journal Publication

First, it is important to emphasize that not all research articles are empirical. In Astrophysics, for example, experimentation is actually impossible: "One cannot experiment on a star or a galaxy in the way in which one can experiment on a chemical compound or a bean plant" (Tarone et al., 1998, 115). As a result, astrophysicists tend to publish logical argumentation papers that have a general-specific structure (see Unit Two). This form of argument moves typically from known principles to observations, and then to equations designed to account for the observed phenomena. Such papers can be common in Theoretical Physics, in Mathematics, in Theoretical Linguistics, and in fields that rely on computer modeling (e.g., certain areas of Economics, Biostatistics, and Engineering).

Papers that are more theoretically oriented tend to not follow the standard Introduction-Methods-Results-Discussion (IMRD) pattern that is used in many research papers.[1] To compensate for the lack of a fixed IMRD structure, these papers often contain a considerable amount of *metadiscourse* (Unit Four), which "roadmaps" the organization of the paper. Further, because of their theoretical nature, the use of first-person pronouns is more widely accepted. We will not deal with this type of paper in great detail in these last two units; nevertheless, much of what we will discuss still applies.

Another kind of journal publication that we will only briefly mention here is the *review article, state-of-the-art paper*, or *meta-analysis*.[2] Such articles are usually written by senior scholars at the invitation of journal editors. The aim of these invited papers is often to clarify the state of the art in a particular field.

Some review articles, known as *systematic reviews*, follow a very strict method for choosing the research to review in response to a carefully chosen research question. Adhering to the same kind of rigor as would be expected in any other kind of research is thought to prevent bias that could emerge when authors are free to select articles. Moreover, with a transparent methodology in place, others should be able to replicate the work and obtain

---

[1] These four sections of the research paper are capitalized when we are discussing them in broad terms or offering details about writing them.

[2] Although the terms *review* and *meta-analysis* are often used interchangeably, they differ in important ways. While a systematic review summarizes literature, a meta-analysis involves combining the results of many separate studies and synthesizing conclusions to determine the effectiveness of a treatment, procedure, or process. Meta-analyses first require a systematic review to be done. However, not all systematic reviews include a meta-analysis.

the same results. Systematic reviews, unlike review articles, generally follow the IMRD pattern. Increasingly, in many graduate programs, students are expected to write systematic reviews. Even if you are not expected to write a systematic review, keep in mind that state-of-the art papers, whether systematic or not, are invaluable since they provide an in-depth overview of the important literature of a field and a snapshot of where the field is at a particular moment.

According to Noguchi's (2001) study of 25 review articles published in the *Proceedings of the National Academy of Sciences,* such pieces are likely to have a primary focus of one of these four types.

Focus	Aim
History	Presenting a historical view of (part of) the field
Current work	Describing the current state of knowledge
Theory/model	Proposing a theory or model to account for the available data
Issue	Calling attention to an important issue in the field

TASK TWO

Read a review article of relevance to you. Does it include one of the aspects proposed by Noguchi? Or is the approach different? What kind of section headings does it have? How long is it? How many references does it have?

There are a few other types of text published in journals. Book reviews (addressed in Unit Six) are found in many journals. Another type of journal publication consists of comments on or responses to published papers. These are not found in all fields but are fairly common in psychology and medical journals. Such critiques were also covered, at least in part, in Unit Six. Then there are editorials in which an editor or invited author makes a case for his or her perspective on an issue, often concluding that a field needs to reassess priorities and directions. Finally, we have *short communications* (also called *brief reports* or *technical notes*) and standard empirical research papers. The main focus of these last two units will be on the latter, but first we will briefly examine one type of short communication (SC), especially because these, along with book reviews, may be among the first items that junior researchers publish.

In fact, most SCs published today in the hard sciences, Engineering, and Medicine now take the form of short articles. In other words, they follow the IMRD format and include an abstract. Indeed, even medical case reports are increasingly taking this form because most today include a comprehensive literature review. Typically, these mini-articles run three to six printed pages. Given their similarity to longer empirical RPs, much of what we have to say about IMRD articles in Units Seven and Eight will apply to SCs as well. However, there is one type of SC that is rather different; this is illustrated in the next section.

Short Communications (SCs) in Disciplines that Report Fieldwork

This type of research communication is widespread but is mostly found in local, regional, or national journals. SCs of this type are part of the writing tradition in disciplines that are engaged in field research[3] (e.g., Biology, Archaeology, and Geology) and in such areas as Linguistics, Folklore, Local History, Architecture, and Ethnomusicology.

A principal function of many of these SCs is to report on a rare or unusual phenomenon, whether it is a rare rock formation, dialectal usage, or organism of some kind. In effect, SCs are used for reportable discoveries, and they have a history that extends back to the original founding of scientific journals in England and France in the seventeenth century. The example in Task Three is taken from a small regional journal called *Michigan Birds and Natural History*. This journal is refereed and appears four times a year. It contains many SCs. The topic of this SC is a badger, a mid-sized nocturnal mammal.

---

[3] Research based on firsthand observations made outside a controlled experimental setting such as a laboratory.

TASK THREE

Read the passage and discuss the questions on pages 282–283 with a partner. We have numbered independent clauses as sentences for ease of discussion.

Occurrence of a Badger in
Pictured Rocks National Lakeshore, Michigan
Belant, J. L., Wolford, J. E., and
Kainulainen, L. G. (2007).
Michigan Birds and Natural History, 14(2), 41–44.

❶ North American Badgers (Taxidea taxus) occur throughout the western United States and Great Plains of North America, with the geographic range extending east to central Ohio (Messick, 1987; Whitaker and Hamilton, 1998). ❷ In Michigan, badgers have been verified in all counties, including those in the Upper Peninsula (Baker, 1983). ❸ However, badger presence had not been confirmed in the Pictured Rocks National Lakeshore (PRNL), located in Alger County, northcentral Upper Peninsula, Michigan.

❹ On 16 September 2004, a badger was captured adjacent to PNRL (lat 46032'N, long 86019'W), incidentally in a cage trap (Model 108, Tomahawk Live Trap Company, Tomahawk, WI), during a study of American Marten. ❺ The badger was immobilized using an intramuscular injection of Telazol® (Fort Dodge Animal Health, Fort Dodge, IA) with basic physiology monitored as described by Belant (2004). ❻ The badger received a radio transmitter (Advanced Telemetry Systems, Isanti, MN); ❼ standard body metrics were taken.

❽ A tooth was not extracted for aging; ❾ however, measurements including body length 25 inches (64 cm), total length 30 inches (76 cm), skull length 4.7 inches (12.0 cm), skull width 3.5 inches (9.0 cm), and estimated weight 13 pounds (6 kg) suggested that this individual was probably a yearling (Long, 1973; Baker, 1983; Messick, 1987). ❿ Teeth were not damaged and evidence of staining was not observed. ⓫ Nipple size (2< mm length or width) and coloration suggested this badger had not produced young.

⑫ Six radio telemetry locations were obtained through September 2004 (Fig. 2). ⑬ The badger occupied an area within and adjacent to PRNL's Inland Buffer Zone, 1.9-2.5 miles (3-4 km) southeast of Beaver lake. ⑭ Mean daily movements were 1.1 + 0.6 miles (1.7 + 1.0 km) (SD). ⑮ Little comparative data is available; ⑯ however, badgers have reportedly traveled up to 8.8 miles (14 km) in 4 hr (Hoodicoff 2002). ⑰ Female and male badgers have dispersed up to 40 and 73.8 miles (64 and 118 km), respectively (Messick, 1987).

⑱ Although this is the first verified record of a North American Badger at PRNL, badgers have probably occupied areas within PRNL previously. ⑲ Badgers have been reported in Alger County south of PRNL on the adjacent Hiawatha National Forest (K. Doran, Hiawatha National Forest, personal communication). ⑳ Additional surveys to document badger distribution and abundance within PRNL and adjacent areas are warranted.

Literature Cited

Baker, R. H. 1983. *Michigan Mammals.* East Lansing: Michigan State University Press.

Belant, J. L. 2004. Field immobilization of raccoons (Procyon lotor) with Xelazol and Xylazine. *Journal of Wildlife Diseases* 40: 786–789.

Hoodicoff, L. W. 2002. Landscape movements and conservation of badgers (*Taxidea taxus*) in British Columbia, Canada. Society of Conservation Biology 16th Annual Meeting, Canterbury, United Kingdom. (abstract).

Long, C. A. 1973. *Taxidea taxus. Mammalian species 26.* The American Society of Mammalogists, Lawrence, Kansas.

Messick, J. P. 1987. North American Badger. Pages 587-597 in (Novak, M., J. A. Baker, M. E. Obbard, and B. Malloch, eds). *Wild Furbearer Management and Conservation in North America.* Ottawa: Ontario Trappers Association and Ontario Ministry of Natural Resources.

Whitaker, J. O. Jr., and W. J. Hamilton, Jr. 1998. *Mammals of the Eastern United States.* Ithaca: Cornell University Press.

1. What is the purpose of this SC? Who is the audience?

2. What stylistic features indicate that this is a piece of academic writing?

3. One typical feature of many field SCs, including this one, is that the authors discuss their findings cautiously. For example, on only two occasions do the authors make a claim about their discovery. One occurs at the end of Paragraph 1 where the authors write . . . *badger presence had not been confirmed in* . . . . What is the other one?

4. The SC has no subsections, but its five paragraphs have a clear structure. What is the focus of each?

Paragraph 1: _____

Paragraph 2: _____

Paragraph 3: _____

Paragraph 4: _____

Paragraph 5: _____

5. Would you describe the organization as problem-solution, general-specific, or something else?

6. What is your reaction to the title? Does it seem appropriate for the text? Can you think of any way to improve it?

7. Do you think the conclusion is reasonable based on the information provided? Why or why not?

8. How important is it to give the measurements in both U.S. and metric units?

9. Do you think the authors are amateurs with an interest in Biology or trained biologists? Does this matter? How might you find out?

10. Because of the heavy use of the passive, we do not know which of the authors actually trapped the badger. Does this matter? The paper also does not explicitly say that the captured badger was a female. Why? Is there any information that could have been included to help readers understand?

11. If you work or partly work in a discipline that requires field-work, does this SC look familiar or not? If not, what might be differences, and why?

12. If you were interested in knowing whether this piece has ever been cited, how would you go about finding this information?

Longer Research Papers

When you read an RP, you may think that it is a fairly straightforward account of an investigation. Indeed, RPs are often designed to create this impression so that authors can appear more convincing to their readers. However, we believe that such impressions are largely misleading and may lead novice authors to conclude that writing up research should be an uncomplicated process for those with some experience. A more accurate picture is that RP authors typically operate in a highly competitive environment. They need to establish that their research questions are sufficiently interesting for others to read. They need to demonstrate that they are familiar with the relevant literature to demonstrate that the research questions have not already been answered. And they need to compete against other RPs for acceptance and recognition. As a result, RP authors are very much concerned with positioning—with showing that their studies are relevant and make some new contribution to the field.

The overall rhetorical shape of a typical RP is shown in Figure 14. The arrows indicate that the sections are closely connected. In fact, some journal editors have suggested that authors try to create a strong connection between the Introduction and Discussion. In addition, authors should make sure that every method described is related to some results and all results are related to a method.

Some empirical papers will follow a slightly different pattern in which the Results and Discussion sections appear in the same section. This eliminates the difficult task of deciding in which section authors should interpret or give meaning to their results. In other types of papers, several studies may be discussed, which results in some cycling of the Methods-Results-Discussions sections. Despite these and other variations, the basic format remains relevant.

FIGURE 14. Overall Shape of a Research Paper

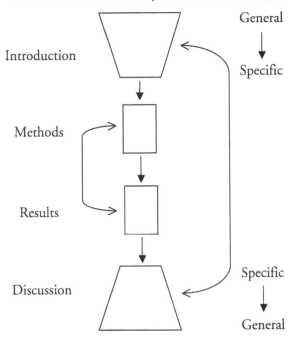

Figure 14 gives a useful indication of the broad-narrow-broad or general-specific-general movement of the typical RP. As the RP in English has developed over the last hundred years or so, the four different sections have become identified with four different purposes.

Introduction (I)	The main purpose of the Introduction is to provide the rationale for the paper, moving from a general discussion of the topic to the particular question, issue, or hypothesis being investigated. A secondary purpose is to attract interest in the topic—and hence readers.
Methods (M)	The Methods section describes, in various degrees of detail, methodology, materials (or subjects), and procedures. This is the narrowest part of the RP.
Results (R)	In the Results section, the findings are described, accompanied by variable amounts of commentary.
Discussion (D)	The Discussion section gives meaning to and interprets the results in a variety of ways. Authors make a series of "points," at least some of which refer to statements made in the Introduction.

We assume that you will be using a typical organizational pattern for your paper—in other words, the IMRD format or some variant of it. Fortunately, many of the units deal with topics that are relevant for this purpose, as shown in this list.

Research Paper Parts	Relevant Topics Covered
Title	Unit Eight: Titles
Abstract	Unit Five: Summary writing
	Unit Eight: Abstracts
Introduction	Unit Two: General-specific
	Unit Three: Problem-solution
	Unit Six: Critiques
Methods	Unit Three: Process descriptions
Results	Unit Four: Location statements
	Unit Four: Highlighting statements
	Unit Four: Qualifications
Discussion	Unit Four: Explanations
	Unit Five: Summaries
Acknowledgments	Unit Eight: Acknowledgments
References	(not dealt with in this book)

As a result of the different purposes given in the box on page 285, the four sections have taken on different linguistic characteristics. We explore some of these linguistic characteristics in this next task.

TASK FOUR

Table 18 shows how the frequencies of selected linguistic features can vary from one section to another. For example, we would normally expect the present tense to appear regularly in the Introduction and Discussion sections, but, depending on the field or type of study, not to be a major tense in the other two sections. Review Table 18 and then do the task.

TABLE 18. Frequencies of Selected Features in RP Sections

	Introduction	Methods	Results	Discussion
Present tense	high	low	low	high
Past tense	mid	high	high	mid
Present perfect	mid	low	low	mid
Passive	low	high	variable	variable
Citations	high	low	variable	high
Hedges	mid	low	mid	high
Evaluative comments	high	low	variable	high

As you can see, there are some similarities between the Introduction and Discussion, on the one hand, and between Methods and Results, on the other. This may suggest a pattern of more "concrete" inner sections and more "conceptual" opening and closing sections.

With a partner, discuss the features of RPs in your field. Would you rate the frequency of the features as high, variable, or low in each of the sections? Use the chart below.

Analyze 3–5 papers in your reference collection (or more, if you have time) to determine whether your perceptions were correct or correspond to Table 18. If possible, add another feature of your own to the final row.

	Introduction			Methods			Results			Discussion		
	High	Low	Variable	High	Low	Variable	High	Low	Variable	High	Low	Variable
Present tense	X					X						
Past tense												
Present perfect												
Passive												
Hedges												
Boosters*												
Citations												
Evaluative comments												
One of your own												

*Boosters consist of language that is chosen to add strength to a claim. They allow authors to indicate a strong conviction to a claim. Examples include *clearly*, *obviously*, and *of course*.

TASK FIVE

Read the eight sentences from a MICUSP research paper from the field of Industrial and Operational Engineering. The paper about a stress ball—a ball made of rubber or a rubber-like substance that is squeezed either to relieve stress or to exercise the muscles in the hand. Can you determine from which of the four sections the sentences come? Mark each one I, M, R, or D. There are two from each section. Work with a partner.

_____ 1. Representative height, weight, comfortable and maximum grip strength values for the participants in terms of means and standard deviations are shown in Table 1.

_____ 2. The test stimuli in this study were the protocols, or instructions for collecting data, that were used in each of the measurement stations.

_____ 3. Anthropometry is a technique for measuring the human body in terms of dimensions, proportions, and ratios.

_____ 4. It should be noted that the recommended dimensions would generate a stress ball that would be best for the study participants, but not necessarily for the larger populations.

_____ 5. If no data is obtained or measurements are inaccurate, products may be designed in such a way that they are either unsafe or unpractical, which most likely would lead to a decrease in sales.

_____ 6. Men participants also had a comfortable grip strength 1.25 kg larger than the women and had a maximum grip strength 8.25 kg larger than the women.

_____ 7. The results of this study might be challenged on the basis that the population tested was small and not random (all participants enrolled in the same course).

_____ 8. Next, the participants visited the grip strength station, which was equipped with a Takei grip dynamometer, to measure their comfortable and maximum grip strength.

Methods Sections

You might have expected us to begin our discussion of RP sections with the Introduction. Instead, we are beginning with the Methods section because this is the section that authors tend to write first. They do this because, in terms of content, it is rather clear what to include. Even so, graduate students often express considerable anxiety about their research methods, especially if qualitative studies are involved. Barton (2002) notes that another source of graduate student anxiety is that the published accounts of Methods sections look perfect, typically because authors avoid discussing what did not work. Finally, reviewers, supervisors, editors, and examiners pay particular attention to Methods sections. A good methodology leads to the expectation that the results will also be good. These two quotations, the first from medical research and the second from Education, demonstrate the importance of the Methods section.

> If an abstract is of interest, the editor next looks at the methods section of the manuscript before deciding whether to reject the paper or pass it on to the screening editor on duty for that day. The screening editor decides whether the manuscript should be sent for external review.
>
> —E. Langdon-Neuner, 2008, 84

> As a reviewer I may find an opening theoretical gambit to be compelling, but if I can't reconstruct the author's means of collecting, reducing and analyzing data, then I will have little faith that the construction of results follows responsible and consistent treatment of evidence and will not likely recommend the paper for publication.
>
> —P. Smagorinsky, 2008, 48

As we will see, there are disciplinary differences in Methods sections; even the heading *Methods* is not always used, as when authors use *The Study* as their section heading or *Materials and Methods*. In some fields, it is common to have subsections in Methods that might deal with materials, the apparatus used, definitions employed, the subjects or participants in the study, or the statistical procedures used. Methods also vary according to how much information and explanation they contain. At one extreme, they may be very condensed; at the other, elaborately extended. Disciplines vary in what needs to be included (Equipment? Statistics? Manufacturers? Sources? Permissions?

Sponsorship? Inclusion criteria?). In some journals, Methods sections are printed in smaller fonts and perhaps placed at the end; in others, they are given the same typographical treatment as the other sections. Finally, as we have seen, in some fields Methods sections are closely examined; in others, especially when standard procedures were used, they may receive less attention. This is especially true when the methods are well known and when a simple reference may be sufficient, as in these examples.

> To identify duplicate gene pairs, we followed the method of Gu et al. (2002a).

> We used the method of surface grating decay [10] to measure surface diffusion on a model organic glass.

> Reverse transcription reactions were performed according to the manufacturer's protocol.

TASK SIX

Work with a partner and decide which of the statements apply to the writing of a Methods section. Write A if you agree or a D if you disagree. If you are unsure, indicate this with a question mark (?).

_____ 1. My Methods section should provide information that helps readers understand how and why my experiments or research was done.

_____ 2. I should include information that would allow other researchers to reproduce my study and obtain largely similar results.

_____ 3. I should describe methods that are standard in my field.

_____ 4. My Methods section should make it easy for readers to understand and interpret my results.

_____ 5. I should write my Methods section in a manner that allows readers to conclude that my results are valid.

_____ 6. My Methods section should constitute a substantial portion of my paper.

_____ 7. I should provide justifications for my choice of methods.

_____ 8. I should discuss the limitations of my method in the Methods section.

_____ 9. In my field, Methods sections typically include references to other studies.

_____ 10. I should mainly use past tense in my Methods section.

If you and your partner are from different disciplines, you may have disagreed on some of the points in Task Six.

Although Methods sections have been somewhat under-researched compared to other parts of RPs, especially Introductions, some interesting disciplinary differences have been highlighted in recent research. For instance, Peacock (2011) examined 288 RP Methods sections in published, data-driven papers from the fields of Biology, Chemistry, Physics, Environmental Science, Business, Language and Linguistics, Law, and Public and Social Administration (36 papers from each field). He proposed the existence of seven "moves" in Methods sections. Simply put, a *move* is a stretch of text with a specific communicative function. Moves are a matter of rhetoric. This concept is addressed in more detail in Unit Eight.

<u>Move</u>

Overview	a short summary of the research method, at or near the beginning of the Methods section
Research aims, questions, or hypotheses	a description of the research goals, the questions to be answered, or the hypotheses
Subjects and/or materials	in Business, Language and Linguistics, Law, and Public and Social Administration, a description of the people (groups of people) in the study; and in the sciences, a description of the materials, equipment, and so on
Location	a description of where the research took place and possibly why
Procedure	a discussion of the process used to obtain the data that was collected
Limitations	a focus on a shortcoming of the method, possibly accompanied by an explanation
Data Analysis	a description of how the data was analyzed

Adapted from Peacock, 2011.

It is important to keep in mind that the moves do not necessarily appear in the order given. In fact, some cycling of moves, particularly materials and procedure, is common in the science fields investigated. In the remaining fields, the move cycle structure may be much more complex and variable. We can see the frequency of the moves in Table 19.

TABLE 19. Frequency of Appearance of Individual Moves: Interdisciplinary Differences (% in which the moves appear)

Moves	Biology	Chemistry	Physics	Environ- mental Science	Business	Language and Linguistics	Law	Public and Social Administration
Subjects or materials	97	100	75	31	92	94	86	86
Location	36	8	0	67	47	58	58	75
Procedure	100	100	100	100	100	100	100	100
Data analysis	86	100	67	78	72	67	56	50
Limitations	6	0	0	69	44	19	28	6
Research aims or questions/ hypotheses	3	0	6	11	36	22	58	67
Overview	3	0	0	50	25	19	42	54

Based on Peacock, 2011.

TASK SEVEN

Discuss these questions about Table 19 with a partner.

1. How might you explain the different percentages for location?

2. Why do you think methods in the sciences do not generally include overviews?

3. Which field, would you say, is most similar to Business in terms of Methods sections?

4. In four fields, limitations were given in less than 10% of the methods. Is this because there were no limitations? Or is there another possible reason?

5. What surprises you most about the table?

Now that we have discussed several aspects of Methods sections, it is time to read and critique one.

TASK EIGHT

Here is the Methods section from a paper investigating hypothetical consumer behavior in buying stolen, pirated, or counterfeit goods from the black market. Read it and then answer the questions on pages 294–295.

Consumer Decisions in the Black Market for Stolen or Counterfeit Goods
Casola, L., Kemp, S., and Mackenzie, A. (2009).
Journal of Economic Psychology, 30, 162–171.

Method

❶ A total of 80 (36 male) participants were recruited at the University of Canterbury (51 participants) and from the general population (29 participants). ❷ Participants from the general public were recruited in four different malls of the local city, representing four different socio-economic levels as indicated by land values. ❸ The overall age range was between 15 and 68 years of age, with a mean of 27 (*SD* = 13). ❹ All participants completed the same questionnaire. ❺ The final sample contained 53 current students and 27 non-students. ❻ All participants were given two $1 "scratch-and-win" lottery tickets in recognition of their help.

❼ The bulk of the questionnaire consisted of nine black market scenarios. ❽ Participants were asked to rate each scenario in terms of how unacceptable they perceived it was for the agent in the scenario to make a purchase from the black market. ❾ Participants circled a value between 1 and 7 on a rating scale where a score of 1 corresponded to "completely acceptable," a score of 4 was "reasonably acceptable," and a score of 7 was "not at all acceptable."

❿ The nine scenarios varied (3 × 3) the need of the agent and the original source of the goods offered in the market. ⓫ The need of the agent could be survival; a need to save money; or not otherwise being able to afford the good. ⓬ The original sources of the goods (victims) were an individual; an organisation or society. ⑬ Two examples of scenarios were:

⑭ "In the days following the Tsunami in Indonesia, isolated places have a food scarcity. ⑮ Ragu has no food to feed his family. ⑯ He has been approached by black market dealers who have offered him food in exchange for money. ⑰ Considering the food has been procured from the burglary of a private home, how acceptable do you think it is for Ragu to buy such food?" (survival need, individual victim).

⑱ "Michael is a student with a passion for music who has been approached and offered state of the art electronic stereo equipment at half the price it sells for in the local stores. ⑲ Assuming that Michael could not otherwise afford such equipment, and that he is aware that the goods have been stolen from a large international electronic manufacturer, how acceptable do you think it is for Michael to buy such equipment?" (cannot afford need, organisation victim).

⑳ Half the questionnaires included scenarios in which all the consumers were depicted as male while in the other half they were always female. ㉑ The only difference between these two question-naires was the implied gender of the names and the pronouns used. ㉒ The order of presentation of the scenarios was varied across participants. ㉓ Finally, a demographic section asked participants their age, gender, occupation and income.

1. Which of the moves described in Table 19 can you find in the method description?

2. Do you think the level of detail is sufficient or insufficient? In other words, is there enough information to allow the study to be adapted or replicated by others? If not, what would you need to know?

3. Do you think the sample scenarios are needed? Should the authors have described how the final sample was derived?

4. How is the information organized? What subheadings could you add to help readers? Where would you place them?

5. What verb tense dominates? Why did the authors choose this tense? Could another tense have been chosen?

6. How do the authors maintain a good flow of ideas in the first paragraph? Do they follow this same strategy in the final paragraph?

7. Does active or passive voice dominate? Why is this the case?

8. What verb tense (past or present) and voice (active or passive) dominates in the Methods sections of the papers that you analyzed? Why?

9. You have been asked to lead a discussion focusing on the method used in this paper. What points would you make?

10. Analyze 3–5 papers from your reference collection in terms of the move structure in the Methods sections. Are the moves the same as those proposed by Peacock or are there others?

Variation in Methods Sections

We have already mentioned that Methods sections can be quite variable in terms of moves and level of detail. Whether the methods are described in considerable detail depends on the type of study being done. Junior scholars are sometimes tempted to over-explain their methods, including information that had little or no bearing on the results. A good rule of thumb is to include steps or procedures that if omitted would cause the experiment or study to fail (Annesley, 2010). The extent to which you describe those steps or procedures depends very much on whether the detail is needed for readers to understand what you did and to perhaps replicate your work. Standard methods may require only a reference plus any modification to the method.

Another consideration has to do with author positioning. How widely acceptable are your methods? To what extent do you need to clarify, explain, and perhaps justify what you did? How much do you need to do to convince your readers that your procedures are appropriate and reasonable? Because of these factors, some Methods sections may be more *condensed*, while others may be more *extended*. According to Peacock's research (Table 19) all Methods sections contain some accounting for procedures. However, how this is done will vary, largely according to discipline. At one extreme, descriptive Methods sections may look like this extract from a MICUSP research paper.

> DNA was extracted from tissue and feather samples using the Qiagen DNeasy Extraction kit. An addition of dithiothreitol was used for samples from feathers. Polymerase chain reaction (PCR) was carried out using two primers pairs for cytochrome B (CytB; Sorenson et al., 1999). PCR and sequencing was done following protocols in Mindell et al. (1997).
> MICUSP File BIO.G2.04.1

As you can see, the extract contains nothing but descriptive statements, consistently using the past passive. There is no chronology here, no use of personal pronouns, and no explanations or justifications for the procedure. Also, notice that the fourth sentence concludes with *was done following protocols in Mindell et al.* Naming procedures by citation (rather than describing them) only seems possible in fields with well-established and standardized procedures, as in some of the hard sciences. We can consider this type of description as abbreviated or condensed.

Now compare the Biology extract with this one from Botany. (We have added bold, italics, and underlining to bring out its features.)

> **To detect groups among the specimens and extract the variables that best diagnose the groups,** we *used* principal components analysis (PCA). <u>Before conducting the analysis</u>, we *standardized* all measurements so that each variable would have a mean of 0 and a standard deviation of 1. <u>For the PCA</u>, we *included* only continuous characters. **To avoid weighting characters,** we *excluded* characters that are probably genetically redundant, as revealed by high values for the Pearson correlation coefficient between all possible pairs of characters.
> Naczi, Reznicek, and Ford, 1998, 435.

We can see here something very different. First, the three authors have adopted the *we* form to describe their procedures. Second, they have added a temporal phrase (underlined) at the beginning of the second sentence and a clarifying phrase at the opening of the third. Third and most importantly, the first and fourth sentences begin with *to* + verb purposive clauses (bolded) that explain and justify the chosen procedures. Such initial clauses have typically an additional rationale; they work to prevent questions and objections arising in the readers' minds. Given the amount of information, we can consider this type of description as *extended.*

On occasion, we may also find cognitive verbs (e.g., *believe*) and/or volitional verbs (e.g., *wanted to*) used in a Methods section to explain or justify more of the thinking behind the procedures, as in this somewhat extreme example (italics added):

> The corpus for this study was constructed *with a number of aims in mind.* Given the preliminary nature of the topic, *we wanted to* cover a fairly wide range of fields (or disciplines) in order to gauge the extent of the phenomenon. *We also* felt *it prudent* to include among the fields those which we guessed would have some use of imperatives, such as statistics . . . geology . . . . *We eventually settled on* the following: . . . .
> Swales et al., 1998.

In effect, *condensed* methods state what the researchers did with little elaboration or justification. *Extended* methods present readers with a rationale of why and how researchers did what they did. You can elaborate your Methods by

- providing useful background knowledge (e.g., through definitions and examples).
- using descriptions of procedural steps, rather than citations and/or acronyms.
- including a number of justifications (e.g., *To determine this value, we . . .*).
- using cognitive or volitional verbs (e.g., *We believed; We wanted to*).
- including *by + –ing* + verb + *how* statements (*This was done by reversing the order*).
- employing a wide range of linking words and phrases (e.g., time expressions, such as *next* or *prior to*).

If your methods are fairly standard you may

- assume readers have relevant background knowledge.
- sometimes use citations or acronyms to refer to processes (e.g., *A corpus was designed following Römer (2010)*).
- have few justifications.
- use few or no cognitive or volitional verbs.
- choose to avoid *by + –ing* + verb + *how* statements.
- employ few linking phrases.

TASK NINE

Looking again at the Methods description in Task Eight, would you say it is condensed, extended, or somewhere in between? Now look at these two extracts from Methods sections. Would you say they were condensed, extended, or somewhere in between? How did you decide?

A. Methods for Analysis and Functional Properties

The standard AOAC methods (AOAC, 1975) were used for the determination of total solids, nitrogen, crude fat, ash, and Vitamin C. Total sugars were determined by the method of Potter et al. (1968), and the total carbohydrates (in terms of glucose) were assayed according to the procedure of Dubois et al. (1956). The method of Kohler and Patten (1967) was followed for determining amino acid composition.

Quoted by Knorr-Cetina, 1981, 157.

B. *Methodology*

The ASTM C127 and C128 procedures were followed to determine the density, specific gravity, and absorption capacity of the fine and course aggregate. To determine the gradation of the candidate Michigan aggregate, dried fine and coarse samples were analyzed using the ASTM C136 method. To determine the unit weight of the candidate Michigan coarse aggregate sample, the ASTM C29 procedure was followed.

MICUSP. CEE. GO.02.1

Read the next Methods section from a paper proposing an approach to identifying genuine and counterfeit currency. Discuss with a partner where it lies on the continuum from condensed to extended.

Counterfeit Money Detection by Intrinsic Fluorescence Lifetime

Levene, M. J., and Chia, T. (2010).
*Lasers and Electro-Optics (CLEO) and
Quantum Electronics and Laser Science Conference (QELS),
2010 Conference on Laser Electro-Optics: Applications*, 1–2, 16–21.

2. Methods

Microscope Apparatus

❶ We used a custom-built two-photon microscope based on an Olympus BX51 WI upright fluorescence microscope (Olympus America, Center Valley, PA). ❷ The excitation wavelength was set to 735 nm with a 100 fs pulsewidth. ❸ The microscope objective was a 4x, 0.28 NA air objective (Olympus, XLFLUOR 4x/340, Olympus). ❹ Samples were held flat on a motorized 3-axis microscope stage (ASI Imaging, Eugene, OR). ❺ Fluorescence lifetime capabilities were made possible through the addition of a multi-channel plate PMT (R3809U-52, Hamamatsu) and a time-correlated single photon counting (TCSPC) card (SPC-150, Becker & Hickl, Berlin, Germany). ❻ The fluorescence was filtered through a 555 nm short-pass filter (Chroma Technologies, Rockingham, VT). ❼ A fluorescence lifetime decay curve was produced by raster scanning the laser beam over a 4 mm^2 area (or frame) and summing the emission photons for 60 seconds (~0.8 seconds/frame). ❽ Fluorescence lifetime decays, F(t), for genuine Federal Reserve Notes were fit to the two-component lifetime model (Eq. (1)),

$$F(t) = a_1 e^{t/\tau 1} + a_2 e^{t/\tau 2} \tag{1}$$

by obtaining the best X^2 fit value. ❾ Counterfeit samples were fit to either a one-component or two-component model depending on its X^2 fit value.

Samples

⑩ The U.S. one hundred-dollar bill was chosen as the primary focus of this study because it represents the largest value on the counterfeit market. ⑪ Therefore, one control group included genuine $100 Federal Reserve Notes from the printing series 1996 and later (n = 10). ⑫ Additional control groups included $50 Federal Reserve Notes (n = 5, Series 1996–2004), $20 Federal Reserve Notes (n = 5, Series 1996–2006), and $1 Federal Reserve Notes (n = 54, Series 1999–2006) in order to test for fluorescence lifetime variations between banknote denominations. ⑬ All control samples were genuine Federal Reserve Notes, in circulation, non-sequential, and untreated prior to lifetime measurements.

⑭ Three types of known counterfeits were tested in these experiments: 1. Copies made by digitally scanning a bill into a computer followed by printing on both sides using a consumer-grade color inkjet or laser printer (herein referred to as "digital"). 2. Traditional counterfeits made with a cotton and linen blend and printed using more sophisticated methods. ⑮ These bills are often produced by foreign organized crime groups (herein referred to as "traditional"). 3. Bleached (or "washed") bills made by removing the ink from a lower denomination bill and then reprinting a larger denomination over the ink-less paper (herein referred to as "bleached"). ⑯ Three counterfeits bills of each type were tested. ⑰ Fluorescence lifetime measurements were also obtained from several control materials. ⑱ These include printer paper made from wood pulp, 100% cotton stationary paper, and swatches of 100% linen cloth.

Although research is still ongoing, we are beginning to get an idea of how fields might differ in terms of the condensed-to-extended continuum, as shown in Table 20. Do you agree?

TABLE 20. Disciplinary Variation in Methods Section

Condensed	Intermediate	Extended
Chemistry	Public Health	Psychology
Materials Science	Political Science	Sociology
Mycology	Systematic Botany	Education
Molecular Biology	Medical Research	Applied Linguistics

However, it should be noted that the Methods section will probably need to be more extensive if any of these conditions apply.

- The paper is aimed at a multidisciplinary audience.

- The methods chosen are new or controversial.

- The paper is essentially a "methods paper."

Language Focus: Linking Phrases in Methods Sections

It is common in academic writing for purpose statements to occur at the beginnings of sentences, as shown in these examples.

> *To detect groups among the specimens . . .*, we used . . . .
> *To avoid weighting characters*, we excluded . . . .

Another way to avoid monotony is to use linking phrases related to time.

> *Before conducting the analysis*, we . . . .
> *After incubating for 48 hours*, the cells were harvested and analyzed.

You may also consider adding a linking phrase to justify a step in the methodology.

> *Based on previous reports of HR mutations in APL*, we performed direct DNA sequencing analysis.
> *Because of its hygroscopic properties*, the dye was stored and handled in ethanol solution.

It is also possible to include cognitive and volitional verbs in order to reveal the thinking behind the procedural decisions:

> The first approach *was considered*, and consequently dismissed. It *was thought* that this method would increase the likelihood of ambiguity and error (for example, there may be more than one political party with the title of The Labour Party).

Here we provide a few more linking phrases that operate to tie sections together and to add some stylistic variety. We have divided them into three groups. How many of these can you turn into complete sentences?

A. Initial Purposive Clauses or Phrases

1. *In an effort to evaluate*
2. *In order to establish*
3. *To further test this hypothesis,*
4. *To determine the cost,*
5. *In the interest of obtaining useful data,*

B. Phrases making temporal links

1. *During the data collection,*
2. *Prior to collecting this information,*
3. *On arrival on campus, the participants*
4. *In the follow-up phase of the study, we*
5. *After the interview, subjects were*

C. Causal or connective phrases

1. *Based on the feedback from the pilot study,*
2. *On the basis of the literature review,*
3. *Because of privacy issues, we*
4. *In spite of these issues, we*
5. *In light of these unexpected findings,*

Frequency of Purpose Clause Types and Verbs

In the Hyland corpus of research articles (80,000 words from 80 research articles in Biology, Physics, Electrical Engineering, Mechanical Engineering, Marketing, Applied Linguistics, Sociology, and Philosophy), the two most common verbs to occur in initial purpose clauses are *determine* and *test*; these are followed by a closely clustered group of six: *avoid, establish, illustrate, obtain, reduce,* and *understand.* Overall, sentence-initial *to* + verb is about three times more common than *in order to* + verb.

Placement of Purpose Clauses

First, if the purpose clause is essentially metadiscoursal, it needs to be placed first.

> To clarify matters, there appear to be five different approaches
> . . . .
>
> To phrase it somewhat differently, one can define . . . .

Otherwise, the decision partly depends on the length of the main clause. So, we might have a choice between these two sentences.

> Contrastive analysis of written discourse in itself will not be sufficient to answer these questions.
>
> To answer these questions, contrastive analysis of written discourse in itself will not be sufficient.

However, in the next case, only initial position seems possible.

> To answer this question, we may draw upon a data set of 4,689 rural "events," episodes in which some collectivity openly seized or damaged the resources of another party or defended themselves against another party's claims upon them that took place between June 1, 1788, and June 30, 1793.

Rationale behind Purpose Clause Use

We suspect that initial purpose clauses are on the increase. After all, if you give your reasons for a decision before stating the decision itself, your reader may be less likely to question that decision, as in "Why did they do that?"

Writing Up a Methods Section

Task Nineteen in Unit Three (page 136) included an interview with a student planning her first research paper for her master's in social work. Mei-Lan's research was on Chinese elderly living in the United States. She had chosen this topic because of some "prevailing myths" that the Chinese communities would always look after their elderly and that such elderly would not accept help from outsiders. She further noted that all the research to date had been conducted in the large Chinese communities in big cities on the east and west coasts and that therefore it would be useful to study smaller communities in the midwest. She was then asked her about her methodology. Re-read the interview transcript.

Later, Mei-Lan and her advisor decided to attend a regional panel discussion on research into elderly minorities in the midwest. For this, they were required to circulate a 500-word summary of their research beforehand. Mei-Lan was given the task of writing up the Methods section. This is her draft.

Semi-structured interviews were employed to investigate current relationships between elderly Chinese and their immediate families. The study-site consisted of three small communities in the American midwest because the available research on this topic has been restricted to the larger communities on the east and west coasts (Yang & Yang, 2007; Olsen & Chang, 2009). Ten elderly Chinese were interviewed. These interviews were conducted on a one-on-one basis (i.e., without the presence of family members who might have impeded the interviewees from expressing their true feelings). Interviews usually lasted about an hour and were conducted in the interviewees' preferred language. Although questions had been prepared in advance by the interviewer, they were not always followed in strict order or in their entirety. On occasion, the conversations moved into new and unexpected territory and so produced new information. Prior IRB permission was obtained for the procedures.

TASK TEN

Choose one task to complete.

1. Mei-Lan's advisor says, "This is good, but I am afraid your draft is too long; it's nearly 150 words. 100 words would be much better. Can you shorten it, focusing more on what you did?" Edit Mei-Lan's draft for her.

2. Write (or re-write) your Methods section for some of your own research.

3. Alternatively, write up your method for how you created your reference collection of articles.

Results Sections

The other section we deal with in this unit is the Results section. As we will see, this section has much in common with the material that was covered in the unit on data commentary (Unit Four). Many of the concepts discussed there are directly relevant, such as

- using location statements
- rounding numbers and making generalized comparisons
- judging the right strength of claim
- highlighting key findings from the data

Before revisiting some of these concepts, we first need to explore the difference between *data* and *results*.

Data versus Results

To begin, although we often use the terms *data* and *results* interchangeably, they are, in fact different (Annesley, 2010). This distinction is important because novice writers may include data in the Results section but fail to provide results, which may lead to a negative evaluation of a study. Data consists of facts and numbers, and these are generally presented in tables and figures. Results, on the other hand, are "statements in the main text that summarize or explain what the data show" (Annesley, 2010, 1067). Data can be manipulated to obtain a result. A result is a message that can, for instance, give readers a sense of whether one value is higher or lower than another or some data differs from other data in some significant way. A result is supported by data (Wright et al., 1999). Here are two examples of results statements that are derived from data.

> After 80 visits, bees visited iridescent disks *more frequently than* after their immediate introduction to the arena [first 10 visits = 4.7 ± 0.5 (mean ± SE); last 10 visits = 8.1 ± 0.4; Student's t-test, t(9) = 4.96, P < 0.001] (Fig. 4B).

> The surface morphology at 65°C (Fig. 5(h)–(j)) *was smoother than* that at 35°C and 55°C (Fig. 5(e)–(g)).

Results versus Discussion

Another important consideration is the difference between results and discussion. As you may know, many guidelines for writing the Results section specify that this section should present only results and include no interpretation or discussion. If, however, you have ever tried to strictly adhere to this, you know it is hard to avoid commenting on the results as you present them. This, of course, is not a problem if you are writing for a journal that combines Results and Discussion sections. However, when Results and Discussion are separate sections, a major challenge is determining what to include in each, what level of generality is appropriate for each, and what type of commentary works best in each. To help with this, we turn to Task Eleven.

TASK ELEVEN

Here are parts of the Results (Section 3.1) and Discussion sections (Section 4) of an article reporting on how divided attention affects a pedestrian's ability to safely cross a busy street. The study was conducted in a simulator where students walked on a treadmill. While crossing a virtual street, students were distracted by a cell phone conversation or by listening to music on an MP3 player. What significant ways do the texts in the two sections differ? In what ways are they similar? Create a list highlighting your findings.

Pedestrians, Vehicles, and Cell Phones
Neider, M. B., McCarley, J. S., Crowell, J. A.,
Kaczmarski, H., and Kramer, A. F. (2010).
Accident Analysis & Prevention, 42, 589–594.

3.1. Crossing success rate

Is the likelihood of safely crossing a street influenced by the number or types of tasks a pedestrian is concurrently engaged in? To answer this question we analyzed the percentage of trials in which observers successfully crossed the road (Table 2). If listening to music or conversing on a cell phone impaired performance, then we would expect success rates in those conditions to be lower than in the no distraction condition. An ANOVA performed with distraction as a within-subjects factor partially confirmed this prediction, $F(2,70)=3.96$, $p<0.05$, $\eta_p^2 = 0.1$. Participants crossed successfully approximately 84% of the time when undistracted and nearly 85% of the time when listening to music, compared to 80% of the time when talking on a cell phone; listening to music induced no performance cost relative to the no distraction condition ($p = 0.53$). Conversing on a cell phone produced significantly lower success rates than listening to music ($p < 0.01$). Participants trended towards poorer performance when conversing on a cell phone compared to the no distraction condition, but the post hoc comparison did not reach significance ($p = 0.09$).

Table 2. Mean Overall Trial Duration(s), Crossing Success Rates, Collision Rates, and Rate of Errors from Time Outs

	Trial Duration	Success Rate	Collision Rate	Time Out Rate
No distraction	11.73 (0.62)	83.85 (1.81)	14.49 (1.73)	1.65 (0.47)
Cell phone	13.27 (0.52)	80.20 (2.32)	15.45 (2.03)	4.34 (1.01)
iPod	11.47 (0.57)	84.98 (1.83)	13.67 (1.60)	1.65 (0.56)

Note. Values in parentheses indicate one standard error of the mean.

[The remainder of the Results section has been omitted.]

4. Discussion

Field studies (e.g., [Hatfield and Murphy, 2007] and [Nasar et al., 2008]) have observed that pedestrians make more unsafe street crossings when conversing on a cell phone than when undistracted. Our findings provide partial experimental confirmation of these observations. Participants were less likely to successfully cross the street in our task when they were conversing on a cell phone than when they were listening to music on an iPod. Furthermore, engaging in a cell phone conversation while crossing the street led to higher time out rates in our virtual street-crossing task than did listening to music or performing the task undistracted. Additionally, participants took more time to initiate a crossing when conversing on a cell phone, and walked more slowly during crossing. The last result is consistent with data from field studies of pedestrian street crossing that have observed slower walking during cell phone conversations (e.g., [Hatfield and Murphy, 2007] and [Nasar et al., 2008]).

The fact that our successful crossing rates were somewhat low (one would certainly hope that in the real-world pedestrians successfully cross the street more than 84% of the time) might suggest that our task was artificially difficult, and hence not representative of the real world. As noted, though, most of the failures to cross successfully were the result of the trial timing out, not the result of collision. The low rate of successful crossing, therefore, does not suggest that the simulated environment or task was unduly hazardous. Pilot data collected in preparation for the current study (identical task but with vehicles traveling at a constant speed and distance from each other), moreover, found similar effects of distraction, even when the crossing task was substantially easier. In the pilot testing, parameters for car movement and density allowed participants to successfully cross the road 99% of the time in the no distraction and music listening conditions, success rates far higher than observed in the present study. Nonetheless, successful crossing rates declined in the cell phone condition, falling to 97% (differences not significant), resulting in a pattern of data that was somewhat similar to that which we report in the current study.

[The remainder of the Discussion section has been omitted.]

As Task Eleven indicates, Discussion sections differ from Results sections in that the Discussion section explains why the results are meaningful in relation to previous, related work and the research question that was explored. More on this can be found in Unit Eight.

When reading the street crossing text, you might have noticed two important characteristics of the Results sections: the use of location statements and comparative language.

Language Focus: Another Look at Location Statements

This Language Focus section further investigates references to non-verbal material (tables, graphs, figures, photographs, etc.). There are four patterns here.

Pattern A	The high rates are shown in Table 3.
Pattern B	Table 3 shows the high rates.
Pattern C	The rates were high (see Table 3) or (Table 3) or (shown in Table 3).
Pattern D	The rates were high, as shown in Table 3. As shown in Table 3, the rates were high.
Pattern E (other, not A–D)	The results, given in Table 3, show the high rates. Figure 3 is a photograph of the bridge.

We reviewed 20 recent articles from a journal in our own field, *English for Specific Purposes: An International Journal,* to find out which patterns were more common. Two of the articles made no reference to non-verbal material; in the remaining 18, 76 references were found (averaging 3.8 per paper), ranging from a minimum of one to a maximum of 11. The results are shown in Table 21.

TABLE 21. Location Statements in *English for Specific Purposes*

Pattern A (. . . *are shown in Table 3*)	22
Pattern B (*Table 3 shows* . . .)	29
Pattern C (*see table 3*)	9
Pattern D (*As shown in Table 3,*)	13
Pattern E (*other*)	3
Total	76

Of the four main patterns, Pattern B was the most common and Pattern C the least common.

We next turned to a very different field to compare our results and chose a journal called *Computer-aided Civil and Infrastructure Engineering.* As might be expected, location statements were more frequent in these articles because they contained much more visual material. We examined recent articles until we collected a total of 100 location statements (this amounted to six articles). The results are shown in Table 22.

TABLE 22. Location Statements in *Computer-aided Civil & Infrastructure Engineering*

Pattern A	22
Pattern B	33
Pattern C	22
Pattern D	15
Pattern E	8
Total	100

As can be seen, Pattern B was again the most frequent. At this juncture, it should be noted that in Pattern B the reference to the non-verbal material is more grammatically prominent because it is placed as the subject of the clause, while in the other three cases the prominence is reduced because they occur in a prepositional phrase (A), in parentheses (C), or in a subordinate clause (D). One possible hypothesis is that in an essentially language-oriented discipline like Discourse Analysis, location statements will be downplayed, producing larger proportions of patterns like C and D. On the other hand, in Engineering, with its stress on figures and calculations, there may well be an understandable preference for Patterns A and B.

In undertaking this small research project, we also discovered some other useful tendencies. First, although individual authors—or groups of authors—obviously had their preferences, all varied their location statements; in fact, all the Engineering author groups used at least four of the five patterns. Second, there was a tendency to use "stronger" statements (A and B) in the earlier parts of their papers and "weaker" ones (C and D) later. Third, there was some preference for placing Pattern D (e.g., *as shown in Table 3*) at the end of the sentence rather than the beginning.

TASK TWELVE

Take your small collection of research articles from your own field, and scan them for location statements, coding them as done in Tables 21 and 22. Make a table and write up your results; include comparisons with Tables 21 and 22 as appropriate. Finally, consider whether or not your results support our preliminary hypothesis.

Some very different results are shown in Table 23. They come from a simple search in MICUSP. The search totaled all occurrences of the word *data* in each of the 16 disciplines covered. Overall, the word *data* occurred 1,901 times in 324 papers (out of total of 830). The results for each discipline have been normalized for 10,000 words so that comparisons can be made.

TABLE 23. Search Results for the Word *Data* in MICUSP

Discipline	Frequency per 10,000 Words
Biology	14.4
Civil/Environmental Engineering (CEE)	8.6
Economics	16.2
Education	7.0
English	0.0
History	0.1
Industrial/Operations Engineering (IOE)	21.8
Linguistics	9.0
Mechanical Engineering	8.2
Natural Resources & the Environment (NRE)	4.4
Nursing	12.6
Philosophy	0.5
Physics	6.3
Political Science	3.8
Psychology	3.3
Sociology	5.1

TASK THIRTEEN

Now read these three versions of a partial write-up of the results for this search. What are the strengths and weaknesses of each? What do you like and not like? Discuss with a partner.

A. Table 23 shows the search results for the noun *data*. It occurred 1,901 times in 324 out of the 830 papers collected in the Michigan Corpus of Upper-level Student Papers (MICUSP). In other words, it was found in fewer than half of the papers. In some fields, it occurred hardly at all, these disciplines being English, History, and Philosophy. On the other hand, it occurred 21.8, 16.2 and 14.4

times per 10k in IOE, Economics, and Biology, respectively. All the other disciplines fell between these two extremes.

B. We next turn to a more technical word *data*, as shown in Table 23. Here we find the expected skewed distribution, with almost no occurrences in the humanities and the highest counts in IOE and Economics. Interestingly, the figures for CEE are much lower, being below those for Biology, Economics, and Nursing. We have no explanation for this finding at the present time. Also, the frequency for Linguistics suggests it is not a humanities discipline, although it is often classified as such.

C. The results for *data* are shown in Table 23. The results broadly reflect how "technical" a discipline tends to be. Frequencies are, on average, highest in Engineering and Science, lowest in the humanities, with the social sciences falling in the middle. Exceptions to this overall finding are the relatively low frequency for Physics (6.3 per 10,000 words) and the high numbers for Economics (16.2 per 10,000). In the former case, it should be borne in mind that much of Physics is highly theoretical; in the latter, that Economics has become much more mathematical in recent decades.

As it turned out, the MICUSP results for *data* are much what we might have expected. Others are not so easy to predict.

Write up your own results for Table 23, selecting, if you like, parts from A, B, and C.

TASK FOURTEEN

What might you expect to be the results for the following searches in MICUSP?

1. *Language*—It is no surprise that Linguistics would have the highest frequency among the 16 disciplines. But which disciplines might be second and third?

2. *If*—This is a common function word; as such it might be expected to have a fairly even distribution. However, the average use of *if* in one of the sixteen disciplines is much higher than that of the other disciplines. Which one is it?

3. *Time*—At least at first sight, your results here may be perplexing. Which three disciplines might you expect to be the top three?

4. *Work*—What do you think are the three disciplines that use *work* the most?

5. *Life*—Neither Biology nor Nursing has the highest frequency for *life*. Which field do you think might use this noun the most?

6. *Should*—This modal auxiliary is used to express obligation or requirement. In your opinion, what field might use this word most frequently?

Language Focus: Special Verb Agreements

This sentence follows the standard rule whereby the verb agrees with the subject noun (in this case *set*) and not the second noun (in this case *questionnaires*).

A set of 200 questionnaires was distributed.

Note that this important rule does not apply in a few exceptional cases, such as when the first noun is a fraction, a proportion, or a percentage. In these special cases, the verb agrees with the noun closest to the verb. Notice the agreement of the subject and verb in these sentences.

A large proportion of students are distracted when they cross a street while talking on the phone.

Only a minority of the cells were alive four hours after antibody administration.

A small fraction of the emitters were contributing significantly to the overall emission current from the array.

TASK FIFTEEN

Fill in the blank with *was* or *were*.

1. A total of 45 undergraduates from a single introductory psychology course _____ recruited for the study.

2. The average score of all the results _____ 69.4%.

3. Well over half of the participants _____ unable to accurately estimate their logical reasoning ability relative to their peers.

4. Nearly 95 percent of the participants _____ unable to estimate how many questions they answered correctly.

5. Approximately 90 percent of the bottom-quartile participants _____ unaware of that their perceptions of ability were grossly out of line with their true ability.

6. One-quarter of the participants who scored in the bottom quartile _____ less able to gauge the competence of others than were their top-quartile counterparts.

Another interesting grammar point arises in sentences beginning with *a . . . number of / the . . . number of.* Which form of *be* would you choose here?

A small number of high performing students _____ able to predict their test scores.

The small number of student errors _____ attributable to their solid preparation.

Language Focus: Making Comparisons

When writing up the results, you may want to include statements of comparison. The street crossing text included a number of statements that compared the different outcomes of the experiments. Here is one such example.

> Conversing on a cell phone produced significantly lower
> success rates than listening to music ($p < 0.01$).

This example is a fairly straightforward comparison. Sometimes, however, the comparisons can be more complex and thus require some careful attention. For instance, we can start with this sentence.

> The median wage of a college graduate is *now higher than* the
> median wage of a high school graduate.

For stylistic reasons, we may then opt to not repeat *the median wage* and instead use *that*.

> The median wage of a college graduate is *now higher than*
> *that* of a high school graduate.

To make matters more complex, we may know roughly how much higher the wage of college graduates is and then produce this sentence.

> The median wage of a college graduate is *now more than 70*
> *percent higher* than *that* of a high school graduate.

We can then include a hedging element.

> The median wage of a college graduate is *now slightly more*
> *than 70 percent higher* than *that* of a high school graduate.

Although the final sentence is rather complex, the basic form of this sentence looks something like this.

> _____ is (more than %) _____ *–er* (comparative adjective form)
> than that of _____.

Another type of complex comparison involves *as much* _____ *as* and *as many* _____ *as* expressions, as in these examples.

> China produces *four times as many engineers as* the United States does.
>
> The nanoscale TBs impart *as much strengthening as* conventional high-angle GBs by blocking dislocation motion.

Here are a few more potentially useful ways to make comparisons.

> *X times the* _____ *of* _____ *as* _____

> Women typically require twice the dosage of morphine as men to achieve the same degree of pain relief.
>
> Turfgrass is the main cultivated crop in Florida with nearly four times the acreage as the next largest crop, citrus.

> *more/less than X times the* _____ *of* _____ *as* _____

> The paired metal chlorides yield more than three times the amount of product than the $CuCl_2$ catalyst (Fig. 2).
>
> Greece consumes more than double/more than two times the amount of cheese as Denmark.

> *more/less than X times the* _____ *of* _____

> The alkaline phosphatase level is usually less than two times the upper limit of normal.
>
> The guarana seed contains more than two times the caffeine of a coffee bean.

> *more than X times* _____ *–er than the* _____ *of* _____

> Each year, the average probability of dying from motor vehicle accidents in France was more than 12 times higher than the risk of drowning.
>
> Although any country can implement smoke-free laws, the proportion of high-income countries with smoke-free restaurants (12 of 41 or 29%) is more than three times higher than the proportion of low- and middle-income countries with similar measures (12 of 139 or 9%).

more than X times _____ –er than that of _____

The density of water is more than 800 times greater than that of air.

The potency of this compound is more than 1000 times greater than that of previously reported inhibitors of the enzyme.

Here are some other ways that authors can signal similarity/equivalence and difference/non-equivalence.

Sentence connectors	Since the six phases of emergency measures were implemented, SO_2 concentrations have dropped a significant 33% to 80µg/m3; *however*, PM10 concentrations decreased just 8% to 162µg/m3.
Subordinators	Analyses showed that 70.5% of students had access to both a desktop and a laptop computer, *while* only 0.6 % of students (n = 11) had access to neither.
Phrase linkers	*In contrast to* the false positives, the false negative rate improves when the distance threshold increases.
Conjunctions	The results of some observers were poor, *but* those of others were satisfactory (Table 5).
More likely than/ less likely than	Women are *more likely than* men to have given the most "pro neighborhood" answer, and men *more likely than* women to have given the most "pro transportation" answer.
Like	The results shown in Figure 8 are very much *like* those of Experiment 5.
Alike	During the study period, real household income rose in both cities and suburbs *alike*, but more so among suburban households.
Similar to/the same as	The observation of smaller magnetization and coercivity at low thickness *is similar to* results obtained for the Fe_3O_4 thin films.
Verbs such as *compared with/ compared to*	Women had a mean score of 3.89, *compared with* a mean for men of 4.76.

TASK SIXTEEN

Complete the alternative formulations. Make some complex statements similar to those in the examples discussed in the Language Focus section.

1. Group A produced 15 fewer errors than Group B but required 20 minutes more time to complete the task.

   Group B _____

   _____.

2. Thailand exported 8.8 million metric tons of rice, while India exported 2.2 million metric tons.

   The amount of rice exported by Thailand was _____

   _____.

3. Sweden consumed 328,000 barrels of oil daily. In contrast, Spain consumed 1,482,000 barrels of oil each day.

   The number of barrels of oil consumed by Spain was _____

   _____.

4. The 1958 tsunami that occurred in Lituya Bay, Alaska, reached a height of 524 meters, but there were only two recorded casualties. However, the 2004 Indian Ocean tsunami, which reached 100 meters, killed over 230,000 people in fourteen countries.

   The height of the Lituya Bay tsunami was _____

   _____.

   The death toll of the Indian Ocean tsunami was _____

   _____.

Commentary in Results Sections

The question of whether the Results section should include commentary— and of what kind—is not easy to answer. In fact, you will find different answers in different writing manuals; further, you may get different views from your instructors, advisors, and supervisors. The more traditional view is that the Results section of an RP should simply report the data that has been collected; that is, it should focus exclusively on simply describing the actual results and should do so using the past tense. Another view would accept some interpretation of results but would suggest that more wide-ranging observations should be left until the Discussion or Conclusions. A third view accepts the fact that authors often include commentary in their Results section because they are aware of their audience. They can *anticipate* that their readers may be thinking, "Why did they use this method rather than that one?" or "Isn't this result rather strange?" For obvious reasons, authors may not want to postpone responding to such imagined questions and critical comments until the final section.

The issue is further complicated by the type of material expected in the final section. In some disciplines, the Discussion section will be extensive and may be the longest section of the RP (as is often the case in medical research, and sometimes the case in the areas of Social Psychology and Education). Elsewhere, the final section may provide little more than a summary conclusion. Because of this uncertainty, it is not surprising that some researchers prefer to offer a combined Results and Discussion section. Bruce (2009) notes that this is a trend in leading chemistry journals, and we have noticed a similar trend in Applied Linguistics.

In a pioneering paper, Dorothy Thompson, herself a biochemist, investigated whether Biochemistry articles contained various types of commentary in their Results sections (Thompson, 1993).

TASK SEVENTEEN

Which of Thompson's types are acceptable in a Results section, or do you think the category is better placed in the Discussion section? If acceptable for Results, write R; if it is better for Discussion, write D.

_____ 1. Admitting difficulties in interpretation

_____ 2. Calling for further research

_____ 3. Citing agreement with previous studies

_____ 4. Commenting on the data

_____ 5. Interpreting the results

_____ 6. Justifying the methodology

_____ 7. Pointing out discrepancies

Table 24 presents Thompson's research (1993) on Results sections.

TABLE 24. Commentary Found in Results Sections in Biochemistry Papers

Type of Commentary	Number of Papers (max. = 20)
Justifying the methodology	19
Interpreting the results	19
Citing agreement with previous studies	11
Commenting on the data	10
Admitting difficulties in interpretation	8
Pointing out discrepancies	4
Calling for further research	0

As can be seen, the first four types of commentary were used by half or more than half of her authors; indeed, only the Calling for Further Research category was universally postponed to the Discussion. Here is part of Thompson's conclusion.

My research demonstrates that scientists—in this case biochemists—do not present results only in a factual expository manner; they also employ a variety of rhetorical moves to argue for the validity of scientific facts and knowledge claims. (126)

How did your responses to Task Seventeen match Thompson's findings?

TASK EIGHTEEN

Complete one of these tasks. Discuss your findings in class.

1. Carefully read a fairly short Results section that you have written, marking any commentary elements. In your estimation, which of the four types is the section most like?

2. Choose Results sections from three to five of the papers in your reference collection and determine which of the four types they most closely resemble.

Type 1

Gives a straightforward description of the author's results; includes no commentary at all (no comparisons with the work of others, no justifications, no—or very few—obvious highlighting statements).

Type 2

Is mostly restricted to present findings but includes a few minor uses of commentary.

Type 3

Consists of both description of findings and a number of commentary elements; uses several of the categories mentioned by Thompson.

Type 4

Makes heavy use of commentary; uses most of the categories found by Thompson; could almost be taken for a discussion.

The Organization of Results Sections

Longer Results sections may have subsections. Some subsections may simply reflect the different stages or parts of the investigation. Consider the case of an article published in the *International Journal of Nursing Studies* entitled "Hospitalized Children's Descriptions of Their Experiences with Postsurgical Pain Relieving Methods." This article, which we will be exploring more closely later, has four subsections in the results.

5. Results

5.1. Children's self-initiated use of pain relieving methods

5.2 Nurses' use of pain relieving methods

5.3 Parents' use of pain relieving methods

5.4 Children's suggestions to nurses and parents

However, in another article from the same journal (entitled "Inflammatory Bowel Disease: Developing a Short Disease Specific Scale to Measure Health Related Quality of Life"), the subsections are very different.

3. Results

3.1 Disease specificity

3.2 Factor analysis

3.3 Reliability

3.4 Validity

Doubtless, in all fields the specifics of the investigation (including the methodology adopted) will determine subsection headings (if any). However, beyond that, the available research suggests that there are some regularities in the organization of Results sections. We present summaries of studies in Sociology (Brett, 1994), Applied Linguistics (Yang and Allison, 2003), and Biochemistry (Kanoksilapatham, 2005) in Figure 15.

FIGURE 15. Outline of Results Sections in Three Fields

Sociology	Applied Linguistics	Biochemistry
location-statement	preparatory information	restating methods
↓	↓	↓
finding	reporting results	justifying methodology
↓	↓	↓
further support for finding	commentary	announcing results
↓	↓	
commentary	commenting on results	

It is useful to note the following.

1. Brett's research shows that *further support* will likely include comparisons and/or examples.

2. Yang and Allison's results indicate that *preparatory information* includes reminders and connectors between sections, location statements, and previews.

3. Typically, there are more result statements than comments. Often two or three result statements are followed by a comment statement.

4. Typically, the components shown in the figure are recycled; sometimes a complete cycle constitutes a paragraph and then the cycle begins again.

5. Typically, the major findings are presented before the more minor ones.

TASK NINETEEN

Here we provide the first of four Results subsections from the article on children's pain entitled "Hospitalized Children's Descriptions of Their Experiences with Postsurgical Pain Relieving Methods." The authors, Pölkki, Pietilä, and Vehviläinen-Julkunen, are from Finland and conducted the study in a hospital there. Suppose this was a draft, can you offer some suggestions for improving the text?

5. Results

5.1 Children's self-initiated use of pain relieving methods

The children reported 13 successful types of self-initiated pain relieving methods. As shown in Table 2, most of the children reported using distraction, resting/sleeping, positioning/immobility and asking for pain medication or help from nurses when they experienced pain.

Table 2. Children's Self-Initiated Use of Pain Relieving Methods after Surgery

"How have you tried to manage pain/what have you done to help yourself when you had pain?"

	N	%
Distraction	51	98
Resting/sleeping	42	81
Positioning/immobility	27	52
Asking for pain medications/help from nurses	27	52
Imagery	16	31
Walking/moving/doing exercises	11	21
Just being and trying to tolerate pain	10	19
Eating/drinking	6	12
Relaxation	4	8
Thought-stopping	1	2
Breathing technique	1	2
Thermal regulation (cold application)	1	2

The most common methods of distraction by which the children tried to focus their attention away from pain included reading, watching TV/videos, and playing games. For example, a 10-year-old boy described his experiences as follows.

> "I have read Donald Duck comics . . . this helps me forget the pain. I can also get my thoughts elsewhere by playing Nintendo games. When I concentrate on playing I don't have much time to think about anything else." (7)

Another method of drawing attention away from pain included the use of imagery in which the children reported thinking about some pleasant action/happening (e.g., getting home), important people (e.g., mother/father, friends), or pets in order to forget the pain. The method of thought-stopping was used by only one child. A 12-year-old boy described this method as follows without utilizing specific replacement thoughts.

> "Then I have kept on thinking that I am not hurting, there is no pain, there is no pain." (11)

Children who used positioning typically associated this method with immobility or restricting movement, as one 12-year-old girl described after undergoing an appendectomy.

> "I have attempted to determine the best possible position to be in . . . either on my side or in a crouched position. I have tried to be without moving so that it would not hurt more." (15)

All children reported using at least one self-initiated pain relieving method. The majority of them claimed to use four of these strategies during their hospitalization. The mean number of strategies identified was 3.8 with a range from 1 to 8.

TASK TWENTY

Produce a Results section from your own work (or part of a Results section if your work is extensive).

Unit Eight

Constructing a Research Paper II

In this final unit, we deal with the remaining parts of a research paper in this order:

Introductions

Discussion sections

Titles

Abstracts

Acknowledgments

Introductions

It is widely recognized that writing Introductions can be slow, difficult, and troublesome for many writers. A very long time ago, the Greek philosopher Plato remarked, "The beginning is half of the whole." Indeed, eventually producing a good Introduction section always seems like a battle hard won.

Writing the Introduction of an RP is particularly troublesome. In some kinds of texts, such as term papers or shorter communications (including case reports), it is possible to start immediately with a topic or purpose statement, as in these examples.

> The purpose of this paper is to . . . .
>
> This paper describes and analyzes . . . .
>
> My aim in this paper is to . . . .
>
> In this case report, we discuss . . . .

However, this kind of opening is increasingly uncommon in longer and more substantial RPs (only a small percentage of contemporary published RPs start in this way). In fact, statements like these typically come at or near the end of an RP Introduction. Why is this? And what comes before?

We believe that the answer to these questions lies in two interconnected motivations. The first part of the answer lies in the need to appeal to the readership. When a paper is written to fulfill a course requirement, the reader is set and known. (Indeed the reader is *required* to read and evaluate your paper!) On the other hand, a paper that is designed for the external world needs to appropriately situate the work within the existing body of related research and attempt to attract an audience. We can illustrate the importance of these purposes by taking the case of one of those few published papers that actually does start by announcing the present research. Here is the opening sentence of the Introduction.

> In this paper, we address the problem of scheduling and balancing sports competitions over multiple venues (Urban and Russell, 2003).

The Urban and Russell paper, "Scheduling Sports Competitions over Multiple Venues," was published in a journal called the *European Journal of Operational Research*, a journal whose audience is researchers and practitioners working in the area of Operational Research/Management Science. Doubtless, the very specific opening to the Urban and Russell paper will appeal immediately to those researchers actively involved in this specific topic. On the other hand, it may "turn off" many other readers of the journal—readers who have no direct interest in the actual scheduling of sporting events.

To explain the second half of the answer as to why simple purpose statements are uncommon first sentences, we believe a metaphor—that of *competition* as it is used in Ecology—is relevant for the writing of RP Introductions. Just as plants compete for light and space, so writers of RPs compete for acceptance and recognition. In order to obtain this acceptance and recognition, many writers will employ a widely used organizational pattern. In this first task, we would like you to try to identify this pattern.

TASK ONE

Read the Introduction and then discuss the purposes of the sections on page 330 with a partner.

Who Says We Are Bad People?
The Impact of Criticism Source and Attributional Content on Responses to Group-Based Criticism
Rabinovich, A., and Morton, T. A. (2010)
Personality and Social Psychology Bulletin, 36, 524–526.

❶ Criticism is an important tool for stimulating change within groups. ❷ Criticism provides objective information about the behavior of one's group, and—provided that criticism is taken on board—it has the potential to initiate reform of sub-optimal behavior and practices. ❸ However, previous research has noted that criticism is often met with defensiveness and rejection, meaning that criticism is more often a "missed opportunity" for creating positive change (see Hornsey, 2005). ❹ This is because criticism threatens the group's positive self-image and may undermine collective self-esteem. ❺ Other research, however, suggests that threat to the public image of one's group can elicit actions intended to reform the group rather than simply defend its current practices (e.g., Iyer, Schmader, & Lickel, 2007). ❻ Thus, it seems that group-directed criticism might sometimes provoke negative reactions but that at other times it might stimulate positive change. ❼ From both theoretical and practical points of view, it is important to understand the factors that determine which of these two responses occurs in response to group-directed criticism.

❽ One key factor that determines responsiveness to criticism is the identity of the critic. ❾ Research on the intergroup sensitivity effect shows that ingroup critics are generally received more positively than outgroup critics—even when the content of their criticism is identical (Hornsey, Oppes, & Svensson, 2002). ❿ The reason behind this effect is that ingroup critics are perceived to have different motivations than outgroup critics (Hornsey & Imani,

2004). ⑪ Ingroup critics are attributed with constructive motives (i.e., genuine desires to improve the group), facilitating acceptance of their message. ⑫ Outgroup critics are instead attributed with destructive motives (i.e., attempting to demoralize the group or struggling for inter-group supremacy), leading to resistance and rejection. ⑬ Thus, responses to criticism are said to be driven not by what people say but by why they are perceived to be saying it.

⑭ In most situations, however, this process of attribution is likely to go in both directions; just as targets make attributions about their critics' motives, critics typically make attributions about the causes of the targets' behavior. ⑮ These attributions may be explicitly communicated, or they may be merely implied by the criticism. ⑯ Although previous research has examined the attributions that targets make about their critics, research has not yet investigated the attributions that critics make about and communicate to their targets. ⑰ With this in mind, the primary aim of the present research was to explore how the attributional content of criticism might further moderate responsiveness to group-directed criticism.

Sentences 1–2   _____

Sentences 3–13   _____

Sentences 14–15   _____

Sentence 16   _____

Sentence 17   _____

How would you evaluate the flow of information? Does the organization seem familiar to you? Does it resemble the Introductions in your field in any way? Does it resemble the moves in Figure 16 on page 331?

Creating a Research Space

As you may have discovered in Task One, the Introductions of RPs typically follow the pattern in Figure 16 in response to two kinds of competition: competition for readers and competition for research space. This rhetorical pattern has become known as the create-a-research-space (or CARS) model (Swales, 1990).

FIGURE 16. Moves in Research Paper Introductions

Move 1—Establishing a research territory
> a. by showing that the general research area is important, central, interesting, problematic, or relevant in some way (optional)
>
> b. by introducing and reviewing items of previous research in the area (obligatory)

Move 2—Establishing a niche[**]
> by indicating a gap in the previous research or by extending previous knowledge in some way (obligatory)

Move 3—Occupying the niche
> a. by outlining purposes or stating the nature of the present research (obligatory)
>
> b. by listing research questions or hypotheses (PISF[***])
>
> c. by announcing principal findings (PISF)
>
> d. by stating the value of the present research (PISF)
>
> e. by indicating the structure of the RP (PISF)

---

[*] The one exception to this occurs in certain RPs that deal with "real world" problems, as in Engineering. In some cases, Move 1 deals with these problems without a literature review and the previous research on attempted solutions is postponed to Move 2 (see the text on pages 335–336).

[**] In ecology, a niche is a particular microenvironment where a particular organism can thrive. In our case, a niche is a context where a specific piece of research makes particularly good sense.

[***] PISF = probable in some fields, but rare in others.

TASK TWO

We begin our more careful analysis with an Introduction to an RP from the humanities. The paper has been adapted from one John wrote for a History of Art seminar he audited on nineteenth-century realism. Read it and answer the questions on page 333.

Thomas Eakins and the "Marsh" Pictures

❶ Thomas Eakins (1844–1916) is now recognized as one of the greatest American painters, alongside Winslow Homer, Edward Hopper, and Jackson Pollock. ❷ Over the last thirty years, there have been many studies of his life and work,[1] and in 2002 there was a major exhibition devoted entirely to his art in his home city of Philadelphia. ❸ His best-known pictures include a number of rowing and sailing scenes, several domestic interiors, the two large canvasses showing the surgeons Gross and Agnew at work in the operating theater, and a long series of portraits, including several of his wife, Susan McDowell. ❹ The non-portraits are distinguished by compositional brilliance and attention to detail, while the portraits—most of which come from his later period—are thought to show deep insight into character or "psychological realism."[2] ❺ In many ways, Eakins was a modern late nineteenth century figure since he was interested in science, in anatomy, and in the fast-growing "manly sports" of rowing and boxing. ❻ In his best work, he painted what he knew and whom he knew, rather than being an artist-outsider to the scene in front of him. ❼ Among Eakins' pictures, there is a small series of scenes painted between 1873 and 1876 showing hunters preparing to shoot at the secretive marsh birds in the coastal marshes near Philadelphia. ❽ Apart from a chapter in Foster (1997), this series has been little discussed by critics or art historians. ❾ For example, these pictures

---

[1] Book-length studies include Hendricks (1974), Johns (1983), Fried (1987), Wilmerding (1993), Foster (1997), and Berger (2000).

[2] The question of what actually makes a work of art "realistic" is, of course, one of the most discussed issues in the history of art, and will not be directly addressed in this paper. For analyses of realism, see, among others, Nochlin (1990).

were ignored by Johns in her pioneering 1983 monograph,[3] per-haps because their overall *smallness* (physically, socially and psy-chologically) did not fit well with her book's title, *Thomas Eakins: The Heroism of Modern Life.* ⑩ These pictures are usually thought to have come about simply because Thomas Eakins used to accom-pany his father on these hunting/shooting trips to the marshes.[4] ⑪ However, in this paper I will argue that Eakins focused his atten-tion on these featureless landscapes for a much more complex set of motives. ⑫ These included his wish to get inside the marsh landscape, to stress the hand-eye coordination between the shooter and "the pusher," and to capture the moment of concentration *before* any action takes place.

1. Divide the text into the three basic moves.

2. How many paragraphs would you divide the text into? And where would you put the paragraph boundaries?

3. Look at Figure 16 again. Where in this Introduction would you divide Move 1 into 1a and 1b?

4. What kind of Move 2 did you find?

5. What kind of Move 3a did you find?

6. Underline or highlight any words or expressions in Sentences 1 through 4 that have been used "to establish a research territory."

7. How many citations are there in the text and footnotes?

8. Footnotes and endnotes are widely used in the humanities. Consider carefully the four footnotes in this Introduction. Do you think that this information is rightly footnoted, or do you think sometimes it would have been better in the main text? Conversely, is there material in the main text that you would have put in footnotes? What do your decisions tell you about the use of notes?

---

[3] Johns' book is an example of the "new" art history with its detailed attention to the *social* conditions and circumstances that give rise to a particular form of art.

[4] Eakins contracted a bad case of malaria on one of these trips, and this brought his visits—and this series of paintings—to an end.

In the opening section of Unit Seven, we argued that RPs were not simple accounts of investigations. If you now look back at the Introduction to the Eakins paper, you will note that it does not explicitly state the motive or rationale for the study. Rather, the study seems to emerge as a natural and rational response to some kind of gap in the literature on Thomas Eakins.

In fact, this is not how the study started at all. The course John audited was an advanced seminar in nineteenth-century realism, and he was already familiar with the paintings of Thomas Eakins. John is also a keen amateur birdwatcher. As he started to read the books on Eakins, he noticed that the critics sometimes misidentified and mislabeled the birds in Eakins' marsh pictures and sketches. This then was what made him focus on these pictures; however, he soon realized that the mistakes about the birds would not make a suitable main theme for a history of art paper—they could only be a small part of the story.

TASK THREE

What is your response to these questions? Discuss them with a partner.

1. Do you think the "true" story behind the paper should be built into the Introduction? If so, where and how?

2. Alternatively, do you think it should be made part of the Discussion? Or dropped in a footnote? Or could it be omitted altogether?

3. Do you have comparable experiences to relate—perhaps stories about how pieces of research started almost by accident but are described as if they were planned?

4. In any investigation, certain events take place in a certain order. Do you think it is necessary to keep to that order when writing an RP, or is an author free to change that order to construct a more rhetorically effective paper?

The Introduction we have just examined is firmly located in the scholarly world of Art History. The rationale for the paper is found in John's belief that art historians had given insufficient attention to one group of Eakins' pictures.

Elsewhere, the rationales for journal articles may lie in problems, issues, or uncertainties that have arisen in the real world. So next, we look at an Introduction of this type from an Engineering journal. Read the adapted text and the analysis.

Durability Monitoring for Improved Service Life Predictions of Concrete Bridge Decks in Corrosive Environments

Cusson, D., Lounis, Z., and Daigle, L. (2011).
Computer-aided Civil and Infrastructure Engineering, 26, 524–541.

I INTRODUCTION

❶ Many reinforced concrete (RC) bridges in Canada and the northern United States are short- and medium-span bridges that exhibit serious deterioration due to the use of de-icing salts during winter. ❷ Approximately 25% of them are considered deficient in terms of structural capacity and functionality (U.S. DOT et al., 2007) as a result of increased traffic loads, changing environmental conditions, and more stringent design codes.

❸ The widespread deterioration and some recent collapses of highway bridges (Inaudi et al., 2009) have highlighted the importance of developing effective bridge inspection and maintenance strategies, including structural health and durability monitoring, which can help identify structural and durability problems before they become critical. ❹ The implementation of structural health monitoring (SHM) programs can provide useful information on the physical health of bridges and their structural performance (Cruz and Salgado, 2009; Moaveni et al., 2009; Soyoz and Feng, 2009; Huang et al., 2010). ❺ Durability monitoring can supply valuable data that can be used to calibrate service life prediction models.

❻ Currently, the majority of highway bridges are inspected at regular intervals through visual inspection, which is followed by a mapping of the observed damage to a qualitative rating scale. ❼ More detailed and in-depth inspections using non-destructive evaluation methods are conducted less frequently to supplement the data obtained from visual inspection, especially for critical bridge elements, to assess the level of corrosion-induced deterioration.

The Introduction for this paper has other sections, which we have not included so that we can focus on the move structure. The omitted sections are *1.1 Toward multi-objective management of highway bridges; 1.2 Toward structural health and durability monitoring of highway bridges;* and *1.3 Objectives.*

Sentences 1–2 establish the research territory. They do this by providing information about the seriousness of the problem, largely without references.

Move 1a

> Sentence 1: *Many reinforced concrete (RC) bridges . . . exhibit serious deterioration . . . .*
>
> Sentence 2: *. . . 25% are considered deficient . . . .*

The next five sentences establish the niche.

Move 2

> Sentence 3: The widespread deterioration and some recent collapses of highway bridges . . . *highlighted the importance of* effective . . . inspection and maintenance
>
> Sentence 4: SHM programs *can* provide useful information
>
> Sentence 5: Durability monitoring *can* supply valuable data
>
> Sentence 6: Current visual inspection procedures
>
> Sentence 7: Rarer, more in-depth on-site inspections

Implications (not explicitly stated in Move 2)

1. SHM and durability monitoring could be improved
2. Inspection procedures could be improved (especially when we learn that this article appeared in a journal called *Computer-aided Civil and Infrastructure Engineering*).

Sections 1.1 and 1.2 are quite extensive and quite technical. The final section of the Introduction (*1.3 Objectives*) is short.

TASK FOUR

Given what you now know, write two or three sentences for Move 3 in order to complete the Introduction to the bridges text. Use your imagination if necessary.

Our third illustrative Introduction section offers a social science approach to the provision of health care.

TASK FIVE

Reconstruct these sentences from the Introduction into their original order, numbering them from 1 to 11? Work with a partner.

University-Community Agency Collaboration: Human Service Agency Workers' Views
Tiamiyu, M. (2000).
Journal of Multicultural Nursing and Health, 6, 29–36.

_____ a. Furthermore, governments, foundations, non-profit organizations, and other stakeholders continue to work on how to provide cost-effective community-based services to members of the society including the elderly.

_____ b. In particular, the study sought to provide an avenue for them to communicate their understanding of university–community agency collaborations and identify how their agencies can work collaboratively with the university.

_____ c. According to the U.S. Bureau of the Census, it is anticipated that if this trend in growth continues, by the year 2030 there will be approximately 70 million Americans aged 65 or over.

_____ d. One approach has been an emphasis on community collaborations to address the planning and delivery of such services.

_____ e. Little, however, is known about participants' views of university-community collaborations.

_____ f. Several studies have examined issues related to the present and future provision and quality of community-based services for the elderly (Kelly, Knox & Gekoski, 1998; Buys & Rushworth, 1997; Damron-Rodriguez, Wallace, & Kington, 1994; Krout, 1994; Kuehne, 1992; Benjamin, 1988; Soldo & Agree, 1988; and Mahoney, 1978).

_____ g. Human-service agency workers are major participants of university-based collaborations; hence, the purpose of this study was to investigate their views of community-based services to the elderly in northwest Ohio.

_____ h. Funding agencies (e.g., U.S. Department of Housing and Urban Development [HUD]) have encouraged university-community collaborations.

_____ i. The growing size of America's population of seniors has drawn attention to its economic and social well-being.

_____ j. America's population is growing older.

_____ k. An example is HUD's Community Outreach Partnership Centers initiative, which involves university faculty, staff, students, and community residents and agencies/groups as partners in the development and implementation of research/community programs.

Which sentences were the most difficult to place? Why?

TASK SIX

Examine the Introductions to 3–5 journal articles from your reference collection. To what extent do their Introductions follow the CARS model presented in Figure 16? If they do not, do you have an explanation for this? Keep in mind that there may be good reasons for alternative structures. Be prepared to discuss one of the Introduction sections with a partner.

Claiming Centrality

In the "University-Community Agency Collaboration" passage, *claiming centrality* (Move 1a) was achieved by stressing the *growing* problem of coping with the elderly in Sentences j, c, and i. In the Eakins text, centrality was created by stressing the artist's growing status and the growing amount of literature devoted to his work (Sentences 1–2). In the bridges text, the authors assert centrality by establishing the "serious corrosion-induced deterioration" in many concrete bridges in northern North America (Sentences 1–3).

In Move 1a certain fixed phrases (or small variants of them) tend to recur. In many cases, the present perfect is used, often with a time expression such as *In recent years*. We list some with the number of Google Scholar hits we found in May 2012.

TASK SEVEN

Update the numbers in the table, and try and find two more opening expressions with more than 1,000 hits.

Phrase	Hits Spring 2012	Hits Now
. . . has been extensively studied . . .	214,000	
. . . there has been growing interest in . . .	17,800	
Recent studies have focused on . . .	17,400	
. . . has become a major issue . . .	7,290	
. . . remains a serious problem . . .	7,280	
. . . there has been increasing concern . . .	4,680	
. . . has been investigated by many researchers.	4,270	
. . . has become an important aspect of . . .	2,470	
		Number of Hits
One of your own		
One of your own		

Now look at the Introduction openings in your reference collection. How many have a Move 1a? Do they use any of the phrases in the table or similar ones? If not, how do your authors *claim centrality*?

Reviewing the Literature

The CARS model states that Move 1b is the place to assemble and review items of previous research relevant to the topic. In fact, in the original version of the CARS model, back in 1981, this was the only place where citations were thought to occur. However, we now know (e.g., Samraj, 2002) that citations can occur anywhere in an Introduction, partly as a consequence of the huge increase in the number of researchers and research papers in recent decades. You may have noticed in the Introduction of the bridges text, for example, that there are more citations in Move 2 than in Move 1.

TASK EIGHT

Once more, review three Introduction sections in your reference collection, highlighting all the citations. (This highlighting will also be useful later.) How are they distributed? Be prepared to discuss your findings with a partner.

Motives for Citing

There are, in fact, a surprisingly large number of theories about the role and purpose of citations in academic texts. These include

- acknowledging the intellectual property rights of earlier authors
- showing respect for previous scholars
- giving your arguments greater authority
- helping (promoting) your friends and colleagues
- showing that you are a member of a particular disciplinary community

However, a more recent consensus among those senior scholars who have studied citations for many years, such as Blaise Cronin and Howard White, suggests that the primary motive for citing remains *perceived relevance.* As Cronin neatly puts it, "Content counts for more than connections" (2005, 1506).

Of course, citation is a surface phenomenon, and there may well be in some cases social and psychological motivations that are not apparent. Even so, in the great majority of situations, it seems clear that well-known scholars and researchers are cited because they have done important work, not simply because they are famous.

Swales and Leeder (2012) studied the citations to the 154 articles published in the 1990s in the *English for Specific Purposes Journal*—a journal that incidentally figures prominently in the references in this volume. They found that the two most-cited articles

- were written by women.
- were written by non-native speakers of English.
- were not by authors working in Anglophone countries.
- were not by authors working at famous universities.

In other words, Swales and Leeder found no evidence of bias; rather, the two papers were highly cited because they had something important and something new to say.

If the role of citations is better understood and accepted these days, this is not true of a subclass of references usually known as *self-citations*. These are citations to an author's own previously published or presented work. In an era when numbers of citations are becoming increasingly important in the evaluation of individuals, self-citations remain controversial. There are two main reasons for this: one is whether they should "count" in evaluations; the second is whether the motives for self-citing are somehow different from those of citing others.

TASK NINE

Read these eight summaries of research papers on self-citing. Then organize a literature review.

1. **Snyder and Bonzi (1989)**
   Patterns of self-citation in six disciplines were examined. 9% of all citations were self-citations: 15% in the physical sciences, 6% in the social sciences, and 3% in the humanities.

2. **Bonzi and Snyder (1991)**
   A study of 51 authors in the natural sciences revealed only a few differences in motivation between citing oneself and citing others.

3. Phelan (1999)

   A study of the citing practices of 56 highly cited authors in the
   field of Education was conducted. Only 2 of the 56 did not cite
   themselves over a 12-year period. At the other extreme, 154
   out of 280 citations (55%) received by one author were the
   outcome of self-citations.

4. White (2001)

   The most important citer motivation is to project one's own
   writing (and reading) by linking earlier work to later work. In
   this sense, a certain amount of self-citation is both natural
   and inevitable.

5. Hyland (2003)

   Self-citations may arise from three kinds of motivation:
   (1) a natural result of the cumulative nature of an individual's
   research; (2) a need for personal gratification; and (3) its value
   as a rhetorical device to increase an author's visibility and
   reputation.

6. Medoff (2006)

   This study of 400 Economics articles showed that an author's
   self-citations did not have a statistically significant effect on
   that article's total number of citations.

7. Falagas and Kavvadia (2006)

   Seventeen percent of references in Clinical Science were self-
   citations, a figure that rose slightly to 20% in Basic Science.

8. Fowler and Aksnes (2007)

   A macro study of more than a half million citations to articles
   by Norwegian scientists in the 1981–2000 period was under-
   taken. The average citation rate was 11%, although there were
   wide individual variations. They then showed that the more
   authors cite themselves the more likely they are to be cited by
   others. However, they note that there are currently no penal-
   ties for frequent self-citing. These results, they conclude,
   question the use of citations to evaluate performance.

As you will have noted, these eight studies have been listed in chronological order. Unless a topic has a clear, linear development over time, a chronological structure is rarely the best way of organizing a literature review, although it may work well enough with some subsets of the material. More generally, the key point about reviews of the literature is that they should clearly show an *organizing mind at work*. Several ways of organizing may be possible, but what readers, reviewers, and editors want to see is an author who imposes order on the material, rather than producing simple undigested lists of what has been done.

Now here is one student's approach to organizing self-citation material in an Introduction.

- I am going to do this specific-general, starting with basic facts.
- I will start with the self-cite percentages: so I'll start with references 1, 7, and part of 8.
- Then I will cover the explanations for self-citing and will use references 4 and 5.
- Then I will focus on individual variation and draw from reference 3 and mention 8.
- After this I will discuss research on self-citation effects using references 2, 6, and 8.
- Finally, I should say something about policy implications and the need for further studies.

Is this how you would do it? Can you suggest a better alternative? Discuss with a partner.

Language Focus: Citation and Tense

Tense choice in reviewing previous research is subtle and somewhat flexible. (It is also not very much like the "rules" you may have been taught in English classes.) The following, therefore, are only general guidelines for tense usage.

Several studies have shown that at least two-thirds of all citing statements fall into one of these three major patterns.

Pattern 1

Past—researcher activity as agent

> Huang (2007) *investigated* the causes of airport delays.
>
> The causes of airport delays *were investigated* by Huang (2007).

Pattern 2

Present Perfect—researcher activity not as agent

> The causes of airport delays *have been* widely *investigated* (Hyon, 2004; Huang, 2007; Martinez et al., 2010).
>
> There *have been* several investigations into the causes of airport delays (Hyon 2004; Huang, 2007; Martinez et al., 2010).
>
> Several researchers *have studied* the causes of airport delays.[1-3]

Pattern 3

Present—no reference to researcher activity

> The causes of airport delays *are* complex (Hyon, 2004; Huang, 2007, Martinez et al., 2010).
>
> Airport delays *appear to have* a complex set of causes.[1-3]

Note the common uses of these patterns.

    Pattern 1—reference to single studies—past
    Pattern 2—reference to areas of inquiry—present perfect
    Pattern 3—reference to state of current knowledge—present

Also note that in Patterns 1 and 2, attention is given to what previous researchers did, while in Pattern 3 the focus is on what has been found.

Finally, note that different areas of scholarship have somewhat different preferences. Patterns 1 and 2 are most common in the humanities and the social sciences and least common in the areas of science, engineering, and medical research. However, all three patterns tend to occur in many extensive literature reviews since they add *variety* to the text.

We have said that these three patterns cover about two-thirds of the cases. The reason this proportion is not higher is because writers of literature reviews can have certain options in their choice of tenses. This is particularly true of Pattern 1. The main verbs in Pattern 1 can refer to what a previous researcher *did* (*investigated, studied, analyzed,* etc.). By and large, in these cases the past is obligatory. However, the main verbs can also refer to what the previous researcher *wrote* or *thought* (*stated, concluded, claimed,* etc.). With this kind of reporting verb (see Unit Five), tense options are possible.

> Rogers (2004) *concluded* that business failure may be related to reduced working capital and retained earnings.
>
> Rogers (2004) *has concluded* that . . . .
>
> Rogers (2004) *concludes* that . . . .

The differences among these tenses are subtle. In general, moves from past to present perfect and then to present indicate that the research reported is increasingly *close* to the writer in some way: close to the writer's own opinion, close to the writer's own research, or close to the current state of knowledge.

The present tense choice is sometimes called the *citational present* and is also used with famous or important sources.

> Aristotle argues that . . . .
>
> Confucius says . . . .
>
> The Bible says . . . .
>
> The Constitution states . . . .

Comparable options exist in the subordinate clause.

> Rogers (2004) found that business failure *was* correlated most closely with reduced working capital.
>
> Rogers (2004) found that business failure *is* correlated most closely with reduced working capital.

The first sentence shows that the writer believes that the finding should be understood within the context of the single study. In the second, the writer implies that a wider generalization is possible. (However, it should be noted that some editors disapprove of the use of present tense here.)

TASK TEN

Review the previously highlighted citations in your reference collection. Which tenses are the most frequent? How does your data fit with the three patterns we have identified?

Variation in Reviewing the Literature

In the Language Focus on pages 344–345, we concentrated on the three main citation patterns. There are, of course, some others.

> According to Suarez et al. (2010), the causes of business failure are closely related to the ratio of working capital, retained earnings, and sales.

> Fang's research shows that reduced working capital and retained earnings are interrelated (Fang, 2007).

Can you come up with others?

Good writers of literature reviews employ a range of patterns in order to vary their sentences. Another form of variation involves the use of integral and non-integral citations. When the cited author is grammatically part of a sentence, the citation is referred to as integral. When the cited author is given in parentheses or referred to by a number, the citation is non-integral. Pattern 1 on page 344 contains integral citations. Non-integral citations appear in Pattern 2.

Most citations are non-integral. Under what circumstances would an integral citation be preferred?

TASK ELEVEN

Choose one of these tasks.

1. Write up a review of the self-citation literature.
2. Revise this passage.

The passage uses only the first citation pattern. As you can see, using the same structure all the time can cause the reader to lose interest. Re-write it to add more variety and provide a more apparent organization structure. Your version will probably be shorter than the original—another advantage!

The Origins of the First Scientific Articles

Banks (2011) describes the founding of the first scientific journals in London and Paris in the 1660s. Obviously, the first scientific articles had no direct models to build on, and several scholars have discussed possible influences. Ard (1983) and Valle (2000) suggest that the first articles developed from the scholarly letters that scientists were accustomed to sending to each other. Sutherland (1986) showed that early articles were also influenced by the newspaper reports of that time. Paradis (1987) described the influence of the philosophical essay. Shapin (1984) claimed that the scientific books of Robert Boyle were another model. Bazerman (1988, 1997) argued that discussions among the scientists themselves made their own contribution to the emergence of the scientific article. Finally, Gross (1990, 2008) ascribes their origins to inventories of nature and natural products.

Move 2: Establishing a Niche

In many ways, Move 2 is the key move in Introductions to longer research papers. (However, this move may not be needed in shorter communications.) It is the hinge that connects Move 1 (what has been done) to Move 3 (what the present research is about). Move 2 thus establishes the motivation for the study. By the end of Move 2, the reader should have a good idea of what is coming in Move 3.

Most Move 2s establish a niche by indicating a gap—by showing that the research story so far is not yet complete. Move 2s then function as a *mini-critique* (see Unit Six). Usually Move 2s are quite short, often consisting of no more than a sentence or two. Let us examine the Move 2s in the first three Introductions we have seen so far.

Thomas Eakins

Apart from a chapter in Foster (1997), this series *has been little discussed by critics or art historians.* For example, these pictures *were ignored by Johns* in her . . . .

Durability Monitoring (bridges)

The widespread deterioration and recent collapses of highway bridges . . . *have highlighted the importance of developing effective bridge inspection and maintenance strategies.*

University-Community Agency Collaboration

Little is, however, known about participants' views of university-community collaborations.

As you can see, the first and third are straightforward gap indications. The second is rather more subtle. It implies, but does not directly state, that current bridge inspection strategies need to be improved.

A fuller range of options for Move 2 is presented in Figure 17.

FIGURE 17. Options for Establishing a Niche

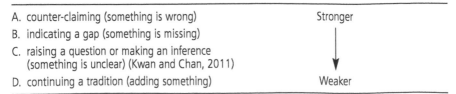

A. counter-claiming (something is wrong)	Stronger
B. indicating a gap (something is missing)	
C. raising a question or making an inference (something is unclear) (Kwan and Chan, 2011)	
D. continuing a tradition (adding something)	Weaker

TASK TWELVE

Here are eight Move 2 statements regarding the self-citation research. Would you characterize them as A, B, C, or D from Figure 17? There are two of each.

_____ 1. These findings suggest that the number of co-authors might affect the self-citation rate.

_____ 2. However, in all three cases, the methodologies used for analyzing self-citations are flawed.

_____ 3. One discipline that has been neglected in self-citation studies is history.

_____ 4. Studies so far lead to a question that has as yet no clear answer: Do self-citations pay?

_____ 5. It would therefore be interesting to have further information about the citation practices of Norwegian scientists.

_____ 6. That said, little is known about how many times individual authors cite their earlier publications.

_____ 7. Recent arguments (e.g., Fowler and Aksnes, 2007) for excluding self-citations from performance assessments rest on a number of false assumptions.

_____ 8. There is obviously value in extending these studies to cover more disciplines.

Of the four Move 2 options, gap-indications are very common in many fields. Option D, however, is typically chosen by research groups in sciences and Engineering as they offer refinements and extensions of their previous work. This is a case of the common "adding another brick to the wall of knowledge" metaphor. At the other pole, regular employment of *counter-claiming* is only likely in contested areas such as Philosophy and Law. Since Option B is widely used, we now explore it a little further.

🌀 Language Focus: Negative Openings in Move 2

Probably the most common way to indicate a gap is to use a "quasi-negative" subject. Presumably, such subjects are chosen because they signal immediately to the reader that Move 1 has come to an end. Note the uses of *little* and *few*.

Non-count	However, little information . . .
	Little attention . . .
	Little work . . .
	Little data . . .
	Little research . . .
Count	However, few studies . . .
	Few investigations . . .
	Few researchers . . .
	Few attempts . . .

Note the differences in the following pairs.

There is little research. (negative, i.e., not enough)

There is a little research. (neutral, i.e., maybe enough)

The department has few computers. (negative, i.e., not enough)

The department has a few computers. (neutral, i.e., maybe enough)

Note also the use of *no/none of.*

No studies/data/calculations to date have . . . .

None of these studies/findings/calculations have . . . .

Use *no* when your conclusion is based on (but does not directly refer to) the cited literature. If you want to refer directly to the previous research, use *none of.*

However, you may want to avoid using a full negative like *no studies;* chances are that somebody will find an exception to your strong statement. Alternatively, you could add *To the best of our knowledge, . . .*

TASK THIRTEEN

Here are some "negative" verbs and adjectives that tend to cluster in Move 2. Work with a partner and decide how "negative" they are. Mark them as seeming definitely or strongly negative (- -) or only slightly negative (-).

Verbs

However, previous research on deforestation has _____ . . . .

____ a. concentrated on   ____ g. neglected to consider

____ b. disregarded   ____ h. overestimated

____ c. failed to consider   ____ i. overlooked

____ d. ignored   ____ j. been restricted to

____ e. been limited to   ____ k. suffered from

____ f. misinterpreted   ____ l. underestimated

Adjectives

Nevertheless, these attempts to establish a link between dental fillings and disease are at present _____ .

____ a. controversial   ____ e. questionable

____ b. incomplete   ____ f. unconvincing

____ c. inconclusive   ____ g. unsatisfactory

____ d. misguided   ____ h. ambivalent

Of course, not all RP Introductions express Move 2 by indicating an obvious gap. You may prefer, for various reasons, to avoid negative or quasi-negative comment altogether. In such cases, a useful alternative is to use a contrastive statement.

> Research has tended to focus on . . , rather than on . . . .
>
> These studies have emphasized . . , as opposed to . . . .
>
> Although considerable research has been devoted to . . , rather less attention has been paid to . . . .

Cumulative and Recycling Move 2s

Sometimes, however, Move 2s can be quite complicated. Consider, for example, the Move 2 from the Introduction section of a paper by Schwer and Daneshvary (2000) entitled "Keeping Up One's Appearance." After an opening paragraph that claims centrality, Schwer and Daneshvary devote the next five short paragraphs to a literature review, concluding that "there appears to be an economic incentive to appear attractive" (209). Now here is their seventh paragraph (italics added).

> *Previous research has not addressed* whether or not people who are employed in some occupations rate the maintenance of overall appearance more important than do people who are employed in other occupations. *Moreover, research has not fully considered* the behavioral consequences of individuals putting more or less emphasis on physical appearance (e.g., does it affect grooming habits or maintenance rituals?). *Nor has it addressed if* they patronize a beauty shop, a barbershop, or a beauty salon in maintaining their appearance.

Notice the strategy here—as shown by the italicized stretches of text—of making a series of quasi-negative statements about "previous research." Also, notice that as the three sentences progress, they increasingly narrow down to the precise research question that Schwer and Daneshvary will be attempting to answer. This type of Move 2 we have called *cumulative* because the gap statements form a series.

The other type involves chopping the more specific earlier references to the previous research into sections and then making a series of Move 2 comments about them. We can illustrate this by introducing the text in Task Fourteen, which focuses on energy harvesting.

As you will see, discussion of previous work is spread out and handled in two paragraphs. One method is discussed in Sentence 3 and critiqued in Sentence 4, while the second method is critiqued in Sentence 11.

TASK FOURTEEN

Read part of the Introduction section for the energy harvesting text (containing Move 2) and then answer the questions on page 354.

Soft Capacitors for Wave Energy Harvesting
Ahnert, K., Abel, M., Kollosche, M.,
Jørgen Jørgensen, P., and Kofod, G. (2011).
Journal of Materials Chemistry, 21, 13392–14497.

❶ The problem of adequately supplying the world with clean, renewable energy is among the most urgent today. ❷ It is crucial to evaluate alternatives to conventional techniques. ❸ One possibility is energy harvesting from ocean waves, which has been proposed as a means of offsetting a large portion of the world's electrical energy demands.[1] ❹ However, the practical implementation of wave energy harvesting has met with obstacles, and the development of new methods is necessary.[2] ❺ Oceanic waves have large amplitude fluctuations that cause devices to fail due to excessive wear or during storms. ❻ A strategy to overcome these catastrophic events could be to base the harvesting mechanisms on soft materials.

   ❼ Soft, stretchable rubber capacitors are possible candidates for energy harvesting,[3–8] that have already been tested in a realistic ocean setting.[9,10] ❽ They were originally introduced as actuators,[11–14] capable of high actuation strains of more than 100% and stresses of more than 1 MPa. ❾ With a soft capacitor, mechanical energy can be used to pump charges from a low electrical potential U to a higher one, such that the electrical energy difference can be harvested.[3] ❿ This is made possible by the large changes of capacitance under mechanical deformation. ⓫ Although the method is simple and proven,[3–10] it is still not clear to what extent the approach is practically useful, which is the concern of this paper. ⓬ Of the many electro-active polymers, it appears that soft capacitors could have the highest energy densities.[15]

1. How many "critique" expressions can you find in the passage? Underline or highlight them.

2. Look back at Task Thirteen. Are these phrases strongly negative or slightly negative?

3. What word signals that Move 1 has ended and Move 2 has started? What other words or expressions could also indicate this shift?

4. Can you now anticipate what Sentence 13 will do?

We can see a slightly different case in the Move 2 of the bridges Introduction (see pages 335–336).

Do you agree (A) or disagree (D) with these comments? Mark (?) if you are unsure.

_____ 1. The first reference (Inaudi et al., 2009) helps to establish the seriousness of the problem and therefore has a different function to the others.

_____ 2. Earlier Swales and Feak said that this Move 2 paragraph was a subtle form of gap indication. In fact, it fits better with the "continuing a tradition" option. SHM monitoring in Sentence 4 contains references, but durability monitoring in Sentence 5 does not. This is because

     _____ there is no published research on this topic.

     _____ the authors simply forgot.

     _____ durability monitoring is the topic of this paper.

     _____ or some other reason.

3. The use of *can* in Sentences 4 and 5 indicates

     _____ that both kinds of monitoring are able to get the job done.

     _____ that both kinds only have a potential to get the job done.

Occupying the Niche

The third and final step in the typical RP Introduction is to make an offer to fill the gap (or extend the tradition) that has been created in Move 2. The first element in Move 3 is obligatory. It has two main variants:

Purposive (P)   The author or authors indicate their main purpose or purposes.

or

Descriptive (D)   The author or authors describe the main feature of their research.

TASK FIFTEEN

Here are the beginnings of ten opening Move 3 sentences. Decide in each case whether they are purposive (P) or descriptive (D). The first two have been done for you. Complete at least three of the sentences.

_P_   1. The aim of the present paper is to give . . . .

_D_   2. This paper reports on the results obtained . . . .

____   3. In this paper we give preliminary results for . . . .

____   4. The main purpose of the experiment reported here was to
        . . . .

____   5. This study was designed to evaluate . . . .

____   6. The present work extends the use of the last model . . . .

____   7. We now report the interaction between . . . .

____   8. The primary focus of this paper is on . . . .

____   9. The aim of this investigation was to test . . . .

____   10. Our primary objective in this paper is to provide . . . .

Note that Move 3 is typically signaled by some reference to the present text, such as the uses of *this, the present, reported,* and *here.* If the conventions of the field or journal allow, it is also common for the authors to switch from the impersonal to the personal by using *we* or, more rarely, *I.* Also note that metadiscoursal references come early in the sentence. It is more common to find

In this paper we present the results of three experiments.

rather than

We present the results of three experiments *in this paper.*

Language Focus: Purpose Statements and Tense

Students sometimes ask us whether they should use *was* or *is* in purpose statements. Indeed, both were used in the phrases in Task Fifteen. The answer to this question depends on how you refer to your work. You have two choices.

1. Referring to the type of *text* (or genre)—paper, article, thesis, report, research note, etc.

2. Referring to the type of *investigation*—experiment, investigation, study, survey, etc.

If you choose to refer to the type of text, present tense is quite common. If you write *The aim of this paper was to . . .* in some fields, this would mean that you are referring to an original aim that has now changed. In other fields, such as Biomedical Research, *was* is typical and simply refers to the aim when the research was conducted.

If you choose to refer to the type of investigation, you can use either *was* or *is.* However, there is an increasing tendency to choose the present, perhaps because it makes the research seem relevant and fresh and new. A safe rule here is to check the journal in which you want to publish your paper to determine the tendency.

Completing an Introduction

Sometimes more than one sentence is necessary to complete Move 3a, as in Sentence b from the paper in Task Five. Here are two examples of Move 3, one from a paper entitled "The Development of Culturally-Sensitive Measures for Research on Ageing" and the other from an Aerospace Engineering article entitled "High Angle-of-Attack Calculations of the Subsonic Vortex Flow in Slender Bodies."

> In this paper, I describe a field test of Krause's multi-method approach to the construction of a culturally-grounded measure for older people in Thailand. A step-by-step elucidation of the approach is presented, as well as an examination of the benefits and problems associated with this mixed-method approach. In addition, the paper discusses issues that gerontology researchers should consider when deciding whether and how to develop a measure that is grounded in the culture for which it is intended.
> Ingersoll-Dayton, 2011.

> The present work extends the use of the last model to asymmetric, body-vortex cases, thus increasing the range of flow patterns that can be investigated. In addition, an effort is made to improve the numerical procedure to accelerate the convergence of the iterative solution and to get a better rollup of the vortex lines representing the wake.
> Almosnino, 1984.

These secondary statements are often introduced by such language as

> *In addition, . . .*
>
> *Additionally, . . .*
>
> *A secondary aim . . . .*
>
> *A further reason for . . . .*

TASK SIXTEEN

Revise your Move 3a (Task Four). Be creative in terms of the research project you might undertake.

Read the table, which provides the Google Scholar hits for some Move 3a expressions obtained in May 2012. Then update the results for today's date. What might you conclude from both sets of figures? Look at some of the first examples for the *was to* and the *has been to* entries. Can you draw any conclusions?

Expression	Hits Spring 2012	Hits Now
The purpose of this paper is to . . .	340,000	
The purpose of this paper was to . . .	19,300	
The purpose of this paper has been to . . .	6,300	
The purpose of this paper will be to . . .	1,780	
The purpose of the present paper is to . . .	66,000	
The purpose of the present paper was to . . .	2,410	
The purpose of the present paper has been to . . .	248	
The purpose of the present paper will be to . . .	65	

In Figure 16 we listed four other elements that can be found at the end of Introduction sections. (There may be others, such as a depiction of the statistical measures employed.) The four elements are arranged in the most likely order of occurrence.

3b. by listing research questions or hypotheses

3c. by announcing principal findings

3d. by stating the value of the present research

3e. by indicating the structure of the RP

In all cases, remember the acronym PISF (probable in some fields but not in others).

TASK SEVENTEEN

In your field, is it probable or improbable that an RP would have any or all the elements listed under 3b–e? What does your reference collection indicate? Be prepared to discuss your conclusions.

Listing Research Questions

Here is Move 3 from the article entitled "Keeping Up One's Appearance," which includes this element. The authors' Move 3 includes both 3a and 3b.

Move 3a

> This paper uses a sample to investigate whether one's (a) occupational status influences the importance one attributes to maintaining overall appearance, and (b) occupation influences one's choice of type of hairgrooming establishment.

Move 3b

> Specifically, we test two hypotheses:
>
> Hypothesis 1. . . .
>
> Hypothesis 2. . . .

Announcing Principal Findings

There is some confusion as to whether RP Introductions should close with a statement of the principal results. One early investigation (Swales and Najjar, 1987) found that physicists do this about half the time but that educational researchers hardly ever include such statements. One useful guideline is to ask yourself whether the RP will open with an abstract. If there is an abstract, do you need to give the main findings three times: in the abstract, in the Introduction, and in the Results section? We think not. If there is no abstract, you may wish to reconsider. Another suggestion would be to follow standard practice in your field—or ask your advisor.

Finally, we need to remember that as the number of research papers continues to increase, so does the competition for readers. As a result, the need for promotion has tended to increase this feature, perhaps especially in

Engineering papers. Further evidence for this comes from a recent requirement by a major publisher of scientific journals that all articles now list 4–5 highlights following the abstract.

Stating Value

You may also want to consider whether to mention at this stage anything about the contribution your research will make. Of course, you will do this in the Discussion section in any case. Note that, as is typical of many biomedical papers, the authors of a paper on vaccine monitoring squeeze a value statement into the Introduction.

> We show how this classification system might permit more accurate evaluation of safety concerns for rare immune-mediated adverse events that may occur following vaccination, thus enhancing our ability to properly identify and analyze associations in clinical trials and post-licensure surveillance.

If you opt for a value statement, it might be wise to be cautious and to use qualifications (see Unit Four).

Outlining the Structure of the Text

A final option is to consider whether you need to explain how your text is organized. This element is obligatory in dissertations and theses but is only included in RPs under certain circumstances. One such circumstance arises when your text is unusual in some way, such as not using a standard IMRD format. Such a field would be Economics. Another arises if you are working in a relatively new field. Cooper (1985) and a number of later researchers (e.g., Shehzad, 2007) have found, for example, that outlining the RP structure is common in Computer Technology and in many other technological areas. On the other hand, it is rare in Biochemistry (Kanoksilapatham, 2007). Ask yourself, therefore, whether your anticipated readers need to have the organization of the RP explained.

Here is a useful example of a textual outline, well-motivated by the unusual structure of the paper. Notice how it uses a good variety of sentence structures. The paper is about currency rates in the European Economic Community and was written by one of our students.

> The plan of this paper is as follows. Section II describes the current arrangements for regulating business mergers within the EEC. In Section III a theoretical model is constructed which is designed to capture these arrangements. Experimental parameters are then tested in Section IV. Finally, Section V offers some suggestions for the modification of the current mechanisms.
>
> Pierre Martin, minor editing

TASK EIGHTEEN

Read this textual outline by another of our students. Notice how it is different from the example. What, if any, changes would you make?

> The rest of the paper is organized as follows. Section 2 presents the theoretical concept of fuzzy expert systems. Section 3 discusses fuzzy-interpolative methodology. Section 4 presents the fuzzy-interpolative ADL matrix. Section 5 presents a numerical example of the FI-ADL matrix and graphical representations. Finally, the conclusion discusses how this tool may be implemented in any software environment.
>
> John Lebens, minor editing

We started this section with a complete Introduction from the humanities. We now close it with one from the field of Biostatistics. It comes from a journal called *Controlled Clinical Trials*.

TASK NINETEEN

Read the Introduction and answer the questions on page 363.

Fraud in Medical Research:
An International Survey of Biostatisticians

Ranstam, J., Buyse, M., George, S. L., Evans, S., Geller, N. L.,
Scherrer, B., Lesaffre, E., Murray, G., Edler, G., Hutton, J. L.,
Colton, T., and Lachenbruch, P. (2000).
Controlled Clinical Trials, 21, 415–427.

❶ The public awareness of scientific fraud has increased remark-ably since the late 1980s when a controversy made front-page news, in which a paper investigated for fraud had as co-author a Nobel laureate [1]. ❷ During the 1990s scientific fraud was disclosed on numerous occasions [2]. ❸ In fact, it was recently suggested that fraud now is "endemic in many scientific disciplines and in most countries" [3]. ❹ However, the clandestine character and conse-quential lack of reliable information make it difficult to study scientific fraud. ❺ The characteristics and frequency of scientific fraud, therefore, are generally unknown, and its impact on medical research is unclear.

❻ Biostatisticians routinely work closely with physicians and scientists in many branches of medical research and have unique insight into data. ❼ In addition, they have the methodological competence to detect fraud and could be expected to have a special professional interest in the validity of results. ❽ Biostatisticians therefore could provide unique and reliable information on the characteristics of fraud in medical research.

❾ The objective of this study was to assess the characteristics of fraud in medical research by surveying members of the Interna-tional Society of Clinical Biostatistics (ISCB).

1. Underline all words and phrases in the first three sentences that help establish the research territory.

2. What does *clandestine* in Sentence 4 mean?

3. Identify all the linking words and phrases. What are their functions?

4. Where and how is the gap established?

5. Using the analysis in Figure 16, it is quite easy to show how all of the sentences, except for Sentences 6–8, fit into the model. How would you interpret those three sentences?

TASK TWENTY

Write or re-write an RP Introduction of your own.

Discussion Sections

By the time you have reached the Discussion section stage in an empirical research paper, you might think that all your hard work is largely over. You might, for instance, be thinking: "All I have to do now is sum up what I have done and then make a few general remarks about what I did." Unfortunately, matters are rarely this simple. A main reason is that this part-genre can be very variable, both in labeling and in substance, due to varying expectations regarding what to include. We explore this further in the next task.

TASK TWENTY-ONE

Answer the questions with a partner.

1. The last parts of an RP might be labeled (and divided) in one of these ways. Do you know of any others?

   Results and Discussion (combined)

   Results and Discussion (separate)

   Results and Conclusions (separate)

   Results, Discussion, and Conclusions (all separate)

   Summary and Conclusions (separate)

   Other? _____

   In your reference collection which, if any, are the most common? Are there alternative labels or arrangements? Be prepared to discuss your findings.

2. Do you agree (A) or disagree (D) with these statements?

   _____ a. Discussion sections should be short and to the point. It is better to let Results sections speak largely for themselves.

   _____ b. A long Discussion section shows that the author or authors are able to reflect intelligently on what was found.

   _____ c. A long Discussion section is just an opportunity for authors to promote their own research and thus themselves.

   _____ d. Conclusions are rarely necessary. Readers can draw their own conclusions. If readers want a summary, they can always read the abstract.

   _____ e. In these days of rapidly increasing numbers of published research papers, Conclusions are valuable because they can highlight the "take home message" of the study.

   _____ f. There is no point in trying to decide whether short or long Discussion sections in a particular field are better. It all depends on the piece of research being reported. Some research projects will need an extensive Discussion section; others will not.

It is therefore not so easy to provide useful guidelines for writing Discussion or Conclusion sections. (We will not distinguish between these two terms since the difference is partly conventional, depending on traditions in particular fields and journals.)

A further factor that leads to variation is the position of the Discussion section in the RP. By the time readers reach the Discussion section, authors can assume a fair amount of shared knowledge. They can assume (if not always correctly) that the reader has understood the purpose of the study, obtained a sense of the methodology, and followed the results. Authors can use this understanding to pick and choose what to concentrate on in the Discussion section. As a result, they typically have greater freedom than in the Introduction.

Overall, in published research papers, Results sections deal with factual statements and their interpretation, while Discussion sections deal with the *claims* that might be made, especially *new knowledge claims*. Here is an extract from a recent study of Discussions sections in RPs in the field of Experimental Physics. In fact, the extract consists of the first two sentences in the author's own Discussion!

5. Discussion

I have argued above that the Discussion section provides an argument that leads the reader from the proof of the data (whose meaning is open to inspection in graphs and tables and is, if the author's method is uncontroversial) to the proof of the claim. The claim is not open to inspection by merely inspecting the data and requires careful argument concerning the cause of the results, and the conditions required by the results.

Parkinson, 2011, 174.

Of course, this is Physics, and in most fields we would not expect actual "proof of the claim," but rather "support for the claim."

Discussions, then, often need to be more than summaries. They should go beyond the results. As Weissberg and Buker have noted, "In the discussion section you should step back and take a broad look at your findings and your study as a whole" (1990, 160).

So, in contrast to Results sections, we might expect Discussion sections to be

- more theoretical.
- more abstract.
- more general.
- more integrated with the field.
- more connected to the real world.
- more concerned with implications and applications.
- more likely to discuss the limitations of the study.

TASK TWENTY-TWO

Here is an adaption of the final section of the bridges paper that we discussed earlier in this unit (see page 335). It consists of an opening paragraph and then eight short bulleted sections. (The "case study" referred to concerns a bridge the authors equipped with experimental monitoring equipment.) We have deleted some short sections for ease of discussion. Answer the questions on pages 367–368.

4 SUMMARY AND CONCLUSIONS

❶ The corrosion-induced deterioration of highway bridges can have serious consequences. ❷ This article proposed a probabilistic modeling approach based on durability monitoring for improving the life cycle performance predictions of aging concrete bridge decks built in corrosive environments. ❸ Its application and benefits were demonstrated on a case study of rebuilt RC barrier walls on a highway bridge near Montreal, Canada. ❹ The following conclusions and recommendations are suggested.

- ❺ Given the uncertainties associated with these parameters governing the service life of RC bridges exposed to chlorides, the use of probabilistic analysis methods are [sic] required.

- ❻ The proposed approach can be used on any RC elements of bridge decks as long as the governing corrosion parameters could be monitored on site and fed to the probabilistic mechanistic prediction models.

- ❼ Recommendations were provided for applying the proposed approach to a given network of bridges.
  ❽ A two-level decision process based on two types of deterioration models were suggested, in which critically damaged bridges are first identified by using simplified Markovian cumulative damage models, and then analyzed using the proposed durability monitoring and probabilistic mechanistic modeling approach.

1. In your view, which of the sentences contains the authors' *major claim* (in terms of generality, etc.)?

2. The final section offers recommendations. If there were an additional bulleted section, what might it contain?

3. Would you say that the opening paragraph provides a general re-orientation for the reader to open the final section, a short abstract of the article as whole, or perhaps both?

4. Look at the final short sentence in the opening paragraph. Do you prefer either of these alternatives?

   a. *Below we provide conclusions, followed by recommendations.*

   b. *The following conclusions are offered and then some recommendations are made.*

5. The word *given* occurs at the beginning of Sentence 5 and again in Sentence 7. Do they have the same meaning? If not, how are they different?

6. The second sentence of the opening paragraph starts with *This article proposed . . . .* What do think of this tense usage?

7. One linguistic feature of this text (and of many similar texts) is the frequent use of past participles used as adjectival modifiers. In the opening paragraph, we can find *corrosion-induced* and *rebuilt*. What other examples can you find?

8. It is often said that the closing section of the Engineering papers are becoming increasingly "promotional." Do you see evidence for or against "promotionalism" in this section?

The Structure of Discussion Sections

There have been a fair number of studies on this topic since the original paper by Hopkins and Dudley-Evans (1988), such as Bitchener and Basturkmen (2006) and Parkinson (2011). To date, this research has covered Discussion sections in Biology, Biochemistry, Physics, Applied Linguistics, Education, and fields in the social sciences. These papers largely point to the same kinds of structure, but the terminologies used to describe the moves are rather different. Because of this, we have attempted to consolidate these findings in Figure 18.

FIGURE 18. The Structure of Discussion/Conclusion Sections

Move 1—Background information (research purposes, theory, methodology) ↓	optional, but PISF
Move 2—Summarizing and reporting key results ↓	obligatory
Move 3—Commenting on the key results (making claims, explaining the results, comparing the new work with the previous studies, offering alternative explanations) ↓	obligatory
Move 4—Stating the limitations of the study ↓	optional, but PISF
Move 5—Making recommendations for future implementation and/or for future research	optional
PISF = probable in some fields	

Here are some thoughts on Figure 18.

1. The basic purpose of Move 1 in the Discussion is to contextualize the study and, in so doing, to consolidate the research space.

2. In most Discussion sections, the majority of the space is taken up by Moves 2 and 3. As we saw in Results sections, typically there are recycled sequences of Move 2 and Move 3. Berkenkotter and Huckin (1995) describe this process as working from "the inside out"; writers refer first to their study and then relate to previous work in their field.

3. Basturkmen (2009) found that one of the major differences between published and student work in language teaching research was that the former much more frequently offered alternative explanations. She offers a number of possible explanations for this difference: Published writers have a deeper knowledge of available theories; they are able to come up with cognitively challenging novel explanations; and they can increase the "news value" of their work by extending the narrow focus of their studies in these ways.

4. There is some evidence that in "big science," such as Pharmacology, *suggestions for further research* may be on the decline. Large research groups may not want to give ideas to their rivals!

5. At this point, you might want to observe that Moves 1–3 (except alternative explanations) and Moves 4–5 seem to be working in opposite directions. Why, you may ask, would authors build up something in order to apparently undermine it later? However, if we remember *positioning*, we can see that authors can position themselves very effectively by

   highlighting intelligently the strengths of the study

   and

   highlighting intelligently its weaknesses.

TASK TWENTY-THREE

Take three of the papers from your reference collection. What moves can you identify in the Discussion and Conclusions section? Prepare to discuss your findings with others.

Earlier in this unit we discussed some data from the Swales and Leeder paper that examined which of the articles published in *English for Specific Purposes* during the 1990–1999 period had received the most citations and attempted to explain why.

TASK TWENTY-FOUR

Here are six sentences (some are slightly edited) taken from the Conclusions and Implications section of the Swales and Leeder (2012) paper. Can you re-assemble them into their original order?

_____ a. Further down the rankings, one could also note Myers' important conclusions of what a textbook is educationally good for and less good for.

_____ b. Despite this uncertainty, we can recommend an alternative approach to a well-explored discipline, a standard study but of an under-researched area, or an unusual topic in a well-known genre.

_____ c. Although it is hard in some ways to draw firm conclusions from our data, there is little doubt that three general factors have led to the citational success of the 15 articles in our core group: choosing academic English; using discourse analysis; and having something new to say.

_____ d. Since this paper has investigated part of the story of the *English for Specific Purposes Journal* in the 1990s, comparable stories of the preceding and the following decade will likely turn out to be very different.

_____ e. We can see this in Mauranen's innovative metaphorical contrast between her two groups of economists and in Salager-Meyer's powerful quantitative analysis.

_____ f. In consequence, the implications for today's rising young scholars (both NS and NNS) must remain tentative.

Language Focus: Levels of Generalization

In the Results sections, some statements may be quite specific and closely tied to the data.

> As can be seen in Table 1, 84% of the students performed above the 12th grade level.
>
> Seven out of eight experimental samples resisted corrosion longer than the controls.

On the other hand, in the abstract or in a summary, space restrictions may lead to a high level of generality.

> The results indicate that the students performed above the 12th grade level.
>
> The experimental samples resisted corrosion longer than the controls.

In the Discussion section, we usually expect something in between these two levels. A common device is to use one of the following "phrases of generality."

> Overall,
>
> In general,
>
> On the whole,
>
> In the main,
>
> With . . . exception(s),
>
> The overall results indicate . . . .
>
> The results indicate, overall, that . . . .
>
> In general, the experimental samples resisted . . . .
>
> With one exception, the experimental samples resisted . . . .

Limitations in Discussions Sections

We saw in Introduction Move 2s that extensive negative language was a possible option. In contrast, Discussion Move 4s tend to use less negative language. The main reason is obvious; it is now your own research that you are talking about. Another reason is that many limitation statements in Discussions are not so much about the weaknesses in the research as about what *cannot be concluded* from the study in question. Producing statements of this kind provides an excellent opportunity for writers to show that they understand how evidence is evaluated in a particular field.

Language Focus: Expressions of Limitations

Here are some typical formulations for stating limitations in one's research scope.

> It should be noted that this study has been primarily concerned with . . . .
> This analysis has concentrated on. . . . .
> The findings of this study are restricted to . . . .
> This study has addressed only the question of . . . .
> The limitations of this study are clear: . . . .
> We would like to point out that we have not . . . .

Here are some typical openings for statements that firmly state that certain conclusions should *not* be drawn.

> However, the findings do not imply . . . .
> The results of this study cannot be taken as evidence for . . . .
> Unfortunately, we are unable to determine from this data . . . .
> The lack of . . . means that we cannot be certain . . . .

We said earlier that Move 4s are optional in Discussion sections. If you feel it is unnecessary to comment on your work in either of these two ways, a useful alternative is to place the limitation in an opening phrase. At least, it does express academic modesty.

> Notwithstanding its limitations, this study does suggest . . . .
>
> Despite its preliminary character, the research reported here would seem to indicate . . . .
>
> However exploratory, this study may offer some insight into . . . .

TASK TWENTY-FIVE

Write a short limitations section for either the bridges text or a paper of your own. Be creative.

TASK TWENTY-SIX

Here we return to a paper dealt with in Unit Seven—the paper on how hospitalized children deal with pain by Pölkki et al. (2003). Read the Discussion one section at a time and then discuss the questions for each section (on the righthand side) before moving on to the next.

6.1. Relevance of the results to nursing practice

❶ This interview study indicated that hospitalized children, aged 8–12 yrs. old, are capable of describing the methods for relieving pain. ❷ The results are consistent with earlier studies conducted among pediatric patients (Savedra et al., 1982; Pölkki et al., 1999; Pederson et al., 2000). ❸ In order to achieve the children's own perspective, however, the children should be asked about the methods that could

Questions for 6.1

1. What is the purpose of the opening sentence? Does this kind of opening seem effective or would you suggest something else? For example, should the authors have restated what they did? Explain.

potentially alleviate their pain, as well as their suggestions regarding the implementation of pain relief measures. ④ Due to their tendency to be independent, school-aged children may conceal their pain and be reluctant to request help from others (cf. Lutz, 1986; Woodgate and Kristjanson, 1995). ⑤ This phenomenon in the children requires specific attention, despite the fact that a certain level of cognitive maturity is achieved during the school-aged period, and a much broader array of non-pharmacological methods are appropriate to use at this age (Vessey and Carlson, 1996).

⑥ All of the children reported that the nurses had used at least two pain-relieving methods and that parents used at least one method. ⑦ Almost all of the children related that administering pain medication and helping with daily activities were the methods most frequently used by nurses to relieve their pain. ⑧ Conversely, the methods of distraction, presence, positive reinforcement and helping with daily activities were the most popular methods used by the parents according to the children's descriptions. ⑨ While 38 children reported that the presence of their mother/father helped them to feel less pain, only four children reported that this strategy was implemented by nurses. ⑩ This may be explained by the nurses' lack of time to sit beside the child, but also by different roles between the nurses and the parents in a child's care. ⑪ On the whole the parents seemed to provide more emotional support

2. Why is Sentence 2 important? Can you think of other ways to show how new work favorably compares with old? What could the authors have written if they had found something quite different from previous studies?

3. What seems to be the purpose of Sentences 3–5?

4. What verb tenses are used? Can you explain why each was used? Is this similar to Discussion sections in your field?

5. How many of the sentences in 6.1 refer to previous literature? Does this seem like too many, too few, or just the right amount? Why?

6. How strong are the claims? Does this seem appropriate? Why?

to their hospitalized children than the nurses. [The last two sentences have been omitted.]

⑫ Many children had suggestions to the nurses, but only a few to the parents concerning the implementation of surgical pain relief measures. ⑬ This may indicate that the children expect the nurses to know how to care for them and relieve their pain (cf. Alex and Ritchie, 1992), whereas the children do not have specific expectations of their parents other than simply to "stay with me more." ⑭ In order to improve nursing care for children with postoperative pain the recommendations provided by children to nurses, such as creating a more comfortable environment (especially minimizing noise problems), giving more or stronger pain medication without delay, as well as visiting regularly or staying with the child more, should be taken seriously into account in nursing practice.

6.2 Reliability and Validity

⑮ Use of the interview as a data collection method allowed the children to express their own perspectives regarding the methods of relieving their pain in the hospital; ⑯ however, there were some defects that may potentially prevent the attainment of purpose. ⑰ First, some children may have tried to provide favorable answers during the interview even though the researcher reminded them that there were no right or wrong answers. ⑱ Secondly, there were practical problems that may have disturbed

7. Where do the authors try to clarify what the results mean?

8. How should we understand *cf.* in Sentence 13?

9. How important is Sentence 14? Why?

Questions for 6.2

10. What is gained by including this section? How important do you think this section is?

11. How strongly do the authors present their concerns? Do you think that they have reason to be concerned? Why?

some children's ability to concentrate on relating their experiences. ⑲ For example, practical issues independent of the researcher included conducting the interviews just prior to the child's discharge, and use of the unfamiliar hospital room as the place for conducting the interviews. ⑳ An interesting question is whether the results would have been different if the children had been asked open-ended questions as opposed to forced-choice questions regarding the methods of pain relief (cf. Branson et al., 1990). ㉑ The use of triangulation, such as observing the children during their hospitalization, may have increased the validity of the results. ㉒ Talking with the children after the data had been analyzed may also have increased the validity of the results (face-validity) (Downe-Wamboldt, 1992; Polit and Hungler, 1999). ㉓ However, the children were asked during the interview to clarify unclear responses by questioning such as "What do you mean by this" or "Could you tell me more about this." ㉔ The researcher also often summarized or paraphrased the responses to the children at the end of each theme in order to make valid interpretations of the data.

㉕ In order to improve the validity and reliability of the study the researcher attempted to establish a confidential relationship with the child and minimized noise problems during the interview. ㉖ The researcher personally collected and analyzed the data, and coded the formed categories three times at 1-month intervals

12. Would you characterize their concerns as *defects*? Can you think of any alternatives to *defects*?

13. What is the order of information in Sentence 15 and the clause in 16? Good news first and then bad news, or the reverse? Why did the authors choose this pattern? And why did they choose to use a semicolon between the two points?

14. In Sentence 20 the indirect question is described as *interesting*. Does this sentence state a limitation or a topic worth thinking about? Do the authors offer an answer? Why?

15. In Section 6.1, the authors wrote *This may indicate that . . .* (Sentence 13). In Section 6.2 they wrote *. . . may have*

(intrarater reliability). ㉗ The discrepancies in the categories were resolved through discussion with two independent researchers (panel of experts). ㉘ The data were quantified, which is justified in the use of content analysis, in order to give the reader a tangible basis for assessing what the analyst claims are the important patterns in the data and improve on impressionistic judgements of the frequencies of categories (Morgan, 1993). ㉙ The validity of the formed categories in this study was supported by previous relevant research in the area of pain relieving methods in pediatric patients (Downe-Wamboldt, 1992).

6.3 Challenges for future research

㉚ This study provided new information regarding the implementation of pain relieving methods from the children's perspective in a hospital setting; ㉛ however, more research is required in this area in order to validate and expand on the discoveries of this study. ㉜ More research is required on the children's experiences regarding help received from nurses and parents for relieving pain. ㉝ Also, it would be interesting to investigate the roles of the other family members and friends in the child's pain relief. ㉞ One of the challenges for future research is to test effective interventions for surgical pain relief in pediatric patients, which should not be restricted only to the non-pharmacological methods implemented by nurses in the hospital.

tried . . . (Sentence 17). How do you explain the difference in the verb forms?

16. In Sentences 21–22, are the authors talking about what they *did* or what they *might have done*? How did you decide?

Questions for 6.3

17. How important is this section to the overall Discussion? Can you think of good reasons for and against including such a section?

18. Review the moves provided in Figure 18. Which moves can you find in this Discussion? Do they follow the order proposed in the figure?

If you wish to write a longer Discussion section, follow the shape recommended in Figure 19. Begin with specifics and then move toward the more general.

FIGURE 19. Shape of a Longer Discussion

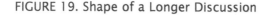
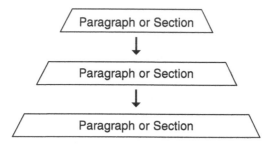

TASK TWENTY-SEVEN

Write or re-write a Discussion section for your own research. If you are working with others, collaborate with them. If your original paper lacked a Move 4 and/or a Move 5, add these to your new draft.

Unfinished Business

Although we have now gone through the four main sections of the RP, there remain some other matters to be attended to. Obviously, there is the question of a title. Then there is an abstract. You may need a short acknowledgments section. Finally, the references have to be in good order.

Titles

Although the title comes first in an RP, it may sometimes be written last. Its final form may be long delayed and much thought about and argued over even if some authors prefer to think of a title early in the writing process to have a clear focus. Regardless of when titles are created, authors know that they are important. They know that the RP will be known by its title, and they know that a successful title will attract readers while an unsuccessful one will discourage readers. What, then, are the requirements for good RP titles? In general, we suggest these three.

1. The title should indicate the topic of the study.
2. The title should indicate the scope of the study (i.e., neither overstating nor understating its significance).
3. The title should be self-explanatory to readers in the chosen area.

In some cases it may also be helpful to indicate the nature of the study (experiment, case report, survey, etc.), but this is not always required. Notice that we have so far not mentioned anything about the language of titles, such as the number of words and the presence or absence of colons or of verbs or of qualifications, such as *A preliminary study of.* . . . This is because there are marked disciplinary preferences when it comes to titles. Further, each journal makes available author guidelines, which may dictate what you can do.

Civil Engineering (and similar fields)

In the journal that published the bridges text, the article titles in more than 90 percent of the cases consist of only noun phrases and prepositions. Here are six examples.

- On-Site Measurements of Corrosion Rate of Reinforcements
- Bridge Reliability Assessment Based on Monitoring
- Chloride Corrosion in Danish Bridge Columns
- An Engineering Approach to Multicriteria Optimization of Bridge Structures
- Influence of Cracks on Chloride Ingress into Concrete
- Chloride Profiles in Salty Concrete

Surgery (and similar fields)

There are 39 original articles in the September 2011 issue of the *Annals of Thoracic Surgery*. Most of their titles are also in the nominal style we saw in Engineering, such as these examples.

- Efficacy and Safety of Aprotinin in Neonatal Congenital Heart Operations
- Thirty-Year Experience with the Artificial Switch Operation

However, there were ten that contained finite verbs and so looked like sentences (or questions). Here are four examples. Note that in the first three the title provides the conclusion of the study and the fourth simply poses a question.

- Long-Term Survival and Quality of Life Justify Cardiac Surgery in the Very Elderly Patient

- Small Prosthesis Size in Aortic Valve Replacement Does Not Affect Mortality

- Anemia Before Coronary Artery Bypass Surgery as Additional Risk Factor Increases the Perioperative Risk

- Should Heart Transplant Recipients with Early Graft Failure Be Considered for Retransplanation?

Applied Language Studies

If we turn to the 15 article references in the Parkinson paper cited on page 365 in our focus on Discussion sections, we see another disciplinary preference—the use of colons. In fact, seven of the 15 article titles cited by Parkinson have colons. Here are four.

- An Exploration of a Genre Set: RA Abstracts and Introductions in Two Disciplines

- Genre Analysis: An Approach to Text Analysis in ESP

- Methods Sections of Management RAs: A Pedagogically Motivated Qualitative Study

- Engineering English: A Lexical Frequency Instructional Model

There are two further options in titles that are worth pointing out. One is the use of verb + *ing* particles, as in these examples.

- Exploring the Deterioration Factors of Bridges

- Analyzing Genres: Functional Parameters

The other is the use of qualifying elements: What differences do you see between the following pairs of titles?

1a. On the Use of the Passive in Journal Articles

1b. The Use of the Passive in Journal Articles

2a. A Study of Research Article Results Sections

2b. A Preliminary Study of Research Article Results Sections

3a. An Analysis of Errors in Period Placement

3b. Toward an Analysis of Errors in Period Placement

4a. The Role of Urban Planners

4b. A Possible Role for Urban Planners

TASK TWENTY-EIGHT

Analyze these ten titles of papers that we have either used or cited in one of the eight units of this book. Record your findings in the chart on page 382. The first one has been done for you.

1. Does Self-Citation Pay?

2. A Duty to Forget? The 'Hitler Youth Generation' and the Transition from Nazism to Communism in Postwar East Germany, c. 1945–49

3. Fog-Water Collection in Arid Coastal Locations

4. A Piezoelectric Frequency-Increased Power Generator for Scavenging Low-Frequency Ambient Vibration

5. Caffeinated Energy Drinks—A Growing Problem

6. Design of a Haptic Gas Pedal for Active Car-Following Support

7. So, What is the Problem this Book Addresses? Interactions in Book Reviews

8. Consumer Decisions in the Black Market for Stolen or Counterfeit Goods

9. The Increasing Dominance of Teams in Production of Knowledge

10. Keeping Up One's Appearance: Its Importance and the Choice of Type of Hair-Grooming Establishment

Title	Number of Words	Any Verbs?	Punctuation	Field
1.	4	does . . . pay	question mark	information science
2.				
3.				
4.				
5.				
6.				
7.				
8.				
9.				
10.				

TASK TWENTY-NINE

Look at the article references in at least one of the papers in your reference collection. What tendencies can you find in the titles of the cited papers?

- Average length in words?
- Presence of finite or +-*ing* verbs?
- Use of colons?
- Use of qualifications?
- Use of questions?

If colons were used in any of the titles you analyzed in Tasks Twenty-Eight and Twenty-Nine, what is the relationship between the pre-colon and post-colon information? You may like to consider these possibilities.

Pre-Colon	Post-Colon
Problem:	Solution
General:	Specific
Topic:	Method
Major:	Minor

Finally, at this stage in your career, we advise against "clever," "joke," or "trick" titles. These can be very successful for undergraduates and for senior scholars, but in your case, such titles may simply be interpreted as mistakes. An example of such a title follows. The author of the paper was Professor Hartley, a well-known professor of Psychology who conducted many experiments on what makes English texts easy or difficult to read. In this instance, he had been comparing texts that have "ragged right" or "unjustified" margins at the end of the lines with those that have straight, or "justified," margins. Here is the title.

Unjustified Experiments in Typographical Research and Instructional Design (*British Journal of Educational Technology* [1973] 2: 120–31)

In this case, we can assume that Professor Hartley, who is a very prolific scholar, is making a joke. But if you wrote it?

Depending on your field, you may wish to consider using qualifications in your titles. In nearly all cases, the process of arriving at the final form of a title is one of narrowing it and making it more specific. Qualifications can be helpful in this process.

TASK THIRTY

Bring the title of one of your papers to class and be prepared to discuss its final form and how you created it.

Abstracts

This penultimate section includes a brief look at RP abstracts. Note that a much more extensive treatment is available in *Abstracts and the Writing of Abstracts*, published by the University of Michigan Press (Swales and Feak 2009).

Unless you are in true humanities, your RP will probably require an abstract. Abstracts have been shown to be very important parts of an RP because of increasing competition to publish. Among certain important journals, manuscripts may be rejected after a reading of the abstract alone. While we need to emphasize that such rejections will be largely based on the perceived lack of research merit, it remains the case that a coherent abstract can only help a manuscript reach the next step of external review. We also know that if readers like your abstract, they may read your paper—or at least part of it. If they do not like it, they may not.

There are two main approaches to writing RP abstracts. One we will call the *results-driven* abstract because it concentrates on the research findings and what might be concluded from them. The other approach is to offer an *RP summary* abstract in which you provide one- or two-sentence synopses of each sections of the paper.

RP abstracts can be characterized as either *indicative* (describe what was done) or *informative* (include the main findings). In some very complex papers or those that are very theoretical (as in mathematics), it may be impossible to report findings and for those we would expect more informative abstracts. Some journals require structured (labeled with section titles), while others may not. However, we should note that structured abstracts have been spreading beyond the medical field (e.g., Hartley and Betts, 2009).

Structured abstracts have subheadings similar to those in a paper.

Background

Aim

Method

Results

Conclusion

Now here is the abstract for a paper we referred to in Task Nine of this unit.

TASK THIRTY-ONE

Read the abstract for the paper in Task Nine and answer the
questions on page 386.

Does Self-Citation Pay?

Fowler, J. H., and Aksnes, D. W. (2007).
Scientometrics, 72, 427–437.

❶ Self-citations—those where authors cite their own works—
account for a significant portion of all citations. ❷ These self-citations may result from the cumulative nature of individual research,
the need for personal gratification, or the value of self-citation as a
rhetorical and tactical tool in the struggle for visibility and scientific
authority. ❸ In this article we examine the incentives that underlie
citation by studying how authors' references to their own works
affect the citations they receive from others. ❹ We report the
results of a macro study of more than half a million citations to
articles by Norwegian scientists that appeared in the Science Citation Index. ❺ We show that the more one cites oneself the more
one is cited by other scholars. ❻ Controlling for numerous sources
of variation in cumulative citation from others, our models suggest
that each additional self-citation increases the number of citations
from others by about one after one year, and by about three after
five years. ❼ Moreover, there is no significant penalty for the most
frequent self-citers—the effect of self-citation remains positive even
for very high rates of self-citation. ❽ These results carry important
policy implications for the use of citations to evaluate performance
and distribute resources in science and they represent new information on the role and impact of self-citations in scientific communication.

1. A first impression suggests that this is an RP-summary type of abstract. Can you show this by aligning the sentences with the IMRD structure?

2. What tense is used consistently throughout the abstract? Is this usage common and conventional in your field? If so, why? If not, why not?

3. The middle portion of the abstract uses first-person pronouns (*we* and *our*). Do you find these in the abstracts in your reference collection?

4. The authors of this abstract approximate their numbers. They refer in the abstract to "more than half a million citations," while the actual number examined was 692,455. What do you think of this?

5. Suppose somebody remarked, "Fowler and Aksnes are really quite promotional in this abstract." What evidence can you find for and against this observation?

6. In November 2011, Google Scholar indicated that this paper had been cited by 45 papers. This is a respectable total for this field. Why do think this is?

It seems clear that tense usage in abstracts is fairly complicated. First, the conclusions are nearly always in the present. Second, RP summary abstracts often use the present or present perfect for their opening statements. Third, there appears to be considerable disciplinary and individual tense variation in sentences dealing with results.

Although descriptions of methods and results are often expressed through the past tense, it is not difficult to find exceptions to this pattern. Here is a short abstract from the "Rapid Communications" section of the journal *Physical Review A* (Vol. 48, R1–R4).

Nuclear-Structure Correction to the Lamb Shift

Pachucki, K., Leibfried, E., and Hänsch, T. W. (1993).

In this paper the second-order nuclear-structure correction to the energy of hydrogen-like systems is estimated and previous results are corrected. Both deuterium and hydrogen are considered. In the case of deuterium the correction is proportional to the nuclear polarizability and amounts to about -19 kHz for the 1S state. For hydrogen the resulting energy shift is about -60 Hz.

Our investigations suggest that the shift to the present tense is more likely to occur in the physical sciences, such as Physics, Chemistry, and Astrophysics, and less likely to occur in the social sciences. We also found that physicists and chemists were—perhaps surprisingly—more likely to adopt a personal stance. Indeed, we have found occasional abstracts, particularly in Astrophysics, which contain sequences of sentence openings like these:

> We discuss . . . .
>
> We compute . . . .
>
> We conclude . . . .

It would therefore seem that choice of tense and person may again be partly a strategic matter in abstracts. Choosing the present tense option—if permitted—can produce an effect of liveliness and contemporary relevance. Choosing *we* can add pace, by making an abstract a little shorter. We have seen, of course, many of these features in the Fowler and Aksnes abstract.

TASK THIRTY-TWO

Draft an abstract for one of your research projects.

Acknowledgments

Acknowledgments have become an integral part of most RPs. Indeed, one well-known professor of our acquaintance reported to us that he always reads the acknowledgments of an RP first. When we asked him why, he replied, "Oh, the first thing I want to know is who has been talking to whom." While we do not think that this is standard reading behavior, it does show that acknowledgments can be more than a display of necessary politeness.

Acknowledgments occur either at the bottom of the first page, following the Discussion, or sometimes at the end of the RP. They provide an opportunity for you to show that you are a member of a community and have benefitted from that membership. Acknowledgments sections, therefore, allow you to "repay your debts" (Giannoni, 2002). At the same time, however, they allow you to highlight that you are also "intellectually responsible" for the content of the publication (Giannoni, 2002). Here we list some of the common elements in an acknowledgments section.

1. Financial support

   Support for this work was provided by [sponsor].

   This research was partially supported by a grant from [sponsor].

   This research was funded by Contract (number) from [sponsor].

2. Thanks

   We would like to thank A, B, and C for their help. . . .

   I wish to thank A for his encouragement and guidance throughout this project.

   We are indebted to B for . . . .

   We are also grateful to D for . . ..

3. Disclaimers (following the first two elements)

   However, the opinions expressed here do not necessarily reflect the policy of [sponsor].

   The interpretations in this paper remain my own.

   None, however, is responsible for any remaining errors.

   However, any mistakes that remain are my own.

We believe that, if permitted, the acknowledgments should be written in the first person—using *I* for a single author and *we* for co-authors. While it is possible to find phrases like *the present authors*, we consider them overly formal for this situation.

As far as we can see, financial support tends to come first, followed by thanks. Disclaimers seem optional. Mentions of other matters, such as permissions or sources of materials, may also occur.

TASK THIRTY-THREE

Write a suitable acknowledgments section for one of your pieces of work. If necessary, invent some forms of assistance to expand the section.

Appendix One:
The Grammar of Definitions

Articles in Definitions

In most definitions, the indefinite article (or no article in the case of non-count nouns) is used before both the term and the class. The indefinite article before the class indicates that you are classifying a term. The indefinite article before the term conveys the meaning that any representative of this term will fit the assigned class. You may ask why *the* is not used in a formal sentence definition. Take a look at the following sentences.

A. A disinfectant is an agent capable of destroying disease-causing microorganisms.

B. A disinfectant is the agent capable of destroying disease-causing microorganisms.

Sentence A classifies the term; it does not refer to a particular representative. Sentence B, however, identifies or describes the term. Further, in Sentence B, it is implied that there has been some previous mention of other agents that are not capable of destroying disease-causing microorganisms and also suggests that there is only one such agent with this capability.[1]

TASK ONE

In the following eight definitions, articles (*a, an,* or *the*) have been omitted before the nouns. Replace them as appropriate, remembering not to do so if the noun is non-count (see Appendix Two).

1. Helium is gas with atomic number of 2.

2. El Niño is disruption of ocean-atmosphere system in tropical Pacific having important consequences for weather worldwide.

---

[1] There is one main exception to the absence of *the* in formal definitions; this sometimes occurs in explanations of fields, as in "Phonetics is the study of speech sounds."

3. White dwarf is star that is unusually faint given its extreme temperature.

4. Rice is cereal grain that usually requires subtropical climate and abundance of moisture for growth.

5. Transduction is technique in which genes are inserted into host cell by means of viral infection.

6. In seismology, liquefaction is phenomenon in which soil behaves much like liquid during earthquake.

7. Disability is physical or mental impairment that substantially limits one or more major life activities such as seeing, hearing, speaking, walking, breathing, performing manual tasks, learning, caring for oneself, and working.

8. Hydrothermal vent is crack in ocean floor that discharges hot (350–400°C), chemically enriched fluids and provides habitat for many creatures that are not found anywhere else in ocean.

Relative Clauses in Definitions

Now let us turn to the grammar of the second part of a sentence definition. The distinguishing information in the restrictive relative clause can be introduced by either a full or a reduced relative clause. There are two common ways of reducing a restrictive relative clause. One involves a simple deletion, while the other involves a change in word form or some larger change. Reduced relatives are often preferred because they are shorter and thus more "economic."

Deletions

You may reduce the restrictive relative cause if

1. the relative clause consists only of the relative pronoun, the verb *to be*, and one or more prepositional phrases

A wharf is a structure *that is along* a waterfront providing a place for ships to load and unload passengers or cargo. →

A wharf is a structure *along* a waterfront providing a place for ships to load and unload passengers and cargo.

In dentistry, enamel is a hard, white inorganic material *that is on* the crown of a tooth. →

In dentistry, enamel is a hard, white inorganic material *on* the crown of a tooth.

(Note how the opening phrase *In dentistry* restricts the scope of the definition.)

2. the relative clause opens with a relative word immediately followed by a passive verb

A theater is a building *that has been* specifically designed for dramatic performances. →

A theater is a building *specifically* designed for dramatic performances.

A collagen is a white, inelastic protein *that is formed* and maintained by fibroblasts. →

A collagen is a white, inelastic protein *formed* and maintained by fibroblasts.

Change in Word Form or Larger Change

You may reduce the relative clause if

1. the relative clause contains the verb *have*. In this case the relative pronoun and *have* can both be dropped and replaced by *with*.

A parliament is a national governing body *which has* the highest level of legislative power within a state. →

A parliament is a national governing body *with* the highest level of legislative power within a state.

2. the relative clause contains an active state verb (a verb that expresses a state or unchanging condition). The relative pronoun is dropped and the verb changed to the *-ing* form. Exceptions to this are *to be* and *have*.

Pollution is a form of contamination *that often results* from human activity. →

Pollution is a form of contamination *often resulting* from human activity.

A moon is a natural satellite *which orbits* a planet. ⟶

A moon is a natural satellite *orbiting* a planet.

Russian is a language *that belongs* to the East Slavic subgroup of the Indo-European language family. ⟶

Russian is a language *belonging* to the East Slavic subgroup of the Indo-European language family.

It is also important to note that a relative clause containing a modal auxiliary cannot be reduced. Look at the following example. What would be the effect on the meaning of the definition if the modal *may* were omitted?

In human resource management, a shock is a sudden and unexpected event that may cause employees to think about how that event will affect their jobs.

Also note it is not possible to reduce a relative clause if it opens with a preposition.

An axis is an imaginary line about which a body is said to rotate.

TASK TWO

Reduce the relative clauses where possible.

1. Aluminum is a lightweight metal that is often used for high-tension power transmission.

2. Phonetics is a branch of linguistics in which speech sounds are studied.

3. A brake is a device that is capable of slowing the motion of a mechanism.

4. A dome is generally a hemispherical roof which is on top of a circular, square, or other-shaped space.

5. Snow is a form of precipitation which results from the sublimation of water vapor into solid crystals at temperatures below 0°C.

6. An antigen is a substance which causes the formation of antibodies, the body's natural response to foreign substances.

7. A piccolo is a small flute that is pitched an octave higher than a standard flute.

8. Membrane permeation is a separation process that involves the selective transport of gas molecules through a permeable polymeric film.

9. A catalyst is a substance that can speed up the rate of a chemical reaction without changing its own structure.

10. A black hole is a celestial body which has approximately the same mass as the sun and a gravitational radius of about 3 km.

Appendix Two: Articles in Academic Writing

Three of the most common words in the English language are also three of the most difficult to use. We are referring to the articles *a*, *an*, and *the*. We will not attempt here to give you every rule of article use in English, but we will provide you with a quick review of some basic rules to guide you in your choice of *a*, *an*, *the*, or Ø (no article needed).

1. Countability

Before deciding if you should use an article, you should determine whether the noun in question is countable (count) or uncountable (non-count) and whether it is generic (representative or symbolic). Count nouns can take the plural; non-count nouns cannot, or can only do so under special circumstances. Let us first take a look at specific nouns and countability. We will take a look at generic use later.

TASK ONE

Mark the following nouns as either count (C) or non-count (NC).

behavior	____	money	____
complication	____	problem	____
crisis	____	progress	____
device	____	proposal	____
discrepancy	____	research	____
energy	____	reception	____
equipment	____	research project	____

Determining whether a noun is countable may not be as easy as it seems. First, you cannot tell whether a noun is countable simply by looking at it. Some nouns that you intuitively think can be counted may not be countable. Money, for example, can be counted; however, the word *money* is a non-count noun. Second, a noun that is countable in one language may not be countable in another and vice versa. *Information*, for example, is a non-count noun in English but a count noun in most of its European equivalents. The following are usually non-count nouns in English.

Names for languages—*Chinese, Korean, French, Arabic* . . .

Names for areas of study—*physics, biology, economics* . . .

Names for solids—*coal, steel, marble* . . .

Names for liquids—*water, nitric acid, oil* . . .

Names for gases—*oxygen, hydrogen, methane* . . .

Names for powders—*salt, sugar, sand* . . .

Third, although you may have learned that nouns are either count or non-count, this is not the whole story. There are quite a number of nouns that can be either. These can be referred to as *double nouns*. There may even be considerable differences in meaning between a count noun and its non-count counterpart. Table 25 lists some double nouns.

TABLE 25. Double Nouns

Non-Count	Count
analysis (in general)	an analysis (a particular one)
calculation (in general)	a calculation (a particular one)
diamond (the hard substance)	a diamond (a precious stone)
grain (in general), i.e., cereal	a grain (a particular one), i.e., a grain of salt
science (in general)	a science (a particular one)
sound (in general)	a sound (a particular one)

An important group of nouns in this category refers to concepts that can be measured or quantified. Examples of these are *temperature, pressure, voltage, growth, density,* and *velocity.* Can you describe the difference between *temperature* and *a temperature?*

> A thermometer measures temperature.
>
> Temperature is expressed in degrees.
>
> A temperature of over 120°C was recorded.
>
> The patient ran a high temperature for several days.

Fourth, some nouns that are non-count nouns in everyday English may be count nouns in technical English. Can you explain the difference in usage between the italicized nouns in the following sentences?

> *Rice* is a staple food around the world.
>
> *A rice* that can resist certain types of diseases should be introduced to the farmers of the region.
>
> *Steel* is critical for the construction of skyscrapers.
>
> The use of *a* light-weight *steel* would improve fuel efficiency.

There are at least two possible explanations for the difference. One is that the second sentence of each set involves a highly specialized use of the term that would most likely only be used by experts in the field. For example, while most non-experts would make a distinction between *rice* and *wheat* or between *steel* and *aluminum,* they would not necessarily distinguish between different types of rice or steel. Experts, however, can and do. Another reason may be for purposes of conciseness. It is simply more efficient for experts to talk of *steels* rather than *different types of steel.* (However, we recommend that you do not shift non-count nouns to count nouns unless you have seen examples from your field of study.)

2. The Indefinite Article and Ø

Once you have determined what type of noun you are using, you can then make some further decisions regarding your choice (or omission) of an article. As you know, *a(n)* indicates that the noun is any single countable item, rather than a specific one. *A* is used before consonant sounds, while *an* is used before vowel sounds. Note that sound, not spelling, is the criterion. This explains why we write *an uprising* but *a university* and *a lead battery* but *an LED display.*

A(n) is typically used with the first mention of a singular countable noun, but not always. There are a number of linguistic contexts that require the use of *the.* (See Section 3, The Definite Article.)

Usually, no article (Ø) is necessary for the first mention of a plural or a non-count noun where none of the special conditions for definite article use apply. (See Section 3.)

3. The Definite Article

The use of the definite article is far more problematic than the use of the indefinite because the definite article is used in a number of different ways. The most important of these, however, is to specify a particular noun, to make clear that reference is being made to a particular singular or plural noun. The definite article should be used in the following contexts.

- Second mention (either explicit or implicit)
    a. The surface is covered by *a thin oxide film. The film* protects the surface from corrosion.
    b. A very lightweight car was developed, but *the vehicle* performed poorly in crash tests.
    c. A new computer was purchased to complete the process, but *the hard drive* was damaged.
- Superlatives or ordinals
    a. *The most-controlled therapy* yielded the best results.
    b. *The first studies* were conducted in early 1993.
    c. *The last security conference* was termed a success.
- Specifiers (e.g., *same, sole, only, chief, principal* . . .)
    a. *The same subjects* were retested at two-week intervals.
    b. *The only research* previously done in this area yielded mixed results.
    c. *The principal causes* of the disaster have yet to be discovered.

- Shared knowledge or unique reference
  a. *The sun* rises in the east and sets in the west.
  b. *The oxygen balance* in the atmosphere is maintained by photosynthesis.
  c. *The stars* are fueled by fusion reactions.
- *Of* phrases or other forms of postmodification (but not with first mention of partitive[2] *of* phrases such as *a molecule of oxygen, a layer of silicon,* or *a piece of information*)
  a. *The behavior of this species* varies.
  b. *The price of gold* fluctuates.
  c. *The results of the investigation* were inconclusive.
- Partitive *of* phrases with plurals
  a. *None of the projects* was satisfactory.
  b. *Some of the subjects* had adverse reactions.
  c. *All of the questionnaires* were returned.
- Names of theories, effects, devices, scales, and so on modified by a proper name used as an *adjective*
  a. *the Doppler* effect
  b. *the Heisenberg* uncertainty principle
  c. *the Hubble* telescope
  d. *the Kelvin* scale

Note, however, that when a proper name is used in the *possessive form*, no article is used.

  a. Coulomb's law

  b. Einstein's theory of relativity

  c. Broca's area

  d. Wegener's hypothesis

---

[2] A partitive phrase is a construction that denotes part of a whole.

TASK TWO

Fill in the blanks with either *a, an, the,* or Ø.

_____ writing is _____ complex sociocognitive process involving

_____ construction of _____ recorded messages on _____ paper or

some other material and, more recently, on _____ computer screen.

_____ skills needed to write range from making_____ appropriate

graphic marks, through utilizing _____ resources of _____ chosen

language, to anticipating _____ reactions of _____ intended readers.

_____ writing as composing needs to be distinguished from _____

simpler task of _____ copying. _____ writing is slower than _____

other skills of _____ listening, _____ reading, and _____ speaking.

It is further slowed by _____ processes of _____ thinking, _____

re-reading what has been written, and _____ revising. _____ writing

is not _____ natural ability like _____ speaking but has to be

acquired through _____ years of _____ training or _____ schooling.

Although _____ writing systems have been in existence for about

5,000 years, even today, only _____ minority of _____ world's

population knows how to write.

4. Generics, Specifics, and Generalizations

Generalizations of various kinds—and often qualified—are obviously important in academic writing. They are more likely to occur in the Introduction and Discussion/Conclusions sections, often as initial (and topic) sentences in paragraphs.

A generic noun or noun phrase can represent an entire class or can be one representative of a class of objects, people, quantities, or ideas. A generic noun is like an archetype in that it manifests what is typical for the class. For this reason, generics are used in formal definitions (see Appendix One).

Compare the specific and general noun phrases in Table 26.

TABLE 26. Specific versus General Noun Phrases

	Specific	General
1.	*The disinfectant* caused an allergic reaction.	*A disinfectant* is an agent capable of destroying disease-causing microorganisms.
2.	*The solar car built at the University of Michigan* won the race.	*Solar cars* that could travel long distances would certainly result in a cleaner environment.
3.	*The computer* crashed while running the program.	*The computer* has replaced the typewriter.
4.	*The water added to the feedstock* is given as a percentage.	*Water* is necessary for all living organisms.

Of the four generalizations in Table 26, Numbers 1 and 3 are generic. As you can see, with generics, a singular formulation represents the whole.

Abstract versus Concrete Generics

Generics can generally be divided into two different types: the abstract generic and the concrete generic. An abstract generic refers to an *entire class* of objects, while the concrete generic refers to *a representative* of a class. Look at the examples in Table 26. Abstract generics, such as Number 3, require *the*, while concrete generics (1 and 4) use either *a* (with a singular count noun) or Ø (for non-count nouns). On this last point, here are two further examples.

Abstract: *The wasp* can detect unique volatile compounds over great distances.

Concrete: *A wasp* can be trained to detect odors.

Abstract: *The computer* has been invaluable in scientific advancement.

Concrete: *A computer* has become standard office equipment in most parts of the world.

Because generics are used to make generalized statements, they are typically used only with the simple tenses, particularly the present. Nevertheless, they can sometimes be used with the present perfect (as can be seen in the *computer* examples) or the continuous.

The elephant *has come* dangerously close to extinction.

Synthetic skin and computer modeling *are replacing* animal skin in the testing of cosmetic products.

TASK THREE

Read this passage and fill in the blanks with either *a*, *an*, *the*, or Ø.

Much has been learned about _____ brain in _____ last 150

years. _____ brain, _____ most complicated organ of _____ body,

contains _____ ten billion nerve cells and is divided into _____ two

cerebral hemispheres, one on _____ right and one on _____ left.

Interestingly, _____ left hemisphere controls _____ movements on

_____ right side of _____ body, while _____ right hemisphere

controls _____ movements on _____ left.

_____ researchers also know that _____ specific abilities and

behaviors are localized; in _____ other words, they are controlled

by _____ specific areas of _____ brain. _____ language, it seems, is

highly localized in _____ left hemisphere. In _____ 1860s, Dr. Paul

Broca discovered that _____ damage to _____ front left part of _____

brain resulted in _____ telegraphic speech similar to that of young

children. Soon thereafter, Karl Wernicke found that _____ damage to

_____ back left part of _____ brain resulted in _____ speech with

_____ little semantic meaning. These two regions in _____ brain are

now referred to as _____ Broca's area and _____ Wernicke's area.

Although there is some debate surrounding _____

specialization of _____ brain, _____ researchers generally agree that

_____ speech is controlled by _____ left side. There is no debate

that in _____ great majority of cases, _____ injuries to _____ left side

nearly always have _____ impact on _____ speech.

Appendix Three: Academic English and Latin Phrases

Nearly all academic languages make occasional use of foreign phrases and expressions, either to add technical precision or to add "color" to the text. English is no exception. Although in many fields the use of expressions or words from French or German may be declining in academic English, the tradition of incorporating bits of Latin remains surprisingly strong. For that reason, Appendix Three (*appendix* is a Latin word!) deals only with Latin. We include it primarily to help you negotiate Latin expressions in your reading. You should consider the preferences of your field when deciding whether to use such expressions in your own writing.

Did you know that *per* in *percent* or *kilometers per hour* is a Latin preposition that originally meant "through" or "by"? *Per* is also used in the Latin expression *per se* meaning "through" or "of itself," and hence "intrinsically."

> Although education conveys important economic benefits, it is also valuable *per se.*

As this example shows, Latin expressions are often set apart from the English language text by italics.

Did you know that all the following abbreviations derive from Latin? How many do you know? How many can you give the full form for?

1. e.g.
2. i.e.
3. N.B.
4. A.M.
5. P.M.
6. P.S.
7. etc.
8. A.D.
9. C.V.
10. ad lib

We have divided the expressions into three groups.

1. Expressions Referring to Textual Matters

TABLE 27: Common Latin Expressions Referring to Textual Matters

Expression	Full Form	Literal Meaning	Modern Use
cf.	*confer*	compare	compare
e.g.	*exempli gratia*	free example	for example
et al.	*et alii*	and others	and other authors
etc.	*et cetera*	and other things	and others
errata	*errata*	errors	list of typographical mistakes
ibid.	*ibidem*	in the same place	the same as the previous reference
i.e.	*id est*	that is	that is to say
infra	*infra*	below	see below
loc. cit.	*loco citato*	in the place cited	in the place cited
N.B.	*nota bene*	note well	take note
op. cit.	*opere citato*	in the work cited	in the work cited
passim	*passim*	here and there	the point is made in several places
P.S.	*post scriptum*	after writing	something added after the signature
sic	*sic*	thus	the error is in the original quote
supra	*supra*	above	see above
viz.	*videlicet*	obviously	namely

2. Latin Expressions Starting with a Preposition

TABLE 28: Latin Expressions Starting with a Preposition

a fortiori	with even stronger reason
a posteriori	reasoning based on past experience or from effects to causes
a priori	deductive reasoning or from causes to effects
ab initio	from the beginning
ad hoc	improvised, for a specific occasion, not based on regular principles (e.g., an *ad hoc* solution)
ad infinitum	to infinity, for forever, or without end
ad lib	at will, so to speak off the top of the head
ante meridiem	before noon, typically abbreviated A.M.
antebellum	before the war, usually before the American Civil War
circa (c. or ca.)	about, approximately, usually used with dates (e.g., c. 1620)
de facto	from the fact, so existing by fact, not by right (e.g., in a *de facto* government)
de jure	from the law, so existing by right
ex post facto	after the fact, so retrospectively
in memoriam	in the memory of a person
in situ	in its original or appointed place (e.g., research conducted *in situ*)
in toto	in its entirety
in vitro	in a glass (e.g., experiments conducted in vitro)
in vivo	in life, experiments conducted on living organisms
inter alia	among other things
per capita	per head, so a *per capita* income of $20,000
per diem	per day, so expenses allowed each day
post meridiem	after noon, typically abbreviated to P.M.
postmortem	after death, an examination into the cause of death
pro rata	in proportion (e.g., *pro rata* payment for working half time)
sine die	without a day, with no time fixed for the next meeting
sine qua non	without which not, hence an essential precondition for something

3. Other Expressions

TABLE 29: Some Other Useful Latin Expressions

Anno Domini (A.D.)/A.C.E.	in the year of the Lord, or the number of years after the beginning of Christianity[3]
bona fide	in good faith (e.g., a *bona fide* effort to solve a problem)
caveat	a caution or warning (e.g., Caveat emptor: "Let the buyer beware")
ceteris paribus	other things being equal (used particularly by economists)
curriculum vitae	summary of one's education and academic accomplishments
ego	literally *I*, the consciousness or projection of oneself
locus classicus	the standard or most authoritative source of an idea or reference
quid pro quo	something for something, to give or ask for something in return for a favor or service
status quo	things as they are, the normal or standard situation
sui generis	unique
viva (voce)	an oral examination

There are further uses of Latin that Appendix Three does not cover. Most obviously, it does not deal with the technical details of Latin names in the life sciences. However, we observe, in passing, that Latin names do not take generic articles (see Appendix One). Compare the following.

The Common Loon breeds in the northern part of Michigan.

Gavia immer breeds in the northern part of Michigan.

Appendix Three also does not address the widespread use of Latin in British and American law, but useful resources can be found on the internet.

---

[3] Today it is preferable to use A.C.E. (After Common Era) and its counterpart B.C.E. (Before Common Era).

References

Since this book is a guide to writing academic English, many of the illustrative texts contain citations. For obvious reasons, we have not included these illustrative citations in this reference list. Every publisher requires its authors to use a particular style for references. We used APA.

References to Academic Discourse and Academic Writing

Annesley, T.M. (2010). Who, what, when, where, how, and why: the ingredients in the recipe for a successful Methods section. *Clinical Chemistry, 56,* 897–901.

Barton, E. (2002). Inductive discourse analysis: Discovering rich features. In E. Barton and G. Stygall (Eds.), *Discourse studies in composition* (pp. 19–42). Cresskill, NJ: Hampton Press.

Basturkmen, H. (2009). Commenting on results in published research articles and masters dissertations in Language Teaching. *Journal of English for Academic Purposes, 8,* 241–251.

Becher, T. (1987). Disciplinary discourse. *Studies in Higher Education, 12,* 261–274.

Belcher, D. (1995). Review of *Academic writing for graduate students* by J. M. Swales and C. B. Feak. *English for Specific Purposes, 14,* 175–178.

Benfield, J. R., and K. M. Howard. (2000). The language of science. *European Journal of Cardio-thoracic Surgery, 18,* 642–648.

Berkenkotter, C., and Huckin T. (1995). *Genre knowledge in disciplinary communication.* Hillsdale, NJ: Lawrence Erlbaum.

Bhatia, V. K. (2004). *Worlds of written discourse.* London: Continuum.

Bitchener J., and Basturkmen, H. (2006). Perceptions of the difficulties of postgraduate L2 thesis students writing the discussion section. *Journal of English for Academic Purposes, 5,* 4–18.

Boggs, J. (2009). Cultural industries and the creative economy—vague but useful concepts. *Geography Compass, 3,* 1483–1498.

Bondi, M. (2007). Authority and expert voices in the discourse of history. In K. Fløttum (Ed.), *Language and discipline perspectives on academic discourse* (pp. 66–68). Newcastle, U.K.: Cambridge Scholars Publishing.

Bonzi, S. and Snyder, H.W. (1991). Motivations for citation: A comparison of self citation and citation to others. *Scientometrics, 21,* 245–254.

Breeze, R. (2005). Review of *Academic writing for graduate students* by J. M. Swales and C. B. Feak. *TESL-EJ, 8.* http://tesl-ej.org/ej32/r1.html

Brett, P.A. (1994). A genre analysis of the Results section of sociology articles. *English for Specific Purposes, 13,* 47–60.

Bruce, I. (2009). Results sections in sociology and chemistry articles: A genre analysis. *English for Specific Purposes, 28,* 105–124.

Casanave, C. (2010). Taking risks? A case study of three doctoral students writing qualitative dissertations at an American university in Japan. *Journal of Second Language Writing, 19,* 1–16.

Chang, Y.Y., and Swales, J. M. (1999). Informal elements in English academic writing: Threats or opportunities for advanced non-native speakers? In C. Candlin and K. Hyland (Eds.), *Writing: Texts, processes, and practices* (pp. 145–164). London: Longman.

Cooper, C. (1985). Aspects of article introductions in IEEE publications. Unpublished master's thesis, University of Aston, U.K.

Cronin, B. (2001). Hyperauthorship: A post-modern perversion or evidence of a structural shift in scholarly communication practices? *Journal of the American Society for Information Science and Technology, 52* (7), 558–569.

Cronin, B. (2003). Scholarly communication and epistemic cultures. *New Review of Academic Librarianship, 9,* 1–24.

Cronin, B. (2005). A hundred million acts of whimsy? *Current Science, 89,* 1505–1509.

D'Angelo, L. (2008). Gender identity and authority in academic book reviews: An analysis of metadiscourse across disciplines. *Linguistica e Filologia, 27,* 205–221.

Dobson, B., and Feak, C. B. (2001). A cognitive modeling approach to teaching critique writing to nonnative speakers. In D. Belcher and A. Hirvela (Eds.), *Linking literacies: Perspectives on L2 reading-writing connections* (pp. 186–199). Ann Arbor: University of Michigan Press.

Falagas M.E., and P. Kavvadia. (2006). 'Eigenlob': Self-citation in biomedical journals. *FASEB Journal, 20,* 1039–1042.

Feak, C. B., and Swales, J. M. (2009). *Telling a research story: Writing a literature review.* Ann Arbor: University of Michigan Press.

Feak, C. B., and Swales, J. M. (2011). *Creating contexts: Writing introductions across genres.* Ann Arbor: University of Michigan Press.

Fowler, J. H., and Aksnes, D.W. (2007). Does self-citation pay? *Scientometrics, 72,* 427–437.

Giannoni, D. S. (2002). Worlds of gratitude: A contrastive study of acknowledgment texts in English and Italian research articles. *Applied Linguistics, 23,* 1–31.

Glänzel, W. (2008). Seven myths in bibliometrics: About facts and fiction in quantitative science studies. *Collnet Journal of Scientometrics and Information Management, 2,* 9–17.

Glänzel, W., Janssens, F., and Thijs, B. (2009). A comparative analysis of publication activity and citation impact based on the core literature in bioinformatics. *Scientometrics, 79,* 109–129.

Glänzel, W., and Schubert, A. (2004). Analysing scientific networks through co-authorship. In W. Glänzel, U. Schmoch, and H. F. Moed (Eds.), *Handbook of quantitative science and technology research: The use of publication and patent statistics in studies of S&T systems* (pp. 257–276). Dordrecht, the Netherlands: Kluwer Academic Publishers.

Hartley, J., and Betts, L. (2009). Common weaknesses in traditional abstracts in the social sciences. *Journal of the American Society for Information Science and Technology, 60,* 2010–2018.

Hopkins, A., and Dudley-Evans, T. (1988). A genre-based investigation of the discussion sections in articles and dissertations. *English for Specific Purposes, 7,* 113–121.

Hoey, M. (1983). *On the surface of discourse.* London: George Allen and Unwin.

Hyland, K. (1999). Academic attribution: Citation and the construction of disciplinary knowledge. *Applied Linguistics, 20,* 341–367.

Hyland, K. (2003). Self-citation and self-reference: Credibility and promotion in academic publication. *Journal of the American Society for Information Science and Technology, 54,* 251–259.

Hyland, K. (2004). *Disciplinary discourses: Social interactions in academic writing.* Ann Arbor: University of Michigan Press.

Hyland, K. (2008). 'Small bits of textual material': Voice and engagement in Swales' writing. *English for Specific Purposes, 27,* 143–160.

Kanoksilapatham, B. (2005). Rhetorical structure of biochemistry research articles. *English for Specific Purposes, 24,* 269–292.

Kanoksilaptham, B. (2007). Writing scientific articles in Thai and English: Similarities and differences. *Silpakorn University International Journal, 7,* 172–203.

Knorr-Cetina, K. D. (1981). *The manufacture of knowledge.* Oxford: Pergamon.

Kragh, H. (2001). Trends, perspectives and problems in the physical sciences. In *Science under pressure proceedings* (pp. 80–94). Aarhus: The Danish Institute for Studies in Research and Research Policy.

Kwan, B., and Chan, H. (2011). An analysis of evaluations of prior scholarship in research articles in two sub-fields of Information Systems. Paper presented at PRISEAL II, University of Silesia, Poland.

Langdon-Neuner, E. (2008). Hangings at the *BMJ*: What editors discuss when deciding to accept or reject papers. *The Write Stuff, 17,* 84–86.

Lillis, T. (1999). Whose "common sense"? Essayist literacy and the institutional practice of mystery. In C. Jones, J. Turner, and B. Street (Eds.), *Student writing in the university: Cultural and epistemological issues* (pp. 127–147). Amsterdam: John Benjamins.

Lillis, T., & Curry, M. J. (2010). *Academic writing in a global context: The politics and practices of publishing in English.* London: Routledge.

Medoff, M. H. (2006). The efficiency of self-citations in economics, *Scientometrics, 69*, 69–84.

Molle, D., & Prior, P. (2008). Multimodal genre systems in EAP writing pedagogy: Reflecting on a needs analysis. *TESOL Quarterly, 42*, 541–566.

Motta-Roth, D. (1998). Discourse analysis and academic book reviews: A study of text and disciplinary cultures. In I. Fortanet, S. Posteguillo, J. C. Palmer, and J. F. Coll (Eds.), *Genre studies in English for academic purposes* (pp. 29–58). Castelló, Spain: Universitat Jaume I.

Noguchi, J. T. (2001). The science review article: An opportune genre in the construction of science. Ph.D. diss. University of Birmingham, U.K.

Okamura, A. (2000). The roles of culture, sub-culture, and language in scientific research articles. Ph.D. diss. Newcastle University, U.K.

Parkinson, J. (2011). The Discussion section as argument: The language used to prove knowledge claims. *English for Specific Purposes, 30*, 164–175.

Peacock, M. (2011). The structure of methods sections in research articles across eight disciplines. *Asian ESP Journal, 7*, 99–124.

Pearson, J. (1998). *Terms in context.* Amsterdam: Johns Benjamins.

Persson, O., Glänzel, W., and Danell, R. (2004). Inflationary bibliometric values: The role of scientific collaboration and the need for relative indicators in evaluative studies. *Scientometrics, 60*, 421–432.

Phelan, T. J. (1999). A compendium of issues for citation analysis. *Scientometrics, 45*, 117–136.

Salager-Meyer, F., Alcaraz Ariza, M. A., and Pabon Berbesi, M. (2007). Collegiality, critique and the construction of scientific argumentation in medical book reviews: A diachronic approach. *Journal of Pragmatics, 39*, 1758–1774.

Samraj, B. (2002). Introductions in research articles: Variation across disciplines. *English for Specific Purposes, 21*, 1–8.

SCImago. (2007). SJR—SCImago Journal & Country Rank from http://www.scimagojr.com

Shehzad, W. (2007). How to end an introduction in a computer science article? A corpus based approach. In E. Fitzpatrick (Ed.), *Corpus linguistics beyond the word: Research from phrase to discourse,* (pp. 243–255). Amsterdam: Rodopi.

Smagorinsky, P. (2008). The method section as conceptual epicenter in constructing social science research reports. *Written Communication, 25*, 389–411.

Skelton, J. (1988). The care and maintenance of hedges. *English Language Teaching Journal, 42*, 37–44.

Smith, F. (2008). Book review: *Academic writing for graduate students: Essential tasks and skills. ESP News, 13*(2).

Snyder, H.W., and Bonzi, S. (1989). An enquiry into the behavior of author self citation: Managing information and technology. *Proceedings of the 52nd*

Annual Meeting of the American Society for Information Science. Medford, NJ: Learned Information, Inc.

Swales, J. M. (1990). *Genre analysis: English in academic and research settings.* Cambridge, U.K.: Cambridge University Press.

Swales, J. M., and Feak, C.B. (2004). *Academic writing for graduate students: Essential tasks and skills,* 2nd ed. Ann Arbor: University of Michigan Press.

Swales, J. M., Ahmad, U. K., Chang, Y. L., Chavez, D., Dressen, D. F., and Seymour, R. (1998). Consider this: The role of imperatives in scholarly writing. *Applied Linguistics, 19*(1), 97–121.

Swales, J. M., and Feak, C.B. (2009). *Abstracts and the writing of abstracts.* Ann Arbor: University of Michigan Press.

Swales, J. M., and Feak, C.B. (2011). *Navigating academia: Writing supporting genres.* Ann Arbor: University of Michigan Press.

Swales, J. M., and Leeder, C. (2012). A reception study of articles published in *English for Specific Purposes,* 1990–1999. *English for Specific Purposes, 3*(2), 137–146.

Swales, J. M., and Najjar, H. (1987). The writing of research article introductions. *Written Communication, 4,* 175–192.

Tarone, E., Dwyer, S., Gillette, S., and Icke, V. (1998). On the use of the passive and active in astrophysics journal papers: With extensions to other languages and other fields. *English for Specific Purposes, 17,* 113–132.

Thompson, D. K. (1993). Arguing for experimental "facts" in science: A study of research article results sections in biochemistry. *Written Communication, 10,* 106–128.

Tse, P., and Hyland, K. (2006). So what is the problem that this book addresses? Interactions in book reviews. *Text and Talk, 27,* 767–790.

Virtanen, T. (2008). Adverbials of 'manner' and 'manner plus' in written English: Why initial placement? *SKY Journal of Linguistics, 21,* 271–293.

Weissberg, R., and Buker, S. (1990). *Writing up research: Experimental research report writing for students of English.* Englewood Cliffs, NJ: Prentice Hall.

White, H. (2001). Authors as citers over time. *Journal of the American Society for Information Science and Technology, 52,* 87–108.

Wolfe, C.R. (2011). Argumentation across the curriculum. *Written Communication, 28,* 193–219.

Wright, T. M., Buckwalter, J.A., and Hayes, W. C. (1999). Writing for the *Journal of Orthopaedic Research. Journal of Orthopaedic Research, 17,* 459–466.

Wulff, S., Römer, U., and Swales, J. M. (2012). Attended/unattended *this* in academic student writing: Quantitative and qualitative approaches. *Corpus Linguistics & Linguistics Theory, 8,* 129–157.

Yang, R., and Allison, D. (2003). Research articles in applied linguistics: Moving from results to conclusions. *English for Specific Purposes, 22,* 365–385.

Sources of Sample Texts and Figures

Ahnert, K., Abel, M., Kollosche, M., Jørgen Jørgensen, P., and Kofod, G. (2011). Soft capacitors for wave energy harvesting. *Journal of Materials Chemistry, 21,* 14492–14497.

Almosnino, D. (1984). High angle-of-attack calculations of the subsonic vortex flow in slender bodies. *AIAA Journal, 23,* 1150-1156.

Amjadi, Z., and Williamson, S.S. (2009). Review of alternate energy storage systems for hybrid electric vehicles, *Electrical Power & Energy Conference (EPEC) IEEE,* 1–7.

Baltruschat, D. (2009). Reality TV formats: The case of Canadian Idol. *Canadian Journal of Communication, 34,* 41–59.

Belant, J. L., Wolford, J.E., and Kainulainen, L. G. (2007). Occurrence of a badger in Pictured Rocks National Lakeshore, Michigan. *Michigan Birds and Natural History, 14,* 41–44.

Casola, L., Kemp, S., and Mackenzie, A. (2009). Consumer decisions in the black market for stolen or counterfeit goods. *Journal of Economic Psychology, 30,* 162–171.

Cusson, D., Lounis, Z., and Diagle, L. (2011). Durability monitoring for improved service life predictions of concrete bridge decks in corrosive environments. *Computer-aided Civil and Infrastructure Engineering, 26,* 524–541.

DePasquale, J. P., Geller, E. S., Clarke, S. W., and Littleton, L. C. (2001). Measuring road rage: Development of the propensity for angry driving scale. *Journal of Safety Research, 32,* 1–16.

DeWitte, S., and Lens, W. (2000). Procrastinators lack a broad action perspective. *European Journal of Personality, 14,* 121–140.

Galchev, T., Aktakka, E.E., Kim, H., and Najafi, K. (2010). A piezoelectric frequency-increased power generator for scavenging low-frequency ambient vibration. *IEEE 23rd International Conference on Micro Electro Mechanical Systems (MEMS),* 1203–1206.

Hall, H. (2011). Review of *The critical assessment of research: Traditional and new methods of evaluation* by A. Bailin and A. Grafstein. *Library and Information Science Research, 33,* 56.

Ichikawa, M., and Nakahara, S. (2008). Japanese high school students' usage of mobile phones while cycling. *Traffic Injury Prevention, 9,* 42–47.

Ingersoll-Dayton B. (2011). The development of culturally-sensitive measures for research on ageing. *Ageing and Society, 31,* 355-370.

Levene, M., and Chia, T. (2010). Counterfeit money detection by intrinsic fluorescence lifetime. *Lasers and Electro-Optics (CLEO) and Quantum Electronics and Laser Science Conference (QELS), 2010 Conference on Laser Electro-Optics: Applications,* 1–2.

Lundberg, S., Romich, J. and Tsang, K. (2009). Decision-making by children. *Review of Economics of the Household, 7,* 1–30.

Lynn, M. (2004). National values and tipping customs: A replication and extension. *Journal of Hospitality & Tourism Research, 28,* 356–364.

Martindale, D. (February, 2001). Sweating the small stuff. *Scientific American,* 52–53.

Maskan, F., Wiley, D. E., Johnston, L. P. M., and Clements, D. J. (2000). Optimal design of reverse osmosis module networks. *American Institute of Chemical Engineers Journal, 46,* 946–954.

McDougall, A. (2008). A duty to forget? The 'Hitler Youth Generation' and the transition from Nazism to Communism in postwar East Germany, c. 1945–49. *German History, 26*(1), 24–46.

Mulder, M., Abbink, D.A., van Paassen, M.M., and Mulder, M. (2011). Design of a haptic gas pedal for active car-following support. *IEEE Transactions On Intelligent Transportation Systems 12,* 268–279.

Naczi, R. F. C., Reznicek, A. A., and Ford, B. A. (1998). Morphological, geographical, and ecological differentiation in the Carex willdenowii complex (cyperaceae). *American Journal of Botany, 85,* 434–447.

Neider, M.B., McCarley, J.S., Crowell, J.A., Kaczmarski, H., and Kramer, A.F. (2010). Pedestrians, vehicles, and cell phones. *Accident Analysis & Prevention, 42,* 589–594.

Noakes, T. D. (2000). Exercise and the cold. *Ergonomics, 43,* 1461–1479.

Pachucki, K., Leibfried, D., and Hänsch, T. W. 1993. Nuclear-structure correction to the lamb shift. *Physical Review A, 48,* R1–R4.

Peskin, M.E. (2011). Review of *Quantum field theory in a nutshell* (2nd edn) by A. Zee. *Classical and Quantum Gravity, 28,* 089003.

Pölkki, T., Pietilä, A. M., and Vehviläinen-Julkunen, K. (2003). Hospitalized children's descriptions of their experiences with postsurgical pain relieving methods. *International Journal of Nursing Studies, 40,* 33–44.

Purvis, A. J., and Cable, N. T. (2000). The effects of phase control materials on hand skin temperature within gloves of soccer goalkeepers. *Ergonomics, 43,* 1480–1488.

Rabinovich, A., and Morton, T.A. (2010). Who says we are bad people? The impact of criticism source and attributional content on responses to group-based criticism. *Personality and Social Psychology Bulletin, 36,* 524–526.

Ranstam, J., et al. (2000). Fraud in medical research: An international survey of biostatisticians. *Controlled Clinical Trials, 21,* 415–427.

Reissig, C.J., Strain, E.C., and Griffiths, R.R. (2009). Caffeinated energy drinks—A growing problem *Drug and Alcohol Dependence, 99,* 1–10.

Ruch, W., Proyer, R. T., and Weber, M. (2010). Humor as character strength among the elderly: Theoretical considerations. *Zeitschrift für Gerontologie und Geriatrie, 43,* 8–12.

Schwer, R. K., and Daneshvary, R. (2000). Keeping up one's appearance: Its importance and the choice of type of hair-grooming establishment. *Journal of Economic Psychology, 21,* 207–222.

Selwyn, N. (2008). A Safe haven for misbehaving? An investigation of online misbehavior among university students. *Social Science Computer Review, 26,* 446–465.

Shah, J., Shah, A., and Pietrobon, R. (2009). Scientific writing of novice researchers: What difficulties and encouragements do they encounter? *Academic Medicine, 84,* 511–516.

Schemenauer, R.S., and Cereceda, P. (1991). Fog-water collection in arid coastal locations. *Ambio, 20*(7), 303–308.

Tiamiyu, M. F. (2000). University-community agency collaboration: Human service agency workers' views. *Journal of Multicultural Nursing and Health, 6,* 29–36.

World Health Organization. (2011). *Manual for the laboratory diagnosis and virological surveillance of influenza.* Geneva, Switzerland: World Health Organization.

Wuchty, S., Jones, B.F., and Uzzi, B. (2007). The increasing dominance of teams in production of knowledge. *Science, 316,* 1036–1038.

Index